PLACIDUS
de Titis

Primum Mobile

Translated by John Cooper
with an introduction by Michael Baigent

Published by
The Institute For The Study Of
Cycles In World Affairs,
36 Tweedy Road,
Bromley, Kent BR1 3PP.

The Institute for the Study of Cycles in World Affairs

The Institute for the Study of Cycles in World Affairs was established in 1980 with the aim of promoting the study of mundane astrology and the history of astrology. Since 1980 the Institute has also issued a periodic bulletin on mundane astrology. Details are available from the Institute at 36 Tweedy Road, Bromley, Kent, BR1 3PP, Great Britain.

© 1983 Michael Baigent

All rights reserved. Quotations of up to one page are allowed, provided the source of the quotation is also added.

ISBN 0 9508412 1 8

Printed in Great Britain by
Calverts Press
55 Mount Pleasant, London WC1

Introduction

The turbulent 17th century presided over profound political and philosophical changes. For those whose lives straddled these years the times were heady with discovery and reform, yet tragic with brutal wars and persecutions. This was though, primarily an era which actively encouraged the divorce of experimental science from its roots which lay deep in the occult. Nevertheless, despite considerable effort on the part of academia and the church, the latter was not removed but simply driven underground. Thrust down into a shadowy world which lay beneath the great men of the century. Here lingered Robert Boyles' "Invisible College", Johan Valentin Andreae's mysterious "Christian Unions" and of course, what reality existed of the brotherhood of Rosicrucians. Once again the Hermetic stream, the mainspring of the Renaissance, was forced to flow beneath the surface of orthodoxy unfortunately eventually taking with it the study of astrology. For the Elizabethan Magus reluctantly gave way before the scientist to the extent that by the end of the century all that remained of the Hermetic or Neo-Platonic world view was maintained only within such discreet societies as the rapidly growing brotherhood of Freemasons.

The great philosophical influence upon this Century came from Rene Descartes. By postulating the concept of a mechanical universe he produced immense changes in man's conception of the heavens. God, he said, was certainly the first cause of motion but following this initial intervention the deity's presence was no longer required, for the cosmos could maintain itself. Hence explanations for phenomena should be sought in terms of physical, measurable causes rather than in the nonquantifiable world of the occult or the spiritual. Astrology, long considered to have an occult basis, thus came under incresing pressure. Academics as well as ecclesiastics now condemned it as more and more universities dropped the subject from their courses. By the mid 17th century only a few continued to teach astrological theory, among them the great centres of Bologna and Padua. The church too reiterated its opposition; in 1631 Pope Urban VIII issued a Papal Bull condemning astrology. This was the direct consequence of an embarrassing debacle in Rome the year earlier. An astrologer of some fame had predicted the imminent death of Urban and as a result, Cardinals began gathering in the eager expectation of a conclave. The Pope, infuriated, vented his wrath upon both the astrologer and his study, gaoling the former and anathematising the latter.

The times grew difficult for astrology as events increased the pressure. Its technical base began to demand reconsideration in the light of the astronomical discoveries of Tycho Brahe and Johannes Kepler. For the invention of the telescope in 1608, coupled with the publication of Kepler's *New Astronomy* the same year had dealt a fatal blow to traditional Ptolemaic cosmology which had long formed the backbone of astrological thought. By the middle of the century astrologers were urgently reviewing their doctrines as a result of the dominance of this 'new' astronomy and the tenets of Cartesian philosophy. *Placidus de Titis* (mis-spelled by the English translators as Titus), or Placido Titi was a major figure in the subsequent reforming movement. According to Lyn Thorndike he became a kind of patron saint for contemporary astrologers.[1]

Placido's theme, developed through his two major works — the *Physiomathematica* of 1650 and *Tabulae Primi Mobilis* of 1657, held that the influence of the stars was natural, manifest and measurable. He theorised that terrestrial phenomena were affected by means of the light coming from the stars, this being the simple and visible causal connection between them and the earth. In this way he was able to distance himself from earlier explanations couched as they were in occult terms.

---

1. Lynn Thorndike, *A History of Magic and Experimental Science*. New York, 1923–34. Vol VIII, p. 302.

Unfortunately, despite his efforts, astrology failed to find a place in the mainstream of scientific thought and was gradually pushed aside.

Placido Titi was born in Italy, possibly Perugia, in 1603, living until 1668. As he reveals in *Tabulae Primi Mobilis* he began his astrological studies when still a young man, learning from teachers sufficiently illustrious to get their work published.[2] It seems likely that one of his teachers was the astrologer Andreae Argoli: Placido, in his *Tabulae Primi Mobilis* uses as an example the birthchart of the Cardinal de Salviatis. This birthchart was first published in 1607 by Magini,[3] who gives the time of birth as 9.36 pm on 21 January 1537. Placido, writing in 1657 however differs slightly, placing the time instead at 9.32 pm. His source for this variant time can be found in a 1639 work by Argoli, *De Diebus Criticis*.[4] *The fact that Placido, despite his many criticisms of Argoli's accuracy, should accept such a revision is an indication of respect for the older man's learning. In addition to this, the bulk of the charts found in Placido's 1657 publication similarly come from Argoli's De Diebus Criticis...* Whatever the truth of the matter at the very least Argoli can be regarded as a major influence on Placido.

Placido joined an ascetic branch of the Benedictine Order, the Olivetans — who were essentially a reformist brotherhood. While not large in number, they had monasteries in several major Italain cities, Padua being one. The Olivetans obviously approved and encouraged his astrological work for his *Physiomathetica* contains an approbation from the Head of the Order. Placido became an accomplished mathematician and astrologer, working it seems, as a teacher. He went first into print with a small collection of horoscopes published in Padua, 1641. Within the year he had issued another collection of horoscopes and a larger astrological text. Some years

---

2. Placidus de Titis, *Primum Mobile*, London, 1814, p. 123.
3. Io Antonii Magini, *De Astrologica Ratione, ac vsu dierum Criticorum*, Venice, 1607, p. 99.
4. Andreae Argoli, *De Diebus Criticis et de Aegrorum decubitu*. Padua, 1639. Book II, p. 45. Published by Paul Frambotti, who was later to print Placido's *Tabulae Primi Mobilis*.

later he produced his two major works — the first appearing in 1650, the second 1657. Between these two, he had printed an annotated edition of Ptolemy's *Tetrabiblos*. If Placido had any intellectual mentor, then it was Ptolemy — always one to acknowledge sources — Placido consistently presented his theories as being essentially those held by that great Alexandrian:

"I desire no other guides but Ptolemy and Reason."[5]

By 1657, when he published his *Tabulae Primi Mobilis,* Placido was connected to the highest ranks of European nobility. His patron — evidenced by his dedication — was Archduke Leopold-Wilhelm von Habsburg, brother of the Austrian Emperor. Furthermore, the year of publication saw the death of the Emperor and Leopold-Wilhelm being offered the Imperial crown. It can be assumed from this connection that Placido was no stranger to the intrigues of European diplomacy. A brief look at the world of the Archduke may serve to throw some light upon that of Placido.

Archduke Leopold-Wilhelm, as the youngest son, followed tradition and entered the church, gaining his first Bishoprics — Strasburg and Passau — by the age of eleven. Similarly, family practice saw him assume in 1642 the rank of Grand Master of the Teutonic Knights. Despite being an ecclesiastic, Leopold-Wilhelm early took up a military career and by 1640 was commanding the Imperial forces fighting in Bohemia. For him to seek advice from an astrologer such as Placido was not out of character for the Archduke was very much a renaissance man, ecclectic in his pursuits and his philosophy. He made collections of paintings, curiosities, even rare plants and at one time became involved in archaeology — the excavation of Frankish king Childeric's grave in 1653. He was described by his contemporaries as having a superstitious streak — perhaps we can see here an allusion to his astrological interests.[6] However, a more

---

5. *Primum Mobile, op cit*, p. 47.
6. William Coxe, *History of the House of Austria*. 2nd edition, London 1820. Vol III, p. 90.

obvious influence upon his decision to patronise an astrologer can be found from a study of his military experience during the 1620's. At this time Leopold-Wilhelm was serving as an officer under the enigmatic Imperial Commander, Albrecht von Wallenstein — both a general and an accomplished astrologer.

Wallenstein had mastered the art of astrology during his stay in Padua, beginning in 1600.[7] His travelling companion and tutor was the astrologer Peter Virdungus, a friend of Kepler.[8] While in the great university city Wallenstein studied under the prominent astrologer Argoli — later to be an influence on Placido. Subsequently, when Wallenstein was commander of the Imperial forces he employed various astrologers as advisors, a group of whom, it seems, constantly accompanied him on campaign — the name of one, Gianbattista Zenno, has survived.

However, without doubt, the best known of Wallenstein's astrological advisors was Johannes Kepler himself. From initially calculating and reading Wallenstein's birthchart, Kepler gradually became drawn into the great man's circle, giving advice and finally being supported financially by him. Kepler did not accompany the commander on the military campaigns but advised from a distance, no doubt Placido later performed similarly with regard to Leopold-Wilhelm's astrological queries.

In passing it is pertinent to comment upon Kepler who, while being a sound methodologist and scientist, nevertheless was a committed astrologer.[9] He maintained curious and as yet unexplored connections with the shadowy esoteric underside of the 17th century. For Kepler moved in the circle of Johann Valentin Andreae, author of the Rosicrucian Manifestos. Also Kepler seems later to have been associated with Andreae's curious 'Christian Unions'. Considerable evidence exists to suggest that Andreae was the leader of

---

7: For a life of Wallenstein see Francis Watson, *Wallenstein. Soldier under Saturn*, London, 1938.
8: Kepler in 1601 began working for Emperor Rudolph II at his "Rosicrucian" court at Prague.
9. See J Bruce Brackenridge, *A Short History of Scientific Astrology*. Appleton, Wisconsin, 1980.

a discreet Hermetic society known to history as the Priory of Sion, which had both philosophical and political aims while remaining firmly underground. The 'Christian Unions' seem to have been a branch of this society.[10] Frances Yates writes that Kepler had a very close association with the "Rosicrucian" world and suggests that a new historical approach to his life needs to be made.[11] As this short review indicates the web of the esoteric was not broken but continued to spread far across the learned world and so it is difficult to establish exactly what blend of occultism and science really existed during this century. However, with the existence of such a web established, if not precisely delineated, it is not at all unlikely that the figures mentioned — Kepler, Wallenstein, Andreae, Leopold-Wilhelm and Placido — had connections between them, other than those which history has recorded.

— Michael Baigent, London, 1983.

---

10. Michael Baigent, Richard Leigh, Henry Lincoln, *The Holy Blood and the Holy Grail*. London, 1982. p. 111-114.
11. Frances A Yates, *The Rosicrucian Enlightenment*. St Albans, 1975. p. 267.

Primum Mobile

This book with the additions of a birthchart for Urban VIII and revised tables, is a translation of Placido's *Tabulae Primi Mobilis*, published in Padua, 1657. It was first put rather unsatisfactorily into English by Manoah Sibly (brother of the astrologer Ebenezer Sibly) but eventually, 25 years later, John Cooper produced the present edition.

While Placido had initially presented all the elements of his thesis in *Questionum physiomathematicarum*, published 1650, this work did not apparently find the wide acceptance he sought. In his introduction to *Tabulae Primi Mobilis* he explains that the function of the new publication was primarily to present in a simpler and more concise manner the lengthy arguments of the earlier. Appended were thirty birthcharts which served, as he put it, "to confirm the truth of things".

Placido's first thesis reveals the basis of his scientific approach: as it is impossible for the stars to influence the earth without some connecting link, and as there cannot be effects without causes it follows, he says, that the medium by which the stars affect the earth must be through their light. He takes of course as a self evident fact that such an effect requiring a scientific explanation exists. The only question for him concerns the cause. He rejects definitively any possibility of an explanation which requires some occult connection between the stars and the earth. Instead, by virtue of his theory, he proposes a cause of astrological effects which is measurable, visible and undoubtedly natural.

From this basic position the remainder of his theory develops. His Fourth Thesis presents an ancient idea originally propounded by the Babylonians and much later repeated by Ptolemy. If the stars or other celestial phenomena cannot be seen then they cannot have any effect. For Placido the reasoning is this: if the stars are not visible then their light cannot be falling upon us. If their light is not falling upon us then there is no connection and so there is no effect. As an example, he explains that invisible eclipses can have no influence over the world, in fact, he adds, all celestial phenomena are able to act solely upon those places from where they can be seen. This concept also gave rise quite naturally to the basis for his revision of the mathematical structure of the astrological houses.

Placido is particularly scathing on the subject of the house system of his day, that of the 15th Century astrologer Regiomontanus. Both he and his predecessor, Campanus, used "space" house systems. Campanus working from equal divisions of the *Prime Vertical* and Regiomontanus from equal divisions of the *Celestial Equator*. The system developed by Placido — who claims only to be returning to that of Ptolemy — is completely different, being based not upon spatial division but temporal. His calculations for the House cusps take as their starting point the time each degree of the ecliptic takes to rise above the horizon. He explains this further in Thesis 51: Because the light from the stars is the medium by which they affect us, the stars themselves must be visible. So, as the stars progressively appear above the horizon so does their effect on us similarly appear. Thus it is time alone which separates the celestial influences and so it must be by time, not space, that the houses are delineated.

". . . there is proportional and equal division,
not indeed of the heavenly and aerial space,
but of the successive influx of the stars
and the houses; . . ."

After Sibly's 1789 edition, the present one of 1814 and the textbook by James Wilson in 1819, Placido was taken up by one of the great publishers of astrological ephemerides in the early 19th century, Robert Cross Smith, writing under the name of Raphael. He popularised the Placidian system to such an extent that it swept all others away before it. Even today, while the advent of computers has made the use of a variety of house systems, ancient and modern, a simple matter, that of Placido, with some small adjustments, remains by far the most common.

PLACIDO'S BIRTHCHARTS
An analysis of their accuracy

EXAMPLE CHART ANALYSIS:
Francis I, born 1494

Factor	Placidus	Actual value	Difference
Asc.	5.56 Cancer	5.52 Cancer	+0.14 degrees
MC.	6.00 Pisces	8.16 Pisces	−2.16 degrees
Sun	28.39 Virgo	28.44 Virgo	−0.05 degrees
Moon	27.30 Aquarius	27.29 Aquarius	+0.01 degrees
Merc.	19.10 Libra	24.14 Libra	−5.04 degrees
Venus	15.50 Leo	15.30 Leo	+0.20 degrees
Mars	23.15 Leo	23.44 Leo	−0.29 degrees
Jup.	23.54 Virgo	24.42 Virgo	−0.48 degrees
Sat.	10.22 Pisces R	9.46 Pisces R	+0.36 degrees

TABLE OF DIFFERENCES

Factor	Francis I 1494	Charles V 1500	Henry IV 1553	G. Adolphus 1594	Average
Asc:	+0.14	+1.28	−1.10	+0.06	0.45
MC:	−2.16	+2.59	+0.13	−0.35	1.31
Sun:	−0.05	+0.23	−0.03	+0.01	0.08
Moon:	+0.01	0.00	−0.12	−0.27	0.10
Mercury	−5.04	+14.24	+4.12	+2.59	6.40
Venus:	+0.20	+0.51	+0.21	+0.14	0.27
Mars:	−0.29	−0.15	−0.09	−0.28	0.20
Jupiter:	−0.48	+0.20	−0.01	+0.38	0.27
Saturn:	+0.36	+1.28	−0.11	+0.11	0.37

Conclusion:

From the simple analysis of the charts presented above the trend can be seen easily enough. Remembering that many of these birthcharts date from over one hundred years before Placido, their general accuracy must be considered as good, the Sun and the Moon being the most consistently close to their true value. However, Mercury is an anomaly, being grossly inaccurate on most occasions. This probably reflects the technical difficulty experienced in observing Mercury with any frequency sufficient to give true accuracy.

The birthcharts published by Placido were checked by computer programmed with the Matrix M-65 system.

Note:

Placido follows an early method of indicating the time on birthcharts. The hours following noon on a particular day are given as PM even when the number of hours exceeds 12 — thus running into the following day. For example: in the birthchart of Emperor Charles V, the time given is 15.39 hours PM on the 23rd February. This translates to 3.39 AM on the 24th. Calculations should start from this time. A simple check proves this point. In the birthchart of Charles, the Sun falls in the second house. Hence, according to Placido, the birth took place in the morning.

Placidus de Titis or Placido Titi
Pseud. Didacus Prittus

Bibliography

Date of Publication

1641	*Septem geneses, quas posuit . . . Jo Antonius Maginus . . . in suo de Diebus criticis opere . . .*
	Padua. (Cribellianis)
	(Quarto, 47 pages. Dedication dated 1641)
1641	*Quadraginta geneses prae coeteris, quas posuit . . .*
	Milan. (Io. B. Malatestae)
	(Quarto, 64 pages. Licence to print dated 1641)
(1641)–1642	*De modis directionum coelestium mobilium in genethlialogicis ad medicinae usum compendiolum . . .*
	Milan. (Io. B. Malatestae)
	(Quarto, 33 pages. The printing is dated 1641, the dedication 1642. Publication is assumed to be on the latter date.)
(1646)–1650	*Quaestionum physiomathematicarum libri tres Inquibus ex naturae principijs hucusq: . . .*
	edited by Pietro Paulo Bonetti.
	Milan. (Io. B. Malatestae)
Book One:	*Physiomathematica sive Coelestis philosophia naturalibus hucusq: . . .*
Book Two:	*Quaestionum physiomathematicarum liber secundus de familiaritatibus astrorum.*

Book Three: *Quaestionum physiomathematicarum liber tertius de Siderum ad familiaritates motibus, et numeris.*

(Of the four copies of this book checked considerable differences were found in the order of title pages and inclusion or not of approbations and dedications. While 1650 would appear certain as the publication date, various additional dates are found. The frontispiece (when dated) 1646, a dedication to Cardinal Senogalliae, the introduction and Imprimatur (when present) are dated 1650.)

1650   *Il corriere astronomo prenuntio de gli accidenti dell'anno M.DC.L cioe Ivnario, e giornale calcolato al meridiano d'Italia* . . .

Bologna. (Herede del Benacci)

(A 38 page pamphlet)

1654   *Nuncius astronomicus* . . .

Milan. (Printer unspecified)

1654   *Il corriere astronomico prenuntio* . . .

Padua. (P. Frambotto)

1657   *Tabulae Primi Mobilis cum thesibus ad theoricen & canonibus ad praxim additis in rerum demonstrationem et supputationum exemplum triginta classimorum natalium thematibus* . . .

Padua. (Pauli Frambotti).

1658   *Cl Ptolemaei . . . Opus de siderum iudiciis quadripartitum praepositis ad singula capita breviarijs, vel notationibus D. Placidi de Titis.*

	Padua. (Pauli Frambotti)
	(This is Ptolemy's Tetrabiblos with notes by Placido. It was quickly reprinted in 1660 and 1665.)
1660	*De diebus decretoriis et aequorum decubitu adiuuandam preclaram Artis Medice Professionem iuxta Summor. Pontif . . . Epitome Astrosophica . . .* Volume One.
	Pavia. (Io. A. Magrijin)
1665	*De diebus decretoriis et morborum causa caelesti . . .* Volume Two. (Of *De diebus* . . .)
	Pavia. (Io. A. Magrijin)
	(This work is normally bound with Volume One)
1666	*Ephemeridum caelestium motuum ab initio anni 1661 usque ad totum 1665 juxta hypoteses Philippi Lansbergi ad longit. gr. 35, cum tractatu de transmutationis elementorum causa efficiente . . .*
	Pavia. (J. Ghidinum)
1666	*Tocco di paragone, onde appare che l'Astrologia nelle parti concesse da S. Chiesa e vera scienza naturale. . .*
	Pavia. (Printer unspecified)
1675	*Physiomathematica sive coelestis philosophia naturalibus hucusq. . .*
	Milan. (Francisci Vigoni)
	(A re-publication of the 1650 edition, title page taken from the earlier version's Book One.)

PLACIDUS IN ENGLISH TRANSLATION

1701 *An appendix concerning Part of Fortune . . . printed at the Latter End of the Last and Best Edition of Placidus de Titis. . .*

by John Whalley

Dublin. (J. Whalley)

(This is a 3 page appendix to Whalley's translation of Ptolemy: *Ptolemy's Quadripartite,* London, 1701.)

1789 *Astronomy and Elementary Philosophy translated from the Latin of Placidus de Titus.*

trans. by M. (Manoah) Sibly.

London. (W. Justins)

(This volume contains the Canons from Placidus' *Primum Mobile.*)

1789 *A Collection of thirty remarkable nativities to illustrate the canons. . . from the Latin of Placidus de Titus. . .*

trans. by M. Sibly

London (W. Justins)

(This contains the charts from *Primum Mobile*)

1790 *Supplement to Placidus de Titus: containing the nativity of that wonderful phaenomenon, Oliver Cromwell. Calculated according to the Placidian Canons, by . . . John Partridge.*

by M. Sibly

London. (W. Justins)

1814 *Primum Mobile*

trans. by John Cooper.

London. (Davis & Dickson)

PRIMUM MOBILE,

WITH THESES TO THE THEORY,

AND CANONS FOR PRACTICE;

wherein is demonstrated,

FROM

ASTRONOMICAL AND PHILOSOPHICAL PRINCIPLES,

THE

NATURE AND EXTENT

OF

CELESTIAL INFLUX

UPON

The Mental Faculties and Corporeal Affections of Man;

containing

THE MOST RATIONAL AND BEST APPROVED

MODES OF DIRECTION,

BOTH IN ZODIAC AND MUNDO:

exemplified in

THIRTY REMARKABLE NATIVITIES

OF THE

Most Eminent Men in Europe,

According to the Principles of the Author, laid down in his
" Celestial Philosophy."

Originally written in Latin,

By *DIDACUS PLACIDUS DE TITUS*,

Mathematician to His Serene Highness Leopold William
Archduke of Austria.

---

*The Whole carefully translated, and corrected from the best Latin Editions.
Illustrated with NOTES and an APPENDIX, containing
several useful Additions to the Work,*

BY JOHN COOPER,

Teacher of the Mathematics.

London:

PRINTED AND PUBLISHED BY DAVIS AND DICKSON,
No. 17, St. Martin's le Grand, Newgate Street, Cheapside:
Sold, also, by all Booksellers and Newsmen in the United Kingdom.

A

SHORT ACCOUNT

OF THE

AUTHOR AND HIS WRITINGS.

THE Author of this work, DIDACUS PLACIDUS de TITUS, an Italian Monk, was a native of Bononia, and was Mathematician to Leopold William Archduke of Austria. It is very much to be regretted that we are not in possession of sufficient data to give any very satisfactory account of this most extraordinary Mathematician and Philosopher.

In the year 1647, he published that most elaborate Treatise known by the appellation of his Celestial Philosophy, under the title of " Questionum Physiomathematicarum Libri " Tres, in quibus ex naturæ principiis hu- " jusqui desideratis demonstratur Astrologia " pars illa, quæ ad Metrologiam, Medici-

" nam, Navigium, & Agricultarum spectat;
" cum 12 Exemplis in fine." This valuable Work was printed in quarto, at Milan, and dedicated to Cardinal Fachinette. It is observable that the title-page of this curious book bears the name " Didacus Prittus," although the Dedication is signed Placidus de Titus. In this Work, both the Physical and Mathematical parts of Astrology are most clearly explained, and demonstrated by many curious Diagrams.

It was from this book that Mr. Partridge took all the best of the matter which he inserted in his Opus Reformatum and Defectio Geniturarum, though he very rarely acknowledged the obligation.

In 1657, the present Work was printed at Padua, under the title of " Tabulæ Primi
" Mobilis cum Thesibus ad Theoricen, &
" Canonibus ad praxim, additis in rerum
" demonstrationem, & supputationem Ex-
" emplum Triginta clarissimorum natalium
" Thematibus." This Work was also printed in 4to, and dedicated to Leopold William Archduke of Austria.

A second edition was printed, at Milan, in 1675. The Theses prefixed to this book are, a Synopsis of the former Work, and contain a short abstract of each Chapter, detached from the arguments, reasons, and proofs, upon which those Theses are founded; and after the Nativities, are inserted, a Collection of Tables for Directions, and a Table of Common Logarithms. He likewise published some Ephemerides, known by the name of the Bononian Ephemeris, but for what number of years I cannot say, as they never yet came to my hands. But it appears, from the observations to be found in Partridge's Mene Tekel, that they contain some curious matter applicable to the Mundane part of Astrology. It is rather extraordinary that this great man never published his own Geniture, if he knew the time of birth; perhaps, the only reason was, his singular modesty.

THE EDITOR

To the Reader.

Benevolent Reader!

It is humbly presumed that the extremely imperfect and mutilated state of the former edition of this Work would alone form a sufficient apology for submitting the present Edition to your candid perusal, as every possible care and attention have been bestowed to make it a *fac simile* of the Original, until you arrive at that part of the Work which is composed of Tables, which, from length of time, are now become obsolete, and by far too incorrect to bear investigation by the present improved state of Astronomy, and are, on that account, for the most part omitted; it being in contemplation to publish a more useful collection for this purpose. The Reader will here find their use amply supplied by Trigonometrical Precepts, exem-

THE EDITOR TO THE READER.

plified by the "Requisite Tables" of Dr. Maskelyne, the late Astronomer Royal; and, by attending to these Precepts, he will be enabled to compute his *Data*, and thereby his Arcs of Direction, with more facility, and to a much greater degree of accuracy, than by any set of Tables yet extant.

In order to render this Edition as complete as possible, the Reader will find a variety of useful Notes at the bottom of the pages, and an Appendix containing some curious observations and selections not generally known. The reputation of the Author, and the merits of the Work, being so universally established in the scientific world, entirely preclude the necessity of any eulogium upon either. It is a fact which is well known, that the Original of this Work is so extremely scarce, that fifty Guineas have been refused for a copy; and from this scarcity of the Original we have, in some measure, to regret that it was formerly published so imperfectly.

The manner in which it was before elicited to the public was as follows: About the time of the commencement of Sibly's "Illustration of Astrology," Dr. Browne, of Islington, being in possession of a Latin copy, caused the same to be translated into English; and that translation he lent to Mr. Benjamin Bishop, then Master of Sir John Cass's School, Aldgate, who copied it, and applied to Mr. Browne for the loan of the Latin copy, for the purpose of copying the Tables, but which was refused. Afterwards, a friend of Mr. Sibly's borrowed Mr. Bishop's copy only for a limited number of hours; and, in that time, it was clandestinely copied, without Mr. Bishop's knowledge or consent, and published by Sibly, under the title of " Astronomy and Elementary Philosophy," but in the most incorrect state imaginable; for, in that Work, there is not one single page which is correct, nor had the publishers the means of making it so, as they were not in possession of either the Original Work, or a correct Translation, whereby to rectify the errors committed in the hurry of copying the book.

In this Edition, every line of the Translation has been very carefully compared with the Latin, and made as correct as possible; so that the lovers of science will now be in possession of a book upon which they may rely with confidence, without the danger of being misled.

That this effort to restore PLACIDUS to his primitive purity may tend to the advancement of science, and be of general utility to every candid inquirer after truth, is the sincere wish and desire of their most humble and devoted servant,

JOHN COOPER,
No. 21, Baldwin's Gardens,
Gray's Inn Lane.

N. B. Arithmetic, Algebra, Geometry, Trigonometry, Navigation, Astronomy, Projection of the Sphere, the Use of the Globes, the Art of Directions, &c. taught on moderate Terms.

THE AUTHOR
To the Reader.

WITH regard to the revolutions of the Stars and their efficient power, no candid reader will deny that a genuine and true science may exist, though for a man to make a full acquirement in it, must doubtless be acknowledged no very easy task; and the more particularly, because its object is by nature incorruptible; its properties altogether immutable; and the passions are concluded in an uniform manner.

We learn from the unanimous consent of Philosophers and Professors of Theology, as well as from the *Egyptians, Arabians, Persians, Medes,* and other very extensive nations, that this science was cultivated, in the first place, among all the natural sciences, by kings and the greatest princes, and it was also held in the highest honour; the truth of which is found in several places among their historical annals. Having always had an eager desire from my youth to attain it, I boldly entered upon it, with no less cheerfulness of mind than hopes of acquiring it. In this pursuit I have spent several years, labouring much; but I was greatly offended at many things the professors had lately introduced as discoveries, determining, that, unless they were strictly conformable to reason and experience, and the opinions of the greatest doctors in physics and mathematics, to lay aside entirely their whole works; being, likewise, on the point of bidding adieu to all watchings; therefore, after uniting all the powers of my understanding, I secretly determined to investigate the chief causes and first principles of this science, which, by arguing from reasons, made *pro* and *con;* and as I found them every where to be probable, and agreeable to reason, I gladly communicated my discoveries to the professors and my friends; and, happily, they were not treated as chimerical, or thought to be unreasonable, but, on the contrary, they seemed to be greatly desired : and being frequently entreated to commit them to writing, I have published this short extract, or abstract, comprehending a very concise theory and praxis; to which are subjoined several examples, extracted from very eminent authors, by whom my own reasons were highly applauded. Under the title of CELESTIAL PHILOSOPHY, I exhibited an universal series of disputations, which might represent the reasons and principles as diffusedly as possible, in proportion as time and fortune gave me liberty: wherefore, having offered to the public, and given an explanation of every thing, some were, indeed, surprised at the strangeness of the doctrine; but none have hitherto attempted to oppose the reasons and causes on which they depend.

Some, with their applauses, mingled no small degree of pleasure, by reason that the principles of this most noble science, which were formerly natural, and aptly suited to reason, were now clearly explained, and made evident to the senses: and it is evidently certain, that they wonderfully agree with the true nature of things, and correspond with the accidental effects; and among the philosophical sciences, that of the stars may, and ought, with very good reason, claim the pre-eminence; but because of the difficulty of the calculations, which I have there explained very copiously, being intended for the learned, students are greatly discouraged, I have here given another explanation for general use, more copious and perspicuous, of all and each of the rules, together with the tables that are necessary, premising what related to the knowledge of the theory, in very short theses, that those who had not gone through the labour attending disputations might comprehend, in very few words, the causes and principles which I have laid down, and from which all this construction of numbers is derived.

Lastly: I have added, as well to facilitate calculations as to confirm the truth of things, the examples of thirty famous men, which I have extracted, only from the most learned authors. Yet, let every one remember, that Nature, in her means and effects, conducteth herself so secretly, that a man's understanding cannot trace her footsteps without the greatest labour and industry, which the many differences of opinion maintained among the professors of philosophy, who disagree among themselves concerning the nature of things, must evince: and do not her changes and mighty effects, in this vast construction of the world, appear wonderful, and altogether unsearchable? Without doubt, it must be confessed that the mind of man is too weak to comprehend them; so that no one can be surprised if the method of calculating should be attended with some difficulty. The work of the Efficient Infinite Power and Wisdom is the concord and harmony of nature; but it is like to infinity, at least as to the variety of effects.

In a work, the power and wisdom of the artist are ever perspicuous; what wonder, then, if the understanding of man is utterly unable fully to comprehend the works of God? For who will endeavour to empty with a cup the waters of the deep, which is as a drop in a bucket compared with the *Omnipotence* of the *Creator?* And shall we, with our confined powers of understanding, presume to comprehend, in any shape whatever, the prodigious extent of the heavens, from an idea of the immensity of the surrounding space? The utmost stretch of human thought cannot attain the least notion of it! Admire the rest, which is almost infinite.

Learn, friendly Reader, by experience, that you may have a true enjoyment in the wonderful works of the MOST HIGH — Adieu!

EXPLANATION
OF THE
CHARACTERS USED IN THIS WORK.

SIGNS.

♈	Aries	♎	Libra
♉	Taurus	♏	Scorpio
♊	Gemini	♐	Sagittarius
♋	Cancer	♑	Capricorn
♌	Leo	♒	Aquarius
♍	Virgo	♓	Pisces

PLANETS.

♄	Saturn	♀	Venus
♃	Jupiter	☿	Mercury
♂	Mars	☽	Moon
☉	Sun	⊕	Fortune

ASPECTS.

☌	Conjunction	△	Trine
✱	Sextile	☍	Opposition
☐	Square		

Primum Mobile.

THESES,

From the FIRST BOOK *of the Author's*
"CELESTIAL PHILOSOPHY."

1st. IT is impossible for the efficient heavenly causes (as being so very far distant from things below) to influence sublunary bodies, unless by some medium or instrumental virtue, by which they are united to bodies, subjected, or simple, or both. There can be no action in the subject, which is not affected by some active virtue; for if so, the effect might be produced in the subject, without any efficient cause; which is the reason, we say, that the instrumental cause of the stars is light, and that this only is sufficient to produce all the four primary qualities, by which they arrive at the whole species of natural effects: by motion the stars apply this light, and we reject a secret influence as superfluous, nay, even impossible.

2. The principal properties of the light of the stars are two, (viz.) intension and extension, the less principal colours, which the very senses shew are found in the stars; nor is it to be concluded from thence that the stars are corruptible, at least, with regard to the whole,

PRIMUM MOBILE.

for the strange phenomena, which very frequently appear to us, demonstrate that there are changes in the heavens; for colours may be found in incorruptible bodies: in short, nothing is visible unless it have a colour. The other properties in the stars are figure, local disposition, brightness, and dimness: local motion is a kind of passion wherewith they apply, increase and diminish their light, rise, set, and recede, near and at distance.

3. The stars neither act nor suffer alternately in the heavens; they only receive light from the Sun, which with alteration they communicate to us from the proper colour of each of them: but they vary their actions in the inferior subjects, in proportion as they act together with equal harmony; and this is sufficient for the whole variety of effects.

4. Though the stars, by their motion in the heavens, alternately change their constitutions, and have a determinate degree of intension, and a definite quantity of extension of their light, they do not act upon those inferiors, according to the true and real intension and extension of that light which they have in common, but only according to the apparent; in respect of which they join those passable bodies: for this reason, the stars act upon the sublunaries only according to that degree of intension, and quality of extension of light, by which they are united to those passable bodies: the less are their intension and extension, the greater their distance from the subjected things; but their action is the same, with respect to that extension to which they are opposed, as we very plainly experience in the ☽. They influence according to their situation and proximity to the passable

subject. Invisible eclipses have no influence; new phenomena act only upon those provinces in which they are seen: so that the stars, where they do not rise, are inactive.

5. The stars are indeed the universal cause, and indeterminate, as to their specific and individual effects; but are determined according to the variety of the passable subjects and nearest causes: as the ☉ melts wax, dries up the mud, whitens it, blackens the human skin, with man generates man, a lion with a lion, &c.

6. The stars cannot be the signs of effects, unless they are also the causes; wherefore interrogations, in the manner of the antients, have no place in nature, unless only in eminent effects, in which they move the approximate cause of natural effects; they also move the parts, organs, and members of the passable subject. In the fœtus they respect the parents, sex, number, figure, &c. The present state of the planets bringeth forth the actual effect, according to a pre-ordinate and pre-existent power, and therefore they are the cause or non-cause, not only signs. But the constellations, which for the present bring their effects to act, are the same as the causes of pre-ordination; and so of death, &c. For unlike causes cannot bring to act the *dissimulas* pre-existing, according to the power of the effects.

7. And since, to distinguish and know the effects of any star, it is necessary to know the difference, nature, and order of those effects, according to the soundest philosophy; after laying down the first principles of all things, Matter, and substantial Form, the primary and compound qualities, we distinguish all these into two

principal kinds, viz. into the passive or feminine, and the active or masculine. To the first sort, we again call in matter and quantity, or quality, so far as it is passive, with all the other qualities which are derived from its moisture, dryness, rarity, density, levity, &c. To the masculine kind, substantial and material forms, the qualities which are active, as light, heat, cold, smell, sound, and all the active virtues of the compounds, &c.

8. We call commixion a union of altered miscibles, but we add, perfected by the efficient superiors, Order and Nature, that is, from a celestial quality, on which the concoction of those miscibles depend; whence the compounds, which have a larger and more perfect concoction with those miscibles, and consequently a more intense celestial quality, are more perfect; such as have a less, the contrary.

9. The virtue of the compound, or the qualities, which, indeed, with respect to the great number, variety, and effects, deserve our admiration, we do not call elementary, nor proceeding from the elements, but celestial qualities, which are altogether derived from the celestial light; wherefore, the elementary and celestial qualities are of different kinds: and though the stars may produce elementary qualities in their alternate transmutation, they still produce others more excellent, whereby they attain the production of the whole species of the compounds.

10. The vital heat and radical moisture in animals, we agree with Aristotle in terming qualities entirely celestial, produced from the light of ☉ and ☽, with the concurrence (which cannot be denied) of all the other

stars, from which a distinction is made of the whole diversity of compounds, though of a nature so opposite to each other, that the *luminaries*, with the *malefics*, generate the poisonous, or the hostile, instead of those that engender with the benign, and on the contrary; whence the antipathies and sympathies of things are mutually derived.

11. The qualities, both of the compounds and elements, are at first powerful, at least, according to nature; then active: but those that are active have their existence by successive motion; for they successively come forth to action from their powerful stations: for which reason they are again restored to their co-natural state of actual qualities.

12. From the vital heat and radical moisture of the animal power, arise sensitives, appetitives, digestives, retentives, expulsives, &c. distinct from each other, and each hath its exercise and action; wherefore those powers have first a powerful, then an active existence.

13. Those vital qualities are extinguished in a two-fold manner, naturally, and violently. First, by a final consumption of a pre-existing power in an extreme old age; secondly, by a violent extinction, exhibited by a different concurrent cause.

14. The powers employ their influence on matter, suitable to every one of them; the sensitive on objects, the vegetative on elements; which, the more perfect they are by the concoction of mixture, the greater and quicker is their nourishment; for it is converted with greater ease and perfection into the substance of the animal, &c.

15. There are four principal colours, viz. white, black, light, and darkness: by light, we do not mean that which is diffused from the ☉ and from fire, but that colour which arises from the intension of that light which is almost like gold; by darkness, its privation. But there are some colours which are composed of celestial qualities, others elementary of these elements; but there possibly flow infinite from their alternate permixion. White is a colour merely passive, light an active.

16. The stars, though they never cease from action, and causing an alteration in things below, yet from that change they produce no remarkable effect, unless in familiarities. We call the familiarity of the luminaries, meeting with power, proportional by an influx motion. Under the name of luminaries, we understand not only all the stars, but likewise uncommon phenomena; and we exclude every other place in the heavens which is void of light, for it is by light only the stars influence, as has been said before. By the power of the conjuncts, we exclude from the familiarities those stars which cannot, by any means, be conjoined together; but it is plain that the familiarities have not their being in the heavens, but in the inferior passable subject, namely, according to their mode of receiving them, as is manifest.

17. Authors treat of the various and different distinctions and divisions of the celestial houses, whereof we only approve of that which Ptolemy places, that is by the two temporal hours: we reject all the rest as vain, and quite inconsistent with nature.

18. The signs and houses have not a real distinction

in the heavens, but in the inferior passable subject, according to its manner of receiving the influx of the stars; the signs likewise have a true and certain sex, in the same manner and masculine, by a proportional influx, to the places where the active quality commences; feminine where the passive; which we shall mention hereafter.

19. From the intension of light, proceeds an active quality; from its extension, a passive; in short, every natural principle of an active virtue has its rise from the intension of light; but the principle of a passive virtue, from its extension. For this reason, the substantial and material Forms, and all the qualities active in kind, are referred to the Sun; but to the Moon, that principle, Matter, and all its qualities, passive in kind.

Hence it is manifest, that the Sun has an active virtue, by reason of the intension of his light; but the Moon, a passive, by reason of extension, though, in reality, there are intension and extension in both; but in the Sun, intension is prevalent, and in the Moon intension is inconsiderable, and extension prevails; and as by its increase and decrease, it shews us the various quantity of its light, in things it augments and diminishes matter and moisture.

20. The variety of colours in the stars produces a diversity of effects. Thus the colour of the luminaries — ☉ or of gold, is possessed of an active virtue, the same as the intension of light, for it proceeds from the intension of light, and, as it were, from the approximate cause. White possesses a passive virtue, as does extension; but these two primary colours relate to

effects of a simple nature which are excellent; such as material substances, &c. The other colours in the stars are the cause of specific qualities; so the blue and yellow, such as are in ♃ and ♀, which are a mixture of white and gold, give signs of a temperate nature from heat and moisture; in the blue, heat is predominant; in the yellow, moisture; and therefore these two planets confer that which is good, useful, and pleasant: the former is masculine, by reason of the too great heat; the latter, feminine, owing to excess of moisture. Leaden and fiery colours, such as are in ♄ and ♂, shew an intemperature, cold and dry in ♄, hot and dry in ♂. ♄ is more cold than dry, and therefore masculine; ♂ more dry than hot, and therefore feminine.

21. But in general, effects, according to their nature, properties, passions, motions, &c. imitate their cause; for the manner of acting follows that of being. As the work of Saturn is unpleasant, rigid, cold, dark, and black, his motion slow, &c. nay, more, from the passions of the luminary which proceed from local motion, follow the passions in the effects; as from access and recess, follows the access and recess of the passion and effects; from its near and distant situation, the near and remote action is derived; from its inception, the beginning of the action; from continuity, its continuance; from its increase, the increase.

22. From the access and near situation of the stars follows the increase of their light, according to extension; and from the increase respecting extension, follows a still greater intension of the light, according to the degree, at least in the effect. From

the increase of the luminary, with regard to extension, follows an increase of moisture : from a greater intension of the luminary, follows a greater heat ; and so in every one of them. Aristotle's Second General Treatise, page 56, in his researches into the cause of the perpetuity of the rise and fall of things, informs us, that not only one inference may assign the cause of this rise and fall, but also that which contains different motions, to which the causes accede and recede, are near or distant in their constitution ; and their access, and near situation, are the cause of generation; their recess and distant situation, of corruption.

23. There is a formation of four conjugations of the manner of starry influence, viz. in the luminary's increase and near situation; in its near situation and decrease ; in its decrease and distance ; and in its distance and increase. By these conjugations are constituted four quarters; First, in the world, which are the circuits of the stars by day from east to south, from south to west, from west to the lowest, and from the lowest to the east. Secondly, in the Zodiac, and the annual seasons, from ♈ to ♋, from ♋ to ♎, from ♎ to ♑, from ♑ to ♈.

24. There are four respects of the planets to the Sun ; from the apogee of the epicycle towards the first station (in the ☽ towards the first decatom) ; from the first station to the perigee ; from thence to the second station (in the ☽ towards the second decatom), at least as far as the apogee. From these are derived an excellent reason, why the three superiors are supposed to be stronger : if they are found to be matutine or eastern, from the ☉,

the three inferiors vespertine, or western; for then they have a greater degree of light, in which consists their virtual influence, and then they are called oriental; but occidental, if otherwise. Every one knows how largely, yet to no purpose, authors have treated of the orientality of the planets.

25. From the cardinal points of the world, and the Zodiac, the stars begin to influence the four primary qualities; from the imum cœli and tropic of ♋, moisture; from the ascendant and ♈, heat; from the medium cœli and tropic of ♑, dryness; from the west and ♎, coldness; but by all these means, the stars, though they have their nature absolute in themselves, they nevertheless produce all the four primary qualities, though with a difference, on account of the diversity of the nature of the stars; but they continually increase the qualities they produce, by advancing successively to the opposite points; such is the reason they likewise lessen the contrary quality.

26. From these, it is inferred, that the influx and rays of the stars depend on real motion and illumination, not on the quantity of the celestial spaces nor the situation: and therefore the stars in the cadent houses are weak; in the succeedents strong; in the cardinals strongest, &c.

27. All the active qualities, whether of the elements, or of the compounds, depend on the horary extent of the stars round the world; but because the duration of things is various, annual, monthly, and diurnal, with which Ptolemy agrees in his chapter of those that have no Nourishment, and the Second Stagyrite and

General Treatise, p. 57. They are diurnal, as being the first and immediate in the order of the work; for in the order of perfection they are the lowest, and the annual durations are in the first place, by reason of their perfection.

28. The virtual qualities of the elements depend on the latitudes of the stars in the Zodiac. The vital qualities of such as live through months and years, depend on the Sun's place in the Zodiac, and the Moon, in respect of the Sun, as from present causes, but are preordained by the Sun's motion round the world, and by the Moon round the Earth: whence the motions of the directions and progressions are derived.

29. The differences of the celestial qualities that are in the compounds, both vital and those that are not vital, depend on the various congressions and familiarities of the luminaries, with the other stars both erratic and fixed, and on the different places in the Zodiac, so far as they are of a different nature; for from the simple places, both in the Zodiac, as well as round the world, that is (if they are thus considered), the primary qualities of the elements are derived.

30. The true moment of the day, on which any one is born (laying aside all opinions of authors), is when the fœtus becomes independent on its finitimate cause, or its ministry; an immediate influx then takes place. At the constitution of the celestial moment, there is no need of its longer perseverance, to make the effects the cause of preservation; for that is impossible; but it is sufficient that it concur with the nearest causes, to confer being, and the co-natural qualities: for so it

is, that he who is born, throughout his whole life has a reference to, and, as it were, represents the effects; and as a stamp resembles the seal, so does the constitution of the stars his nativity.

31. The stars insert their power in an animal, and the virtual qualities in certain latitudes of a shorter time: these they pre-ordain with effect. The accidents naturally active, operate at their appointed times to the conclusion of life, and begin at the moment of the nativity; but they are the latitudes of days and months, and pre-ordain successively, therefore orderly, and in co-operation; and they are ready to act at the time pre-ordained, when the favourable constitutions are the same as their causes of pre-ordination; for dissimular present causes cannot produce any effect but what agrees with them.

32. In the constitution of the stars, the nativities are said to continue immoveable, as well as the significators and promittors of effects; and this only, by reason of the retrospect of that nativity's temperament to those places: for while the stars concur with the nearest causes in conferring existence, they imprint on that animal so many degrees of their qualities, as they effect from those places in which they are found; and therefore that animal respects, all its life, the places of the stars of its nativity, as being always immoveable.

33. But as there is a double motion of the stars, that is, under the *primum mobile,* and round the world, by both which, as we have said, they influence, we must consequently suppose, that the significators rule over things subjected to them by this twofold (or double)

motion, to wit, under the *primum mobile*, and round the world. So in the former moderation, the significators remain immoveable in the world, *i. e.* in their horary circles of position; in the latter they are in a state of immobility in their places immediately under the *primum mobile:* the promittors in the former moderation remain immoveable under the *primum mobile*, but are moved with their parts of the Zodiac to the horary circle of position of the same significator. In the latter moderation, they remain immoveable in the world, that is, in the horary circle of position, but are moved in a manner immediately under the *primum mobile*, to the moderator's place taken under the *primum mobile*.

34. We say that the significators continue immoveable in their mundane situation. By mundane situation we mean the horary circle, *i. e.* (according to Ptolemy) of unequal hours, not the circles of position which pass through the common sections of the horizon and meridian, as will appear more fully hereafter. Likewise, when we say that the significators in the former moderation remain immoveable, in such a situation, we do not exclude the change of declination; we mean that the moderators should always continue and advance by their own real and natural way; as if we speak of the Sun in the ecliptic, or the Moon in her circle, constituting the Dragon, in which she is in perpetual motion, and in which she successively alters her latitude.

35. The Sun, when it is found in the space of the crepuscules, before rising and after setting, does not remain there immoveable under the horary circle; but in the crepusculines, parallel to the horizon, in which it

always affords us the same degree of the intension of light, from which equality of the intension of light it is said to continue immoveable; for if it should, with regard to us, vary in the degree of the intension of light, it could not be said to remain immoveable, but would be in a state of motion. In the remaining space of obscurity, the Sun must be directed, with a reference from the limits of the crepuscles to the lowest; as if we should say, from the proportionable division of the obscure arcs, they were seminocturnal arcs. This will be more fully shewn hereafter.

36. Moderators of things are five, viz. the Sun, the Moon, *Medium Cœli*, Horoscope of the Country, and the Lunar Horoscope; every one of these so moderates its own proper species of things, that it cannot attain to that which relates to the other: it is necessary to observe this, that we fall not into error and confusion.

37. The Aphetic places of the world, or those wherein are received the moderators of life, are five, viz. the House of the East, the tenth, the ninth, the seventh, and the eleventh; in any of which the Sun being found, always becomes the moderator of life; but if he is absent, the Moon, &c. according to the doctrin delivered by Ptolemy in his third book, which we ought to follow so rigorously, absolutely, and without the least exception whatever, that whoever, by neglecting the luminaries, if in the Aphetic places, should receive the horoscope as the moderator of life, would be guilty of a very great error, and would be unworthy of the name of a professor of the true and natural Astrology.

THESES
From the SECOND BOOK.

38. There are two motions of the stars, whereby they influence those inferiors, that is, under the *primum mobile*, and round the world; but familiarity is nothing more than a proportional influx, exhibited by the motion, as has been said. It necessarily follows, that there are two kinds of familiarities of the stars; the one under the Zodiac, the other round the world: these two kinds of familiarities are delivered by Ptolemy in several places; first, in the Almagest, Book viii, chap. 4, in these words:

" It remains now to write of their aspects : of these,
" therefore (excepting those that have a mutual forma-
" tion, and are thought immoveable, as when in a
" right line or triangular aspect, and others of the like),
" some are aspected to the planets only, and the Sun
" and the Moon, and parts of the Zodiac; some only
" to the Earth; some to the Earth, together with the
" planets and the Sun and Moon, or parts of the Zo-
" diac," &c. From which words, it is evident, that Ptolemy places these two kinds of familiarity, viz. in the Zodiac, and towards the Earth, that is, towards the world.

In the Quadripartite, in the beginning of the first book, he speaks thus: " There is one which is first,
" both in place and power, whereby we discover the
" configurations of the Sun and Moon, and motions
" of the stars, both towards themselves and the earth."

&c. Again, book first, " The stars are said to appear " in their proper forms, &c. when every one of them " are configurated with the Sun, or even the Moon, in " the same manner as their houses are with those of the " luminaries, as Venus in the Sexangular, configurated " with the luminaries, but the Vespertine with the " Sun," &c. Venus never has the ✶ to the ☉ in the Zodiac, as it can only be extended by it 48°; wherefore, unless any one will say that Ptolemy was ignorant of this (which is absurd), he must of course say, he spoke of the Sextile in the world. Likewise, in the third book, chapter of Aphetic places, he says, " As " we are first to suppose those Aphetic places, in which " it is absolutely necessary to find that which is desirous, " to obtain the jurisdiction of presiding over life, as round " the Horoscope, from the five parts first immerging " above the horizon, to the other twenty-five succeed- " ing; and that which conjoins these thirty parts with " dexter hexagonal rays, is called the place of the Good " Genius. Likewise with quadrangular, or the highest " part of heaven above the earth; and with trigonal, " &c. and from no other places." It is evident, Ptolemy was of this opinion.

39. The familiarity in the Zodiac is the proportionable influx of the stars by local motion, whereby they are able to effect a favourable conjunction. That these familiarities happen, and are powerful only among the stars which are there in motion, but that they are powerful to the cardinals and rest of the houses, we absolutely deny; for omitting other reasons, the stars move not to the cardinals, by advancing in the Zodiac; which

is the reason they do not effect any proportional distances to those cardinals, but the rays are no more than proportional distances, &c.

40. The familiarities of the stars in the world are a proportionate influx of the stars, agreeable to motion round the world; and they happen, and are efficacious in the proportional distances taken by a proportional division of the diurnal and nocturnal arcs, and no other way.

41. But because the stars have a mutual motion under the *primum mobile*, and round the world, it happens that they mutually contract both kinds of familiarity; as Ptolemy, in the place already cited, insinuates. But familiarities, taken in any other manner, and in any other circle, even in the equator (according to the opinion of Maginus), are entirely reprobated, and to be rejected.

42. These two kinds of familiarities being given, we say, that in every kind, neither more nor less than nine species are found, which are ☌, ✱, Q, □, △, Sqq, Bq, ☍, and parallels called by some Antiscions, which Kepler, by an exquisite and plain reason, has selected from their concording harmonies. Of these familiarities, the Sextile, Quintile, Trine, and Biquintile, are benign; the Quadrate, Sesquiquadrate, and Opposition, malign; the rest indifferent, with the fortunate stars good, and equally evil with the unfortunate.

43. The latitudinal stars do not commit all their virtual influence to the ecliptic, but preserve it among themselves; and their greater or lesser proximity to the ecliptic, adds not to nor lessens their power of acting: the ecliptic cannot act without the stars, but the stars

have their activity in themselves wholly independent of the ecliptic.

44. The stars alternately conjoined, do not acquire greater or lesser powers to act in a favourable conjunction, which falls out when another is found within the sphere of the other's activity, from a greater or less alternate proximity; but we only say, that their active virtues are the more or less conjoined. Under the name of the Sphere of Activity, we understand those that Ptolemy has placed, in Jupiter twelve degrees, in Venus eight degrees, &c.

45. But the stars which are found in the same partial longitude, we do not call conjoined in a favourable conjunction, if their alternate distance be greater by latitude, than is their sphere of activity; as ♀ with 8° of south latitude, is not favourably conjoined with ☿, having a northern latitude, though they are found in the same degree and minute of longitude; they may indeed be said to be conjoined by virtual conjunction, if they ascend or descend in the same horary circle, or cardinal, which is one of the species of mundane aspects.

46. The stars therefore should not be cardinally placed; nor even those that are fixed, with the other planets, if the latitude distance from the circles of position be greater than their sphere of activity; nor ought any difference to be made between the aspects of the natural constitution, and those produced by the motion of direction in preserving the latitude, as Argol thinks, there being equal reason in both cases.

47. In defining the intermediate rays, the half latitude in ✶ and △ is not to be observed, nor rejected in quar-

tile, as Blanolinus has taught, whom some authors imitate: but the latitude of both aspects are to be observed; for the rays are to be projected from the body of one to that of another, as it happens that these stars are found by latitude; so that in whatever latitude the planets are, they emit and receive the rays in proportional distances, taken with regard to longitude; as the ✳ in the distance of 60°, the □ in 90, &c. We would have this always observed, both in the daily motions of the planets, and in the directions and progressions, wherein the significators advance by their own real and natural way, on which they receive and emit the aspects; and in all the motions of the stars.

48. The fixed stars that are in a favourable conjunction with the planets, effect with them the other aspects, in the *primum mobile*, which otherwise have no effect. The same must be supposed of their familiarities in Mundo.

49. The rays in their kinds, from the brevity or longitude of the ascension of the signs, do not alter their nature from the fortunate to the unfortunate, or the contrary, as it is generally supposed by authors; yet it may be, that the quadrate in the Zodiac is either △ or ✳ in the world, or the contrary: but then every one has its effect according to its nature in both kinds, or it may be, they alternately moderate each other; but if these rays be found by the favourable stars, they doubtless produce happiness; if by the unfortunate, otherwise.

50. That which is vulgarly termed antiscions, we call parallels in the *primum mobile*; because we would have

them to be nothing else but parallels to the equator, as Ptolemy hints, " as they rise at an equal space of " time, and describe the same parallels," for which reason they are called the antiscions, or parallels in the *primum mobile*, and are equidistant from the equator; and if it be of the same country, it is called the primary parallel, or opposite if of a different country. The North commands, the South obeys; and they are taken from the table of declination, but parallel, in its physical sense, is an equal power of the influence of the stars from the *primum mobile*.

51. The twelve houses or mansions in heaven, authors divide several ways, but they all disagree. Rejecting the opinion of them all, we, with Ptolemy, distinguish them by the two temporal hours; for so it is, that there is proportional and equal division, not indeed of the heavenly and aerial space, but of the successive influx of the stars and houses; and the Mundane rays appear equal and proportional. But it is our opinion, that the division of the houses, by great circles passing through the common sections of the horizon and meridian, and the twelve equal divisions of the equator, which late authors make use of, are, of all, the most remote from and abhorrent to natural truth.

52. As many kinds of aspects as are found in the *primum mobile*, of which mention is already made; so many, we say, are found in the world. Wherefore, besides the usual ray, we likewise place in the world the parallels, which are an equipollence of the influx of the stars round the world.

53. Several resemblances are found between the mun-

dane parallels, and those in the *primum mobile*. (1.) The efficacy of the aspects in both consists in the parity of equal power, and equipollence of the active virtue. (2.) As in the *primum mobile*, they represent the same quantity of the ascension of the signs: for example, the signs ♓ and ♈, also ♊ and ♋, ascend in the same time; and with so much likeness do they exhibit the same quantity of ascension and descension in the world, that the eleventh house causes an ascension equal to the descension of the ninth, and the twelfth house equal to the second, &c. (3.) As the parallels in the *primum mobile* are equidistant from the cardinal points of the Zodiac, so are parallels in Mundo equidistant from the cardinal points of the world. (4.) As in the *primum mobile* they exhibit equal temporal hours, so in the world they exhibit equal temporal hours of the distances from the cardinals. (5.) The parallels in the *primum mobile* are at an equal distance from the pole of the world; the parallels in the world have the same polar elevation; and other resemblances, if required, will be found.

54. The efficacy of all the parallels, both in the *primum mobile*, and in the world, consists in the parity of the degree of quality, which the stars effect when found in the parallels; as it is plainly gathered from those which we mentioned in sect. 25; for by going through intension, and returning through remission, from the cardinal points, it happens, that they effect an equal degree of quality, as well under the *primum mobile* as round the world.

55. As for the *circles of position* in which the signi-

ficators are said to remain immoveable, and upon which they are to be directed, and their oblique ascension to be taken, those great circles passing through the common sections of the horizon and meridian, according to late authors, cannot be received; for this opinion is openly inconsistent with the precepts of Ptolemy; but those seats or parts of the circle are to be received, in which the stars, having a different declination, effect equal temporal hours. From what has been said, this conclusion is drawn, and agrees with the divisions of the houses, through the two temporal hours, and with the mundane rays. For this reason, we call such a seat the *horary situation of position.*

56. The dignity of the planets in the signs and their parts, which are called the bounds and terminations, have a real and natural foundation; to wit, the powerful aspect or proportional influxes to the moveable points in which the stars begin to produce the primary qualities. So that, according to those things we have explained, in the Philosophy of the Heavens, these are found to agree so well with the Egyptian boundaries, that they are highly deserving of admiration.

THESES

From the THIRD BOOK.

57. To speak physically, the stars are moved but by one motion, which is of the *primum mobile,* viz. from West to East; but for the easier explaining astronomical matters, we say in a simpler language, that the

stars are moved by a double motion; of which frequent mention has already been made; nay, more, we say there are many motions in the heavens, by which the stars change their aspects with respect to us.

58. The motion of direction is that which the Sun causes round the world every day, following that of the nativity, in whatever latitude, preordaining in power and virtue, the vital heat with its natural effects, viz. from every day to every year by Order: for it happens, that at the end of the first, after the natal day, when the Sun has returned to the same equal hour of the nativity, the parts of the *primum mobile*, with all the stars, have nearly gone through one degree of the equator; and the same happens every subsequent day: meanwhile the stars, as they advance, apply either by body or rays to the stations of the significators.

59. There is a double motion of direction. The *direct*, which Ptolemy calls *Actinobolium*, and tells us is formed toward the following signs; and the *converse*, which he terms *Horimeany*, and shews us it is formed towards the preceding places.

60. By the direct motion of direction, we direct the angles and all the moderators; but by a converse motion, the angles cannot be directed.

61. The angles only receive the rays in the world, but not the parallels, nor the rays in the Zodiac. The other significators, by a direct motion, receive the rays and parallels both in the Zodiac and in the world; but by a converse motion, the rays only, and parallels in the world, and by no means in the Zodiac.

62. By a converse direction, the significator, if it

descends from the Medium Cœli, strikes against the west, and all the rays that are between the significator and the west; and the rays are to be taken in the world; for in a converse direction, the rays have no place in the Zodiac, as has been said, but the hostile rays of the malignant that lie between, either cut off, or take away, the years from the number of direction to the west; as on the contrary, the rays of the benign either preserve or add the years according to Ptolemy's method, which we shall treat upon in the Canons.

63. It also happens, that when the significator and promittor are both hurried away together, by the rapt motion of the *primum mobile,* that they effect parallels in the world—equally powerful with all the other aspects.

64. In a direct direction, the significators advance by their own real way; as the Sun by the ecliptic, the Moon by her circle, upon which successively she alters her latitude, in proportion to her latitudinal motion. The same is to be said of all, when they become significators.

65. Authors are divided, as to measure in direction; for some take the whole degree of the equator, for all and every one of the years; others, the Sun's motion of the natal day: some, the Sun's mean motion; whilst many more vary in their computations. But we, to the first year after the natal, take that part of the equator in which the Sun ascends in a direct sphere, by the motion of the first day following the nativity; to the second year, that which ascends by the second day's motion; to the third, that which he ascends the third day after

the nativity; and thus of the other subsequent ones: for we would have the directional motion successive, and always formed towards the succeeding places, and the Sun's motion each day to be referred to, as the cause and rule to every year, as to their effects, in the same order and number.

66. But because the primary and principal motion of direction is derived from the motion of the Sun on the days following that of the nativity, as has been said, it consequently happens, that by some secondary means, the aspects that are made to the luminaries and angles on those days, jointly assist the significators of the primary directions; for this reason, we say, that the days whereon these aspects happen are very powerful in those years, which answer to those days, and on which they depend. From those motions, in preference to the rest, appears the true, real, and hitherto unknown, foundation of the critical or climactrical years; for the Moon, almost every seventh day, is placed in the critical place with respect to her place in the nativity; and (which is very important) experience wonderfully proves the truth of it; as may be seen in the examples extracted from Argol and Maginus. We call these motions the secondary directions, to distinguish them from the primary and principal; and we are of opinion, that Ptolemy, speaking of annual places, is to be understood of the places of those motions, and when of the menstrual, hints at the places of the progression.

67. The equal and uniform progressions which are commonly made use of, are supposed to be false; for there appears no reason or foundation to support them;

nay, all the professors with one voice affirm, they do not correspond with the effects. Wherefore, because we think the motions take their rise from the Moon's circuit towards the Sun, by which it pre-ordains in power and virtue, the radical humidity with its co-effects; so in like manner the motion of the direction originates from the Sun, by which it pre-ordains the vital heat; therefore the progressional motions are caused by the Moon in her circuits towards the Sun, and her returns to the same appearance, illuminations, or distance; consequently every one of the circuits, after the nativity, has a reference and respect to as the cause, of each year of the life of the native, and the Moon's progress, through each of the signs, to every month.

68. In the universal daily motions, the stars are continually agitating things of an inferior and material nature; but they produce surprising effects, when they arrive at the places of the moderators: and if they be radical, they are called natural transits. But at the places of the directions and progressions, they are called *ingresses;* for then, if the constellations of those motions be similar to the constitutions of the nativity, or the directions or progressions, they force to action the pre-ordained effects; for in this, and no other manner, the stars act upon inferior objects; that is, according as they find the next in power.

69. Of the ingresses some are active, others passive; the active are caused by the stars, which have an active virtue, when they enter the places of the directions and progressions of the moderators; for then they act upon the moderators. The passive are produced by the

universal moderators in the whole world, viz. by the ☉, ☽, angles, and part of Fortune, when they enter upon the places of the directions and progressions of the stars, whatever they are, which have an active virtue: but the active ingresses, if they be similar to the pre-ordained effects, cause them to influence; if dissimular, they either diminish or retard, as Ptolemy has it in the last chapter of Book IV. The passive ingresses administer nourishment towards the cooling and preserving the vital heat, and refreshing the radical moisture.

70. In like manner of transits; some are active, others passive: and hence it is evident how powerful are the accidental aspects of the luminaries and cardinal signs at their setting; and at other times of the natural accidents, arising from those fortunate or unfortunate stars, both of the nativity and of the place of the direction and progression, agreeably to which, as has been said, we are to reason on uncommon phenomena: for from the extension and intension of light, from the colour, diuturnity, apparition, situation, either in the world, or among the images of the starry orb, and other passions, are gathered their effects, and the provinces under their influence. New phenomena being found in nativities, experience has already shewn the wonders they have performed, chiefly as to the powers of the understanding, inventions, the performing of business, &c. And remember, reader, that art, or the human understanding, according to its ability and industry, is capable of changing, increasing, diminishing, and perverting, any influxes whatever of the stars; especially if the effects are considered, which the power of man is capable of attain-

ing; and therefore, they who are possessed of a more subtle and acute understanding, attain to greater things than those of duller capacities: but they who are entirely negligent, attain nothing. By all that has been said in these Theses, it will not be difficult to understand the questions and explanations of my Celestial Philosophy. And, finally, it is requisite that this doctrine of the stars should be attentively observed, not only in nativities, but also in decumbitures and judgments of critical days, and changes in the air, wherein you will find wonderful effects. For this doctrine is universal, and shews the manner in which the stars act upon these inferiors, whether compound or simple, &c.

Use of the Tables.

PART I.

FOR greater distinction and perspicuity, I have divided the following rules into four parts :—

The first contains the calculation of the places of the stars, in order to know their places under the *primum mobile*, in longitude and latitude, with the situation of each of them in the world, and the distance from the angles and houses, the right and oblique ascension, the horary times, the semi-diurnal and nocturnal arcs, and many things of this kind.

The second consists of methods to compute the directions of the significator to the aspects in the Zodiac, or *primum mobile*.

The third, the calculations of the directions to the aspects received in the world.

The fourth, the observations and precepts of the progressions, ingresses, transits, &c.

But, because all the tables confine their numbers to the whole degree, both of latitude and longitude, as often as the given place is in degrees and minutes, either by longitude or latitude, the proportional part corresponding with those minutes is to be taken with the given place, in both beyond the degree; concerning which, in the first Canon or rule, a method is explained for young beginners; and also, in the Canon of the use of the Sexagenary tables, and several of the Canons, that it might not be sought in vain whenever it happens that the proportional part is to be taken. It is, therefore, to be observed, that the method is always the same as in the first and fourteenth Canon; consequently, it is ever, and on all occasions, to be looked to and observed*.

Canon I.
To take the Declination of the Planets, and from the Declination the Longitude, in the Ecliptic.

The table of declinations contains six signs in the first part, and six in the last; those under the left columns have the degree of longitude descending, but those on the right, ascending: it is divided into two parts, viz. into north and south latitude, the degrees of which latitudes are seen under their denominations. It is likewise divided by the intermediate scale into north and south declination; that in the former place, i. e. above the scale, is north, and below the scale is the southern. If the given place, whose declination you want to know, has no latitude, seek for that under the column of latitude 0°, which is in the ecliptic; and if it be in the integral parts, as, for example, in ♌, 24° 0', under the column of latitude 0°, over against ♌, 24°, you will have the declination 13° 34': but if the given place be in degrees and minutes, suppose in 24° 10' of ♌, the proportional part belonging to the 10' must be taken from the difference, which is between the declina-

---

* For the Trigonometrical Precepts relative to the Canons, see the Appendix.

tion of 24° and 25° of ♌; the declination of 24° of ♌ is 13° 34'. But 25° gives 13° 14' declination: the difference between the two declinations is 20', wherefore, by the golden rule, I say, if the integral part, i. e. 60', gives 20', what will 10' give? Answer, 3', which is to be taken from the declination 13° 34', which is facing 24° of ♌; because the declination is less (but if it should be increased it ought to be added), and there remains for the declination of 24° 10' of ♌, 13° 31'. But if the given place has latitude, and is in the integral degrees both for longitude and latitude, at one view you will have its declination; viz. in the common angle. Suppose, then, the given place 24° of ♌ with 2° north, in the common angle, you will have the declination 15° 27'. But if it be according to longtitude in degrees and minutes, and for latitude in the integral degree, the proportional part is to be taken from the difference of the declination of the greater and lesser degree of longitude, between which is the given minute, under the column of the said latitude.

Let the place be in 24° 10' of ♌, with 2° north, under the column north, latitude 2° to the longitude 24° 0', the declination is 15° 27'; and to the longitude 25° 0', under the same column, the declination is 17° 7'; the difference of those declinations is 20', from which for the 10', 3' is to be subtracted, as before. If the given place be by longitude in the integral degree, and latitude in degrees and minutes, the proportional part must be taken from the difference of the declination of the greater and lesser degree of latitude, between which is the given minute, and to the same longitude; as if the given place be 24° of ♌, with north latitude 2° 51′, under the latitude 2°, the declination is 15° 27′; under the latitude 3°, the declination is 16° 24′, and the difference is 57′; from which, for the 51′, will be found by the golden rule to give 48′ to be added, because the declination is increased by latitude. Lastly, if the given place be by longitude and latitude in degrees and minutes, as in the nativity of Sebastian, King of Portugal, the Moon's place, according to longitude, as in 24° 10′ of ♌, with 2° 51′ north, the proportional part must be taken doubly; wherefore, subtracting the 3′ from 15° 27′, there remains 15° 24′; and by adding the 48′, there remains the Moon's declination 16° 12′. To take the proportional part, you have the logistical logarithms, or sexagenary table: its use is shewn in the fourteenth Canon, though the golden rule may likewise serve; but this method of calculating is to be rightly understood; for in all the tables it would be too tedious always to repeat it. In the scale which divides the northern declination from the southern, care should be taken as often as it happens to pass through the scale, from one part to the other, either in longitude or latitude, to have the declination conjoined, and there will be a very great difference; from which, subtracting the proportional part, if it be less than the declination of the former angle which belongs to the integral degrees, either the longitude or latitude is to be taken from the declination of that angle, and there will remain the declination of the same denomination; but if, on the contrary, the proportional part taken be greater, the former must be taken from the latter, and the remaining declination changes the denomination.

Let the Moon be in 9° 10′ of ♎, with latitude 4° north, I add the 6′ to the 18′, and the difference is 24′; from which, to the 10′, 4′ is due: these, as they are less than 6′, I subtract from the 6′, and there remains the declination 2′ north. Suppose the Moon in 9° 40′ of ♎, from the difference for the 40′, 16′ is due; which, as they are more than 6′, I take 6′ from the 16′, and there remains the Moon's declination 0° 10′ south; but if the Moon in this case should have 4° 30′ north, I add 18′ to the 38′, which are under 4° and 5°, and the difference is 56′; from which, for the 30′, 28′ are due: from these, as they are more than 10′, I subtract the 10′, and there remains the declination 0° 18′ north. Again, if they are less, suppose 5′, I should take these 5′ from 10′, and the declination is 0° 5′ south. The given declination is brought back to the degree in the ecliptic in this manner, however, if it be not greater than 23° 28′, for otherwise it would fall out of the ecliptic. Under the column of latitude 0° 0′, that is, of the declination of the ecliptic, let the given declination be sought for, and above the scale if northern, but below if southern: but if it should be found even to its minutes, the degrees of the signs in the ecliptic corresponding with it are those which are placed opposite on both sides; but if the minutes of the given declination are not expressed, the proportional part is to be taken, instead of the minutes that are wanting to be added or subtracted from the degree in the ecliptic, &c. in this manner:—Let the declination be south 7° 28′ under the scale, and in the column of latitude 0°, I find it opposite to 19° of ♎, or in 11° of ♓, therefore it answers to these degrees. In the nativity of Sebastian, King of Portugal, the declination of ♄ is 7° 47′, which is not expressed in the table; but I take the next less, 7° 28′, then the next greater is 7° 51′; the difference of these is 23′: the declination of ♄ exceeds the less by 19′. I then ask, if the whole difference of 23′ give 60′ of longitude, how many will 19′ give? Answer 50′, which are to be added to the 19° of ♎; so that ♄'s declination corresponds with 19° 50′ of ♎, or with 10° 10′ of ♓: the same happens if the proportional part be taken differently; for the next greater declination exceeds ♄'s declination by 4′, for which the proportional part is 10′, which are added to the 10° of ♓, or the 20° of ♎, from the place of the ecliptic, as before.

Canon II.

The Ascensional Difference.

In the upper part of the table of ascensional differences look for the Pole's elevation in the latitude of the country, and in the first column the declination of the given place; which, if it be with the integral degrees, the ascensional difference required is placed in the common angle; but if the declination be with degrees and minutes, then take the proportional part, as in Canon I. As if the given declination be 12°, at the Pole's elevation 42°, the ascensional difference is placed in the common angle, 11° 2′; but if the declination be given 12° 25′, the ascensional difference at declination 13°, is 12°; wherefore the difference between this and the former is 58′, from which 24′ is due, i. e. to be taken in their room, 25′ to be added, and the ascensional difference becomes 11° 26′.—*Another way:* If you have already by you the tables of oblique ascension of the given place, and the right ascension, subtract the less from the greater, and the remainder is the ascensional difference. In like manner, if you have already the semi-diurnal or nocturnal arc, subtract it from 90°, if it be less; if greater, subtract 90° therefrom, and the remainder is the ascensional difference.

Canon III.
Semi-Diurnal or Nocturnal Arcs.

The semi-diurnal or nocturnal arcs are thus obtained; the semi-diurnal in degrees and minutes, by adding the ascensional difference to 90; when a star has north declination, by subtracting it from 90, when south. On the contrary, the semi-nocturnal is found by subtracting the ascensional difference from 90°, when a star declines to the north; and by adding it to 90, when the star declines to the south; for either the remainder or sum will be the semi-nocturnal or diurnal arc in degrees and minutes. If the declination above given, viz. 12° 25', be northern, the semi-diurnal arc will become 101° 26', by adding the ascensional difference 11° 26' to 90°: if the declination be south, the semi-nocturnal will be the same; if the declination be north, and subtracted from 90, there will remain the semi-nocturnal arc 78° 34'; but if it be southern, the semi-diurnal will be the same. If you would reduce the semi-diurnal or semi-nocturnal arc into hours and minutes (see Canon XI.), you will likewise have the semi-diurnal and semi-nocturnal arc of the places in the ecliptic from the tables of semi-diurnal and nocturnal arcs. At your Pole's elevation, if the sign of the given degree be in the upper part, look for its degree in the descendant degree placed to the left; but if it be at the lower part, in the ascendant degree, which is to the right, and in the common angle of meeting, you will have the arc required, whose denomination you will perceive under the very sign, whether diurnal or nocturnal. And remember, if there are minutes, to take the proportional parts; but if it be denominated semi-diurnal, and you want the semi-nocturnal, or the contrary, subtract the arc found from 12 hours, and the remainder is the other arc required. In the nativity of Charles V. the Sun is in 14° 30' of ♓ : at the Pole's elevation 52°, I find the sign ♓ in the lower part; wherefore, to the 14 ascendant degrees, I take in the common angle the semi-nocturnal arc, 6^h 33'; but because the Sun has above 30', I subtract one minute, and there remains the semi-nocturnal arc, 6^h 32': whereas, if I want the semi-diurnal arc, I take 6^h 32' from 12^h, and there remains 5^h 28'. Of the latitudinal planets, provided their declination does not exceed 23° 28', the said semi-diurnal or nocturnal arc, in hours and minutes, may be had thus: After reducing their declination to the longitude of the ecliptic, in the manner explained in Canon I. with this degree of the ecliptic, I enter the table of semi-diurnal arcs, and take out the hours and minutes corresponding thereto, in the manner we have mentioned, &c. as in the nativity of Sebastian. Saturn hath declination 7° 47', and is reduced to 19° 50' of ♎, or 10° 10' of ♓, whose semi-nocturnal arc at the Pole's elevation 40°, is 6° 27'.

Canon IV.
The Horary Times.

These may be taken several ways; first, the diurnal from the partition of the semi-diurnal arc in degrees and minutes taken by six; the nocturnal from the partition of the semi-nocturnal, likewise by six, which six temporal hours the cardinal signs of the world are mutually distant: let the semi-diurnal arc be 104° 45′, the 104° divided by 6 make 17, and there remains 2; which, reduced to minutes, and these added to the other 45, makes 165; which, when divided by 6, the quotient is 27′, and makes the horary times 17° 27′ diurnal. Secondly, the horary times of the parts of the ecliptic are collected in the proper tables; as to the pole's elevation 45 to 15° of ♉ in the ecliptic, the horary times diurnal are 17° 51′. Thirdly, the semi-diurnal arc taken in hours and minutes, if multiplied by two and a half, is converted into the diurnal horary times; and, in like manner, the semi-nocturnal arc into the nocturnal horary times; as the semi-diurnal arc of 15 of ♉, at the Pole 45°, is 7^h 9′, which, multiplied by 2 and a half, becomes 17° 52′. Fourthly, of the planets having latitude, let their given declination be brought back to the ecliptic in the manner as explained in Canon I, and with that degree of the ecliptic in the table of horary times, they may be taken as above-mentioned; but if the planet has a greater declination than 23° 28′, the horary times cannot be taken any other way, except by the help of the ascensional difference. But if you have the diurnal horary times, and want the nocturnal, or the contrary, subtract your sum from 30, and the rest will be the horary times required: as in the given example, I subtract 17° 51' from 30, and there remains the horary times nocturnal 12° 9'.

Canon V.
Right Ascension.

This you will take from the proper table; and if the given place be in the ecliptic, so as to have no latitude, look for the right ascension under the column 0° 0', and in the common angle you have it, by taking the proportional part for the minutes of longitude, if there are any, as in Canon I. In the nativity of Charles V, the Sun is in 14° 30' of ♓; the right ascension of 14 of ♓, is 345° 16'; for the 30', 28' are due, to be added, and the Sun's right ascension becomes 345° 44'. If the given place be not in the ecliptic, but has latitude from it, and is in the integral degrees, both according to longitude and latitude in the common angle, you will have the right ascension: but if there are likewise minutes, let the proportional part be taken, as in Canon I.

Canon VI.
Right Distance.

To know the distance by right ascension of the stars in a right circle, subtract the lesser from the greater, that is, the right ascension of the preceding place from the right ascension of the following, and the remainder is the right distance required. And this caution is to be observed, that as the right ascension is an arc of a circle, numbered in degrees of the equator, which are 360, commencing at the beginning of the sign ♈, and terminating with the end of ♓, when it happens that the right ascension of the preceding place is less than a circle, as in ♓, ♒, &c. and the following place greater than the beginning of the circle, as ♈, ♉, &c. a whole circle, or 360, must be added to the right ascension of the following places, and from their sum subtract the right ascension of the preceding place. Let the 18° of ♒ be upon the Medium Cœli, whose right ascension is 320° 30′, and the following place be 15° of ♈, whose right ascension is 13° 48′; you cannot subtract 320° 30′ from 13° 48′, unless you add 360°, which makes the sum 373° 48′; from which subtracting the 320° 30′, there remains 53° 18′, the right distance required. And this caution is to be observed in all subtractions of ascensions, whether right or oblique, and whether in degrees and minutes, or hours and minutes.

Canon VII.
Oblique Ascension and Descension,

Will be had by subtracting the ascensional difference from the right ascension of the star, if its declination be northern; but, if south, by adding the ascensional difference to the right ascension, and the sum, or remainder, is the oblique ascension. Lastly, if it has no declination, that right ascension becomes oblique ascension. On the contrary, the oblique descension will be found, by adding; if the declination be northern, by subtracting; if south, to or from the right ascension. Example: to 1° 23′ of ♉, the declination is 12°; its ascensional difference at the Pole's elevation 42°, as we have mentioned in Canon II, is 11° 2'; the right ascension is 29° 13'; but as the declination is northern, subtract the ascensional difference 11° 2' from the right ascension, and there remains the oblique ascension 18° 11'. Now, 1° 23' of ♏, has the same declination and ascensional difference, which is to be added to the right ascension 209° 13', because the declination is southern, and the oblique ascension is 220° 15'; besides, there are extant many tables of oblique ascensions by which they may be gained; as those of Argoll's, and several others.

Canon VIII.

To reduce the Right Ascension, or Oblique, to the Degree of Longitude in the Ecliptic, or to any other Place of Latitude or Longitude.

Look for the given right ascension of the ecliptic in the body of the table of right ascensions under the column of latitude 0° 0', and you will have the places in the ecliptic, corresponding to it, by taking the proportional part for the minutes, if there be any. But if, when the right ascension of a latitudinal planet is given, you are desirous to know to what longitude in the ecliptic it corresponds, look for that right ascension under the column of the given latitude, and in the column of longitude you will have the degree of the ecliptic corresponding to it: as, for example, the right ascension of 157° 48' in the ecliptic answers to 6 of ♍; but if the right ascension 157° 48' be, for example, for the Moon, in latitude 5° southern, it answers to 8 of ♍; but with this caution, because the Moon then mediates the mid-heaven with 6° of ♍, but has the rays in the Zodiac to the other planets from 8° of ♍. In like manner you must reduce the oblique ascension to the ecliptic from the table of the oblique ascensions of the Pole's elevation; as the oblique ascension of the ecliptic 168° 9′ to the Pole's elevation 45° is reduced to 21 of ♍ in the ecliptic; but, if the oblique ascension be of the Moon in south latitude 5°, I say it is reduced to 19° of ♍ with latitude, as is there posited, but with the same distinction; for then the Moon co-ascends in the same circle of position with 21° of ♍, but has the rays to the other planets in 19° of ♍. This revocation is of service, in order to know what longitude and declination the significator encompasses by the direction, and consequently with what planets it contracts the aspect when in the Zodiac, which is, by adding the arc of direction to its right ascension, if it be found in the right circle in the nativity; or to the oblique ascension, if elsewhere.

Canon IX.

Distances from the Cusps of the Angles or other Houses.

The distance from any cardinal sign or house (that is) from their cusp, will be easily obtained after the ascension of that house or cardinal sign, and likewise the ascension of a star is given; for subtracting the lesser, which is the preceding place, from the greater, which is the following, the remainder will be the distance of the star from that house or cardinal sign; but if the house or angle be in the descending part of heaven, taking the descensions of the house, and the same of the star, or the ascensions of the opposite places, and subtracting, in like manner, the lesser from the greater, the remainder will be the distance required. The preceding place is that which is in the lesser degrees; the succeeding in the greater: as the beginning of ♈ precedes, the beginning of ♊ follows; and thus in all. The distances of the stars from the cusps of the houses may be taken without the oblique ascensions; but the right ascension is to be known, together with the semi-diurnal and nocturnal arcs, or the temporary hours; for after taking their primary distance from the culminations, the secondary distances are made at the cusps of the houses; and the ninth and eleventh houses are distant from the meridian, by the double horary times, or the third part of the semi-diurnal arc; the eighth and twelfth, by double gemination, &c. Wherefore, the primary and secondary distance of a star from the meridian being given, always subtract the lesser from the greater, and you will have the star's distance from the given house; by primary distance I mean that which the planets have in a nativity; but the secondary, that which they acquire by direction. There are several examples in the nativities which are shewn farther on.

Canon X.

To describe a Figure of the Heavens.

This we are taught by almost all professors, but in a very different manner; therefore be pleased to take here a very concise method. If the italic hour be given, let the astronomical be made, by adding the semi-diurnal arc. In the tables of houses at the Pole's elevation given, let the place of the Sun be looked for, upon the cusp of the tenth house, and let the time from noon be taken, which is found on the back of it, and added to the astronomical hours found above. Finally, with this sum, when it is found in the same table of houses, directly opposite, will appear the signs and degrees which belong to the six eastern houses, taking the proportional part, when there is occasion. Of the other six western houses, the cusps are described with the opposite signs, and the same degree as the opposite houses.

Another way.—The italic hour being given, let the gree opposite to the Sun of the given day be sought for in the ascendant, and let the time from noon, which shall be found there, be added to the given hour; when this sum is found, let the division of the houses, directly opposite, be taken, &c. From this same sum of the hours, subtract the time from noon found at the degree of the ☉'s place on the same day, constituted in the tenth house, and there will remain the astronomical hour; or, in other words, *post meridian*, as in the nativity of Charles V. The given italic hour is $10^h\ 11'$; which place in the horoscope is 14° of ♏, on the back of which the time from noon is $4^h\ 29'$, to which add $10^h\ 11'$, and the sum is $14^h\ 40'$; which, when I find in the tables of houses, I take their divisions, &c. Again, I place the Sun in the medium cœli, and there I take $23^h\ 1'$, from which reject $14^h\ 40'$, first adding the 24^h (as we have said in Canon VI), there remain the astronomical hours $15^h\ 39'$ *post meridian*.

To place the planets in the figure, let the astronomical hour be equated; first, by the table of equation of natural days, then for the difference of meridians, in the manner they are noted. The places of the planets are very easily calculated to the equated hour, from the Sexagenary table, in this manner:—In the first column on the left hand, to the number 24, for 24 hours, look in the body of the table for the planet's motion; and, directly under the same column, at the given hour, you will have its motion, to be added to the place of the same, at noon; or to be subtracted, if the planet be retrograde, as in the example of Charles V. The diurnal motion of the Moon is 14° 39', which, opposite to the 24th number, I find, in the body of the table Sexagenary, under the 37th column; but because there they do not go so far as minutes, I take the proportional part, and I find it corresponds under 36° 37': with the 15th hour, under the 36° I take 9°; and, for the 37' from the difference which is there made, I add 9'; again, for the 39' of the given hour, I look under 37, and, at 39, in the common angle, I take 24' to be added, and this makes all the Moon's motion 9° 33', to be added to its place, calculated for noon; but as the ☽ is in 27° 12' of ♐, its place immerges to the given hour, 15ʰ 39' in 6° 45' of ♑. As for the other planets, when their motion exceeds 72', whereas in the Sexagenary table at 24, the greater number is 72, make use of half the diurnal motion of the planet, and the product of the given hour must be doubled: as the diurnal motion of ♀ is 75', I use half this number 37, and I find opposite 24, under the column 93; wherefore, opposite 15, under the same column, I take 24', which, doubled, make 48; or use the geminated hours, as 48, for 24'. In the body of the table, I find the

PRIMUM MOBILE. 45

motion of ☿ 75, under the column 94; but opposite 31, for the 15ʰ 39′, I take 48 or 49, as before. In like manner are the latitudes calculated, by reducing the parts to minutes, and looking on the sides for days, and in the body for the difference of latitudes, &c. As the latitude of ☿ to the 20th of February is 3° 16′, to the first day of March it is 2° 11′, the difference is 65′ for the 10 days; from which, for the 4 days, are produced 26, to be subtracted: but, because the Sexagenary table to number 10 is not extended above 30, I look for it at the triplicate of 10, which is 30, and I find 65 under 130; but, at the triplicate 4, *i. e.* 12 under 130, I find 26 as above: I look for 10 at the quadriplicate, which is 40, and I find it either under 97 or 98; for in the one it is deficient, in the other it exceeds in the minutes 20 seconds; and at the quadriplicate 4, *i. e.* 16 under either of the same columns, I find 26 as above. The *Part of Fortune* is placed according to the Moon's distance from the Sun. And you must observe, what rays the Moon has to the Sun, for the latter ought to have the same, and with the same excess or deficiency as the ⊕ to the horoscope. As the Moon is to the Sun, so is ⊕ to the horoscope; and as the Sun is to the horoscope, so is the Moon to the *Part of Fortune;* as in the nativity of Charles V, the Moon applies to the ultimate Sextile of the Sun, but with a deficiency of 7° 45′: I subtract the 7° 45′ from 5° 34′ of ♏, the ultimate Sextile to the horoscope, and the ⊕ is placed in 28° 9′ of ♎. But the partitions of the houses may also be made by the right and oblique ascensions to the polar elevations of the houses; first, you are to bring back the given hour to the degrees of the equator: if the given hour be *Italic*, add these degrees to the oblique ascension of the Sun's opposite place, and the sum will be the oblique ascension of the horoscope of the figure to be erected: if the given hour be astronomical to the Sun's right ascension, add the degrees to which you have reduced the astronomical hours, and the sum will be the right ascension of the medium cœli: the ascensions of the other houses are made by constantly adding 30° for the ascensions of every one of them; and from the tables of oblique ascensions, to the elevation of the houses, are had the degrees of the Zodiac, to be placed in these houses. Finally, directly under the horoscope, describe the latitude of the planets, the declination, horary times, right ascension, &c. Likewise, to every house, draw the Pole's elevation and oblique ascension, which you may do by adding 30 degrees to the right ascension of the *medium cœli;* for the eleventh, likewise add 30, and you will have the oblique ascension of the twelfth, and so for the rest. The elevation of the Poles of the houses is shewn in the proper table, and also in the tables of the houses.

Canon XI.

To convert Hours and Minutes of Time into Degrees and Minutes of the Equator; and, vice versa, the Degrees and Minutes of the Equator into Hours and Minutes.

This is too obvious to require any explanation.

Canon XII.

On the Circle of Position, or the Pole's Elevation of any Planet.

Under the circle of position, later authors are to be understood of the nature of that passing through the common sections of the horizon and meridian; and upon such circles they direct their moderators, and constitute the intervals of the houses. But how frivolous and remote from natural truth this opinion is, may be seen in my Celestial Philosophy, where it is largely and plainly demonstrated; but it is also contrary to the doctrine of the *Prince of Mathematicians*, Ptolemy, who has transmitted to posterity this universal science, founded only on the most sublime principles of Philosophy, which, I think, innumerable examples fully prove. Those who refuse to follow him, doubtless proceed through confused ways, which have no claim to the least commendation whatever. I desire no other guides but Ptolemy and Reason. I have no idea of circles of position which are directed through the common sections of the horizon and meridian, but those that are described by the proportional distances of the stars towards the angles; and we may, by means of a very easy method, know the Pole's elevation upon the Ptolemaic circle of any star whatever. In the first place, let the quantity of the house be taken; which the star, whose polar elevation is sought for, measures by lustration. This quantity of the house may be had several ways: (1.) The horary conditionary times of that star, when doubled, produce the quantity of the starry house. (2.) The third part of the semi-diurnal arc of the star, is the measure of the house above the earth; of the semi-nocturnal, under the earth. (3.) The distance of a star from the preceding house, joined with the distance of the same star from the succedent, taking the distance as mentioned in Canon IX; I say, these distances, added together, produce the space or quantity of the house. I then let the difference of the Pole's elevation be taken, which is between the succedent and preceding houses, as before, between which the star is found by the table of the poles of houses; then let the distance of the star be taken, either from the succedent or preceding houses, as before mentioned. (4.) By the Golden Rule. *Quere*, If the whole quantity of the starry house give the polar difference between the succedent and preceding houses, what part of the difference will the distance of the star from either house give? Let the fourth number, which is the product, if the Pole's elevation be augmented by the house from which the distance of the star is taken, be added to the house's elevation; if diminished, subtracted; and the remainder or sum will be the polar elevation of that star, of which many exampl follow in the nativity of Francis, the first King of France, Cardinal Salvatius, &c. Here we must be cautious, because the polar elevations of the houses are not increased or diminished uniformly; that is, for example, to the latitude of the country $45°$, the polar elevation of the eleventh house is increased $18° 50'$; the twelfth house is augmented $15°$ nearly, and the horoscope is increased $11°$, so that you see they have no equal increase. When a star is about the mean distance from the centres of the preceding and succeeding houses, if any one desire to have a true polar elevation of that star, he ought to avoid this inequality; as, suppose the star to be in the middle distance from the *medium cœli* to the eleventh, where, by the golden rule, the pole increases 9° 25′, which is the half of 18° 50′, to which the eleventh house is elevated. A star in this case hath, in reality, a polar elevation greater than this half, and the reason is, because the difference of the polar elevation is always diminished from the *medium cœli* to the horoscope; and, therefore, in the tenth house, the polar elevation has a greater augmentation in the first moiety than in the latter. The difference of the Pole's of the houses are these, 11, 15, and 19: if we divide 11 into 5 and 6, but 15 into 7 and 8; lastly, 19 into 9 and 10, the division will appear very agreeable to reason, viz. into 5, 6, 7, 8, 9, and 10, which are the difference of the Pole's elevation in the middle of each of the houses; wherefore, to the given star placed in the middle distance from the culmination to the 11th, you will have the Pole's elevation 10. But the caution is only to be observed when a star stops about the mean distance from the cusps, where, first taking the proportional parts, by the golden rule, near one degree, as mentioned above, should afterwards be added or subtracted; but, when it remains about the cusps of the houses, it may be entirely neglected, as it makes but little difference.

Canon XIII.

The Distances of the Aspects both in the Zodiac and World, and the Degrees in them.

In the Zodiac the Sextile has 60°, the Quintile 72°, the Square 90°, the Trine 120°, the Sesquiquadrate 135°, the Biquintile 144°, and the Opposition 180°.

But because every ray is a circle, whose centre is the star projecting the ray, excepting the opposition, doubtless every ray cuts the whole latitude of the Zodiac; wherefore, whenever it happens that another star passes through that ray's section, whatever latitude the other star may have, it receives the ray, and mutually projects the same from that section to another star; and not only from the point of latitude which this star has there, but this manner of receiving and projecting the rays happens in the daily motion of the stars in the directions, progression, and all the motions of the stars; and indeed from the great difference of latitude of such stars as are mutually aspected, there follows some difference of the ray's longitude, but of a very few minutes, which may be omitted; however, those who wish for further investigation, may consult Regiomontanus and Maginus.

At the *medium cœli*, the stars have their SEXTILE from the cusp of the eighth and twelfth houses.

QUINTILE,

When their distance from it is four of the five parts of the semi-diurnal arc, or six parts of five of the *.

QUADRATE,

From the eastern and western points, that is, from the ascendant and seventh.

Trine,

From the centre of the second and sixth houses.

Sesquiquadrate,

From the mean distance between the east and the *imum cœli*, and between this and the west.

Biquintile,

When their distance from the *imum cœli* is two of the five parts of the semi-nocturnal arc, or three of the five parts from east to west below the earth.

Opposition,

From the *imum cœli*.

At the horoscope, the stars have the sextile from the cusp of the eleventh and third houses.

Quintile,

When the distance from the east is four of the five parts of the semi-diurnal arc, or nocturnal; or in other words, when they are distant one part out of five of the above arc from the *medium cœli*, or *imum cœli*, towards the east.

Quadrate,

At the *Medium* and *Imum Cœli*.

Trine,

From the cusp of the ninth and fifth.

Sesquiquadrate,

From the middle distance between the *medium cœli* and west, and between the west and *imum cœli*.

Biquintile,

When the distance is two out of five parts from the west above and below the earth. To the Sun and Moon, existing in the cusp of any house, the rest of the planets have their rays in the world in like manner as towards the angles; that is, if they abide in the cusp of the ninth house, they have

The Sextile,

From the cusp of the eleventh and west.

Quintile,

When the distance from the luminary is beyond the Sextile a fifth part, from a double gemination of the horary times, and diurnal if a star remains above the earth; nocturnal, if below; for the Quintile has twelve parts more than the ✶, which are the fifth part of it.

Quadrate,

From the cusp of the twelfth and sixth houses.

Trine,

From the east and cusp of the fifth.

Sesquiquadrate,

When their distance beyond the Trine is one change in the horary times, in like manner conditionary, *i. e.* nocturnal; I may say, when their distance beyond the Quadrate is the half of the semi-nocturnal arc, because both the Sesquiquadrates to the cusp of the ninth house fall below the earth.

Biquintile,

When they are distant beyond the Trine twice the fifth part of the nocturnal Sextile, *i. e.* when taken below the earth, or when their distance from the opposition of the luminary is two of the five parts of the semi-nocturnal arc; and in like manner, in whatever other place they are found, whether luminaries, or any other star, the rays in the world are taken by a proportional division of the semi-nocturnal and diurnal arc.

Parallels *in the* Zodiac,

Which are commonly called antiscions, are circles equidistant from the equator, and are taken from the equal declination of the stars of what latitude soever, which, if it be of the same name, are called equal in dignty; if one circle be northern, the other southern, the former is said to be of authority, but the latter in subjection.

Parallels *in the* World,

Are distances equally proportional from one of the cardinal houses in both distances; though, indeed, they appear to have distances equally proportionate to all the cardinals; as the eleventh with the ninth and third; and they are taken by a proportion of the semi-diurnal and nocturnal arcs of the stars.

Canon XIV,

Contains the use of the Sexagenary table, to find the part proportional, and is shewn by examples in other parts of this work, to which we refer the reader.

Canon XV.

The Use of the Logarithms*.

We have placed the logarithms of absolute numbers, because in that manner of Ptolemean direction, which we

---

* N. B. Instead of the common logarithms, use Dr. Maskelyne's Proportional Logarithms.

follow, they are of very great service in exhibiting the fourth proportional number; therefore the three numbers being given, whether of parts or hours, if they are minutes, let each of them be reduced to minutes, adding them as they are disposed in their places; then take the logarithms of the 2d and 3d number, add them together; from this sum subtract the logarithm of the first, and look for the remainder in the middle of the table; opposite to which, take the number for the fourth required, which divide by 60, and with the remainder you will have parts or hours with their minutes. For example; let the numbers be given, the first 95° 25′, the second 35° 45′, the third 100° 15′, reduced to minutes are 5725′—2145′—6615′; the logarithm of the first 3.75778, of the second 3.33143, of the third 3.82053. I add the second and third together, and I make the sum 7.15196, from which I subtract the first, and there remains the logarithm 3.39418, answering to the number 2478, which, reduced to degrees, makes 41° 18′, the fourth number required. But because the logarithm consists of eight figures, the six first of these are sufficient for this purpose, and it seemed not good to rescind the rest, by reason of other advantages resulting from them, you may only make use of the six first, provided you think proper, for it is of little use or consequence; but if the seventh figure be five or greater, you should add unity to the sixth figure, which will be your last; and if the seven figures be 4, 3, 2, 1, 0, omit it entirely. In the given example of the first number 5725, the logarithm of eight figures is 3.7577755, I leave out the two last figures 55, and add the unit to the sixth, which make it 3.75778. Observe also, that the logarithms are easier collected by taking two figures for every change; thus first collect 37, then 57, lastly 78.

Canon XVI.

To equate the *Arc of Direction*.

Add the arc of direction to the right ascension of the natal Sun, look for this sum in the table of right ascensions under the ecliptic, and take the degree and minute of longitude corresponding with that sum: then in the best Ephemeris reckon in how many days and hours the Sun from the day and hour of birth, has arrived at that degree and minute. The number of days indicate as many years; every two hours over, reckon a month.- See examples in the following nativities.

PART II.

To calculate the Directions to the Aspects in the Zodiac.

I HAVE divided the Canons into four parts, for greater distinction and perspicuity, that I might not always repeat the same thing under any other title than that of Canons, that is, either in the Zodiac, or in Mundo; wherefore, in this SECOND PART, know, that I treat of the Directions to the Aspects in the Zodiac only; or, in other words, in the *primum mobile*, and of no other. But what the aspects in the *primum mobile* are, and what in the world, together with the cause of this true distinction, I have very plainly demonstrated, from natural principles, in my Celestial Philosophy; for the aspects in the *primum mobile*, which happen between the stars, are mutually independent of the horizon of the country, by reason of their motions in the same *primum mobile;* under which they are in the same situation in all countries and cities of the world, with the difference only of time and polar elevation. The aspects in the world are made dependent on the horizon of every country, because of the motion of the stars towards the world, and cardinal houses. But, as it may be disputed, whether it is proper to say, that the significator is directed to the promittors, and their rays, or the promittors and rays to the significator, know, there is a double motion of directions, direct and converse. I say, that in the direct direction the significator remains immoveable in the mundane situation, always under the same Pole's elevation, but advances under the same *primum mobile* from its more western parts, to the more eastern; the occourses, however, remain immoveable under the *primum mobile*, but are moved with a rapt and universal motion from the eastern quarter of the world to the more western, or the place of the significators. Again, I say, that in the converse motion of direction, the significator remains immoveable under the *primum mobile*, but is moved by an universal rapt motion from the eastern quarter of the world to the more western, towards the place of the promittors in the world; but the occourses remain always immoveable in their mundane situation, or polar elevation. It follows, therefore, that both may have a name, but with a distinction; and, I will say, indifferently, according as I should have occasion to mention them. Finally, as experience in every place ever convinces us, that besides the reason I have advanced in the Philosophy of the Heavens, the aspects of the star to the luminaries and cardinal houses, which happen every day after the nativity, have a very strong influence, viz. from every day to every year, whence, above the rest, are derived the climactrical years, as I shall shew afterwards; and it is likely that Ptolemy, in the last Chapter of Book IV, under the name of Annual Places, means the places of those motions. I thought proper

K

to give these motions the name of Secondary Directions; but the others, which we are going to mention, to characterize under that of Primary Directions.

Canon XVII.

To direct the Sun, being near the Mid-heaven, to the Conjunctions, and all Rays.

The Sun is accounted near the cusp of the house when he is not more than 3° distant. First, take the Sun's right ascension, then that of the aspect, whether it be the conjunction or opposition, or any other intermediate ray, by always taking the right ascensions, and omitting the latitude in this case, even in the conjunction and opposition, if, however, the promittor hath not greater latitude than the orb of his light (for this is the difference between the zodiacal and mundane aspects; the former being caused by a greater proximity to the greater distance of the stars between each other, and upon their real way in the Zodiac, the greater proximity happening in the same partile longitude, though their distance and difference be according to latitude, if the distance of latitude in the conjunction and opposition, as I have said, be not greater than the sphere of activity of light of the stars; for if it be greater, the conjunction is not powerful, nor the opposition in the Zodiac, as I have demonstrated in the Celestial Philosophy). Lastly, subtract the Sun's right ascension from that of the aspects, and the remainder is the arc of direction. *Example:* In the nativity of George Aldobrandinus, the ☉'s right ascension is 215° 58', but the right ascension of Venus, taken in the ecliptic, is 262° 8′, from which, subtracting the Sun's right ascension, there remains the arc of direction, 46° 10′.

Canon XVIII.

To direct the Sun, when found near the Cusp of the Horoscope, or Seventh House, to the Conjunctions, and all the Rays.

Take the Sun's oblique ascension, if in the ascendant under the latitude of the country, or the descension, if in the seventh, or the oblique ascension of the opposite place; then the ascension or descension of the place of the aspect under the same Pole, leaving out the latitude in this case, provided that, in conjunction and opposition, the latitude of the planet does not exceed its orbs, as before mentioned, and take the Sun's oblique ascension from that of the ray, and the remainder is the arc of direction required.

Canon XIX.

To direct the Sun, when found above the Earth, far distant from the Cardinal Houses, to the Conjunction, and all the Rays.

If the Sun remains above the earth, and his distance from the cardinal house is more than 3° from the cusp, first take the Sun's right distance from the meridian; and from the same, the right distance of the aspect which the Sun is to be directed to, which call the primary, the semi-diurnal arc, and that of the aspect; and by the Golden rule say, if the Sun's semi-diurnal arc gives the right distance of the same, what distance will the semi-diurnal arc of the promittor, or occurrent place give: multiply the second and third, and the product divide by the first, which is the secondary distance of the aspect. Then, if both the primary and secondary distance of the aspect be from the same cardinal house, and in the same hemisphere of Heaven, ascendant or descendant, subtract the lesser from the greater, and the remainder is the arc of direction; but if one is in the ascendant, and the other in the descendant, add both distances together, and the sum is the arc of direction. You may take the semi-diurnal arc, both of the Sun and the aspect, either in hours or minutes, or degrees and minutes; or, instead of the semi-diurnal arc, you may use the temporal hours.

Example. In the nativity of Cardinal Fachenetti, I have a mind to direct the Sun to the quintile of Jupiter in the Zodiac, which happens in 19° 41′ ♈, the right ascension of the *medium cœli* being 326° 26′.

	h. m.		h. m.
Semi-diur. arc of ☉	6 0	Semi-diurn. arc of 19° 41′ ♈	6 30
Right ascension .	0 8	Right ascension . . .	18 9
Dist. *a medium cœli*	33 42	Primary distance . . .	51 43 from [*medium cœli.*]

Now, by the Golden rule, if the Sun's semi-diurnal arc, viz. 6ʰ, give its distance from the *medium cœli* 33° 42′, what will the semi-diurnal arc of ♈, 19° 41′, viz. 6ʰ 30′ give? *Answer,* 36° 30′,* which is the secondary distance of the aspect's place. But because both the primary and secondary distances are produced in the ascending part of heaven, I subtract the second-

---

* See Appendix, Use of the Proportional Logarithms.

ary distance from the primary, and the remainder is the arc of direction. Thus,

Primary distance at *medium cœli* is . . 51° 43'
Secondary distance, ... 36 30
                                   ―――――――
                Subtract and arc, = 15 13
                                   ―――――――

For the equation, I add the arc of direction to the Sun's right ascension; and I make the sum 15° 21', which answers to 16° 40' ♈, to which the Sun, from the day and hour of the nativity, arrives in 16 days, and some hours, which are the compass of so many years.

Another way.—To direct the Sun by the oblique ascension, under his Pole of position, take the Pole's elevation, in the manner explained in Canon XII, and the oblique ascension of the Sun, and of the aspect, and subtract the oblique ascension of the one from the other, &c. of which more examples will be given; we having laid down a table of the Pole's elevation of the eleventh, twelfth, second, and third houses, for the latitude of the country, to 60°: also, in the tables of the houses, there is placed, above every house, its polar elevation.

Canon XX.

To direct the Sun, when found below the Earth, in the Space of the Crepuscule, to the Conjunctions and Rays.

The reason why the Sun, when found in the crepuscular space, should be directed upon the circles parallel to the horizon, and not upon the horary circles, as when the Sun is above the Earth, has been given in the Theses, and demonstrated in the clearest manner in the

Celestial Philosophy; but now attend to what pertains to the practice of calculation. If the Sun is found in the morning crepuscule, first direct the Sun to the degree of the aspect, under the latitude of the country, that is, to the elevation of your pole, though indeed the Sun does not remain there, but below, and in a separate place. You must observe the arc of direction, and then take the Sun's distance from the horoscope, by its oblique ascension, which call the Sun's primary distance; and observe, that if this distance be greater than the whole quantity of the crepusculine to the parallel of depression, 18°, the Sun is not in the crepusculines; and, in this case, you are to calculate by the following Canon. But if the Sun is in the space of the crepuscules, with the Sun's distance from the horoscope, above taken, enter the table of crepuscules at your Pole's elevation, placed in your first column; and with the Sun's sign, and degree, according as they are placed, in the beginning or end; and when, in the body of the table, you have found this distance of the Sun from the east on the back of the same opposite to it, you are to observe what degree of the crepusculine parallels the Sun possesses, viz. in the second column, by taking the part proportionate only to the Sun's degree of longitude, as I shall mention afterwards; and under the same parallel see what the distance of the place or occurrent degree is, by direction; that is, what the Sun's distance is from the horoscope, in the same crepusculine parallel, after the direction is finished; and this distance I call the secondary; and if the primary and secondary distances are equal, the true arc is that which you have calculated above, viz. the Sun's arc in the horoscope; but if they are unequal, subtract the lesser from the greater, and the remainder call the ortive difference. Lastly, if the secondary distance be less, and the primary greater, add that remainder, or ortive difference, to the Sun's arc of direction, calculated in the horoscope; but, if the secondary distance be greater, and the primary less, subtract the ortive difference from the arc of direction, and you will have in the remainder the true arc of direction calculated in the crespusculine circle, which is to be equated the usual way, as in Canon XVI. And observe, that in seeking for the Sun's primary distance from the horoscope in the tables of the crepusculine, it is sufficient to take the part proportional to the degree of the Sun's place, which is found at the degree of the crepusculine, or parallel's depression; opposite to which you will find the distance which you have taken, with the proportional part near it, omitting that primary one of the natural Sun; for it is of no consequence to take the degree and minute of the crepusculine depression; but it is enough if you take the integral degree nearest the Sun's longitude distance, taken with the proportional part. For example; In John Duke Rainutius Farnese, the Sun's distance from the horoscope is 18° 56′, to the latitude of the country 44°; opposite to 13° of the depression, under 10° of ♈, the distance is 18° 32′, under 20° of ♈ the distance is 19° 1′, the difference is 29′, from which, for the 6° (for the Sun is in 16° of ♈) 17′ are due, which, when added together, the distance is 18° 49′, but the Sun's distance 18° 56′; yet this is nothing to the purpose, as the distance is but small, therefore make use of the former 18° 49', without any regard to that of the Sun, 18° 56'. To the same depression of the crepusculine 13°, under 0° 0' of ♋, the place of the quartile of Mars, I take the secondary distance, 24° 45', from which I subtract the Sun's distance obtained after taking the part proportional, which is 18° 49'; and I suppose that the Sun in the nativity might have this distance from the horoscope, that I may place it under the crepusculine circle 13° exactly. But if you are desirous to have the crepusculine circle in minutes, take the proportional part; but it would be attended with greater trouble than advantage; for you will find the difference in the ascensions almost imperceptible, and not greater than that which arises from the difference of some minutes of the pole's elevation of the circle of position, in which all professors entirely omit the minutes. Wherefore, when you have occasion to use the ortive difference, do as already mentioned, &c. of which examples follow in Gustavus King of Sweden, Odoardus Cardinal Farnese, Rainutius, of whom we have just now spoken, and John Columna, which are given by Argol. Had I met with more examples of other authors, relating to this point, I would have undertaken to give you a thorough examination. I alledge nothing of my own observations, lest they should be rejected as spurious and false; but from these four, and all examples that Argol gives of this nature, I think, that to any one diligent in searching into the truth of things, my opinion on this subject will appear highly satisfactory. But if, again, the Sun possesses the evening twilight, the same method entirely is to be observed, except only changing the manner. Let the Sun's direction be to the place of the aspect, by the oblique descension, or the oblique ascension of the opposite places under the Pole of the country; then let the Sun's distance be taken from the west, by the same descensions or opposite ascensions; let this distance be required in the table of twilight, which, if it be greater than the whole quantity of the crepusculine to the inferior parallels, 18°, the Sun is no longer in the crepusculine; and then we must make use of the following Canon. Lastly, let the secondary distance under the same crepusculine circle be taken, namely, of the occurrent place, and let the lesser be subtracted from the greater, and the remainder added to the arc of direction found above, if the secondary distance be greater than the primary; but let it be subtracted, if less (that is, in a manner contrary from that we spoke of above); and the sum or remainder is the true arc of the direction.

Canon XXI.

To direct the Sun when found in the Space of the obscure Arcs to the Conjunctions and other Aspects.

When the Sun is under the Earth, and distant from the horizon, either eastern or western, more than the whole Crepuscular Arc, it is then in the obscure arc. First, take the Sun's semi-nocturnal arc, from which subtract the whole crepusculine arc, which you will have at the inferior parallel 18°; and the remainder is the obscure arc, which you must observe in a separate place; then take the semi-nocturnal arc of the place of the occourse, from which subtract the whole arc of crepusculine, that is, that which is found there by the Sun; and this you will have, under the degree of the occurrent place to the inferior parallel, 18°, and there will remain the obscure arc of this place of the occourse. Thirdly, take the Sun's right distance from the *imum cœli*. Lastly, by the rule of proportion, say, if the obscure arc of the Sun gives his distance from the *imum cœli*, what distance will the obscure arc of the occurrent place give? and you will know the secondary distance of the place of the occourse, and you must proceed to the end in the same manner as set forth in Canon XIX, as if the obscure arc were semi-diurnal or semi-nocturnal.

Suppose the Sun to be in 29° 31' of ♑, as in the fourth example produced by Argol in his first edition of Critical Days; if ♃ be in 3° 21' of ♎, with 1 40' north latitude, as it is placed in the more correct tables; in the *imum cœli*, 24° of ♐, whose right ascension is 263° 28'; but as ♃'s declination is 0° 12' north, t happens that its parallel of declination falls in 29° 30' of ♓ in the ecliptic, to which the Sun moves by direction.

	Of the ☉.	h.	m.
From the semi-nocturnal arc		7	23
Arc of the crepuscular, take		1	48
Arc which remains obscure		5	35
Right ascension		301	42
Distance from the *imum cœli*		38	14

PRIMUM MOBILE. 67

Of the Part 29° 30′ of ♓.

	h.	m.
Semi-nocturnal arc	6	0
Crepusculine arc	1	42
The obscure arc	4	18
Right ascension	359	33
Primary distance from the *imum cœli*	96	5

Now, by the golden rule, if the Sun's obscure arc, 5ʰ 35′, gives its distance from the *imum cœli*, 38° 14′, the obscure arc of the aspect gives its secondary distance from the *imum cœli* 29° 26′, which, subtracted from the primary, as both that and the secondary distance of the aspect or place are from the same cardinal house and descendant hemisphere, leaves the arc of direction 66° 39′. Then for the equation, add this to the Sun's right ascension, and it makes the aggregate 368° 21′; from which, subtracting the integer circle 360, there remains 8° 21′, which answers to 9 of ♈, at which the Sun, from the hour of the nativity, arrives in 67 days, comprehending so many years of age, at which time the native shewed himself capable of discharging the highest honours, and accordingly was raised to them; the rays meeting in the place of direction, are the quintile of Venus, and the sextile of the Sun, proper. See another example of *Card. Salviatis*, explained further on to the 47th year, wherein is a calculation of the Sun's direction to the parallel of Jupiter's declination. You may likewise perform these calculations by logistical logarithms. These two examples serve also for the subsequent Canon, and are a convincing proof that I am right in my opinion. See other examples calculated in Charles V, Francis I, King of France, and others.

Canon XXII.

To direct the Sun, wherever found, to the Parallels.

It was thought proper to call those parallels, which are commonly called antiscions, it being necessary to preserve the latitude of the planets in taking them. And, as I have said, those stars only are alternately in the antiscions which describe the same parallel or parallels, as Ptolemy says; that is, those which have the same declination, both in number and name, are called primary antiscions; or only in number, which are places of authority, and subjection; wherefore, if you want to direct the Sun to the parallels of a planet, first take their declination, by observing their latitude, then take the degree and minute of the ecliptic answering to the same declination. Now when the ☉, by the motion of direction, arrives at the same declination, or degree, and minute of the ecliptic, it will be said to have reached the parallel or antiscions of those stars; take, therefore, the right or oblique ascension of that degree and minute of the ecliptic, the semi-diurnal or nocturnal arc, the horary times, and every thing else, according as the situation of the Sun requires. See the example in the former Canon.

Canon XXIII.

To direct the Significator, wherever it is found, accompanied with Latitude, to the Conjunction and Rays.

As the Sun, whilst he is moved in a right direction,

advances on his real way, which is the ecliptic, even so the other moderators, whose motion is latitudinal, whilst they are moved by direction, advance upon their true and real way, which is that of their successive latitude; I say, successive latitude, by reason that it is not always the same as in the nativity, or in the beginning of the direction's motion, but is changed according as such prorogators vary the distance from their nodes, as has been observed; then, as the conjunction in the Zodiac happens when the stars are in the same longitude and become alternately nearer, and the opposition in the greater alternate distance, not omitting their latitude, when it happens to be great; consequently the directions of the prorogators moving latitudinally to the conjunctions and rays in the Zodiac, upon their true and real latitudinal ways, should be calculated, omitting the latitude of the occourses, either through the conjunctions or rays. But the ways of directing differ in nothing from the abovementioned, except that, what has been said of the Sun, constituted below the Earth, is omitted in the other prorogators; for, having found the direction's place, according to longitude and latitude, that is, according to the latitude of the significator in the direction's place, in proportion to the distance there from their nodes, take the right or oblique ascension of that place, the semi-diurnal or semi-nocturnal arc, the horary times, right distance, &c. always in the same manner, both above and below the earth; of which mention has been made. See examples in Charles V, Henry IV, &c. &c.

Canon XXIV.

To direct the Significator with Latitude, wherever it is found, to the Parallels of Declination.

First find the declination of the star, to whose parallel the significator is said to be carried; then in the body of the table of declination, look up or down according to the order of degrees and signs from the significator's place, changing also the latitude in the same manner as the significator varies in his motion, till you come to the declination of the promittor or star found as above; and when you have obtained it, take the right ascension or oblique ascension of that place according to its latitude and longitude, &c. and you will have every thing entirely in the same manner as before explained. You have examples in Sebastian King of Portugal, Ferdinand Gonzagius, Cardinal Salviata, Zachia, Verospus, Spinelli, and others. See likewise the seven nativities, which, for my own purpose, I lately extracted out of Maginus; in all which, by an exact calculation, you will find that the true prorogator of life, when chosen as the doctrine of Ptolemy teaches, arrived at such a parallel of declination, at the time of death. You will know whether the prorogator may fall on the parallels of declination of the stars, by observing the following rule : If the prorogator leaves the tropics, so as to lessen his declination, he will fall on the parallels of those stars, whose declination is less than his; and if it departs from the equinoctial, on the parallels of greater declination.

Canon XXV.

To direct the Significators to their own proper Rays in the Zodiac.

First mark out the proper ray of the significator longitudinally in the ecliptic, if it be the Sun, or latitudinally if the Moon, preserving that latitude which it hath in the place of the ray, according to its distance there from its nodes; then take the right or oblique ascension of the aspect, longitudinally and latitudinally; and work according to the foregoing rule. See an example in Charles V. Meanwhile, observe that the angles are not directed to the planetary rays in the Zodiac; neither to the parallels, nor the proper rays, for they receive only the rays of the stars taken in the world. These we shall mention in the following Part.

PART III.

To calculate the Directions to the Aspects in the World.

ASPECTS in the world are proportional distances acquired by motion round the world; for every star, after leaving the east, when its distance is the third part of its diurnal arc, is in the ✶ to the east, when the half part is in the quadrate; when two third parts is in the △, when the whole diurnal arc is in the ☍, for it is in the west; therefore the first house has the ✶ with the eleventh and third houses, quadrate with the tenth and fourth, △ with the ninth and fifth. The second house has its ✶ with the twelfth and fourth, its quadrate with the eleventh and fifth, its △ with the tenth and sixth. The third house hath its ✶ with the first and fifth, its quadrate with the twelfth and sixth, its trine with the eleventh and seventh.

And thus the houses, always in the same manner, through the diurnal and nocturnal arcs, differ between each other. The stars also have their mutual aspects alternately from those houses, with such rays as are taken in the world, whatever may be their latitude or declination. Farther, as those houses have no real existence, and no distinction, or are proper by nature, force, or limits, but from the stars; so that if they had no existence, and did not move round the world, there could be no place in the heavens for the houses or their partitions, as I have fully demonstrated in the Celestial Philosophy. Now, the houses are not alternately aspected, with respect to one another; but it is the stars that aspect, constitute, and are the measure of the houses; and for this reason they mutually and alternately aspect each other from those houses; and to these and the cardinal signs they direct their aspects. But in the partition of the houses by the duplicate horary times, or, according to Ptolemy, by the two temporal hours, no respect is had to the ecliptic, just as if there was no ecliptic in the heavens; but we respect always the diurnal and nocturnal arcs of the stars. And it follows, that even the aspects of the stars to the houses, and *vice versa*, from the houses, which I thought fit to call mundane, have no respect to the ecliptic, but to the diurnal and nocturnal arc of every single star, or to their motion round the world. All this, if rightly understood, will render every calculation in this Third Part perfectly easy.

Canon XXVI.

To direct the Cardinal Signs to the Conjunctions and Opposition.

If you direct the right cardinal sign, take its right ascension from that of the occurrent star, preserving its latitude, and the remainder is the arc of direction required. In like manner to the opposition, keeping to the contrary latitude. If you direct the cardinal sign of the ascendant, take its oblique ascension from that of the occurrent

74   PRIMUM MOBILE.

star, carrying the oblique ascension of both to the latitude of the country, but always preserving the latitude of the occurrent star, the remainder will be the arc of direction required. To the ☍ use the ascensions of the opposite places. The ascendant may be directed to the stars without the oblique ascension; for if you subtract the semi-diurnal arc from the star's right ascension, and from the remainder take the right ascension of the *medium cœli*, what remains is the arc of direction required. Or, if you subtract the star's primary distance, that is, betwixt it and the *imum cœli*, from its semi-nocturnal arc, the remainder is the arc of direction. But if the star has not reached the *imum cœli*, add its primary distance from the *imum cœli* to its semi-nocturnal arc, and the sum will be the arc of direction.

These calculations are easy, and need no example; and from what will be said afterwards, they will still be easier. To the fixed stars, in like manner, by the ascensions, &c. by taking their oblique ascension, with the help of the ascensional difference, if their latitude be extensive.

Canon XXVII.

To direct the Medium Cœli to the Sextile, Quartile, and Trine.

Now, it is plain from what has been said, that the intermediate rays to the angles are taken by dividing the semi-nocturnal or semi-diurnal arc into three equal parts; or, which is the same, by doubling the horary times of the aspecting stars, by which is known the space of the houses, as to longitude, what the measure in degrees and stay of those stars in their motions round the world is. When this is known, it is very easy to calculate the directions of the angles to the intermediate rays of the stars; for the sextile is the distance of two houses, the square three, the trine four; and these are called secondary distances. So, if you want the ✶ to the *medium cœli*, which begins from the eighth house, add two diurnal houses, that is, the stars diurnal horary times twice doubled to the right ascension of the star. If you want the other Sextile, which is produced by the 12th house, subtract, in the same manner, the two diurnal houses from the right ascension, and from the sum or remainder take the right ascension of the *medium cœli*, and it will give the arc of direction. But if you seek for the Trine, which originates from the sixth house, subtract two nocturnal houses from the star's right ascension: if you seek for the other Trine, which comes from the second house, add the two nocturnal houses to the star's right ascension, and from the remainder or sum subtract the right ascension of the *imum cœli*, the remainder will be the arc of direction of the *medium cœli* to the △ and *imum cœli* to ✶ of the star. Lastly, if you want the arc of direction to the square, direct the star to the horizon, as above mentioned. But if you have already the primary distance of the star from the *medium cœli*, if the star is in the ascending part of heaven, subtract the secondary of the sextile from the primary of the star from the *medium cœli*, and you will have the arc of direction of ✶ to the *medium cœli*; subtract that star's primary distance from the *imum cœli* from the sextile's secondary, and you will have the arc of direction to the trine of the *medium cœli*. But if the star is in the descending part of heaven, subtract its primary distance from the *medium cœli* from that of the sextile's secondary, and you will have the arc of direction to the sextile. Subtract the secondary of the sextile to the *imum cœli* from the stars primary distance, and you will have the arc of direction of the trine. But if the star passes from the ascendant to the descendant part of heaven, or on the contrary, add both distances together, and you will have the arc of direction.

Note. The △ ray to the *medium cœli* is the ✱ to the *imum cœli*, and the ✱ to the *medium cœli* is the △ to the *imum cœli*. Lastly, the rays to the angles are easily calculated by the oblique ascension of every house; for after taking the star's oblique ascension, under the pole of that house, from which it emits the ray to the *medium cœli*, and taking the oblique ascension of the house from that of the star, there will remain the arc of direction required. But if the star goes to project the ray to the descending part of heaven, use the oblique ascension of the opposite place, and this method is of use also in the following Canon, and is, of all, the most expeditious.

Canon XXVIII.
To direct the Oblique Cardinal Sign to the Sextile, Quartile, and Trine.

If you require the rays to the horoscope, which are projected from supra-terraneous places, divide the semi-diurnal arc of the aspecting star into three equal parts, or into two diurnal horary times, and you will have the spaces of the houses that are above the earth. If you add two of these to the star's oblique ascension, taken in the horoscope, and from the sum subtract the horoscope's oblique ascension, what remains is the horoscope's arc of direction to the sextile of the star, produced from the eleventh house; but if you add four houses, and from the sum subtract the horoscope's oblique ascension, you will have the arc of direction to the trine which is caused by the ninth house.

Another way.—Subtract one house from the star's right ascension, and from the remainder take the right ascension of the *medium cœli*, and there will remain the direction's arc to the sextile; add one house to the star's right ascension; from the sum subtract that of the *medium cœli*, and you will have the direction's arc to the trine, that is, to the horoscope.

But if you are desirous to find the rays that are emitted from subterraneous places, divide the star's semi-nocturnal arc into three equal parts, or its double nocturnal horary times, and you will have the space of the houses that are below the earth; of these, for the sextile, which proceeds from the third house, by subtracting two; and for the trine, which is produced from the fifth, by subtracting four from the star's oblique ascension taken in the horoscope; and if from the remainders you subtract the horoscope's oblique ascension, you will have the arcs of direction to the sextile and trine. You may also use the *imum cœli* by the right ascension, as has been said of the *medium cœli*. Quadrate rays are produced by the *medium cœli* and the *imum cœli*; therefore, for these, direct the stars to the *medium* and *imum cœli*, as has been said in Canon XXVI. Let there be an example for both Canons, under the Pole's elevation 45°, the ascendant 13° 30' of ♑. In the *medium cœli*, let us suppose 12° 0' of ♏, whose right ascension 219° 33', the horoscope's oblique ascension 309° 33'. Let the Sun be in 1° 0' of ♑, within the twelfth house, the Sun's right ascension 271° 5', the oblique ascension to the Pole 45°, is 296° 51'; the diurnal horary times 10° 42', which, being doubled, constitutes the diurnal house, or the third part of the Sun's semi-diurnal arc 21° 24'. If I want to direct the horoscope to the sextile of the Sun, I add to the oblique ascension the Sun's horary times, twice doubled, which makes 339° 39'. From which I subtract the horoscope's oblique ascension, and there remains the arc of direction 30° 6'. And observe, that the arc of direction consists of 8° 44' preceding the direction, and likewise of the Sun's duplicate horary times; that is, of one house, or 21.24. Wherefore, from the bare adding of this one house to the computed direction of the sextile to the *medium cœli*, there arises the arc of direction of the horoscope to ✶ of ☉.

I want to direct the horoscope to the ◻ of the Sun: I subtract the right ascension of the *medium cœli* from that of the Sun, and there remains the arc of direction, 51.32; or to the sextile's arc of direction 30.6, above calculated. I add the ☉'s duplicate diurnal horary times 21.24, and the arc of direction is 51.30. In like manner, if to this I add the duplicate, horary times, I make the arc of direction to the trine of the horoscope, 72.54. Again, if I add to this the geminated horary times, the direction's arc of the *medium cœli*, to the Sun's sextile, will be 94.18, and so in all of them. Under the earth, we must make use of the nocturnal horary times, and the semi-nocturnal arc; but the direction both of the cardinal signs and houses to the rays of the sextile, quartile, and trine, are calculated (in a manner much easier than any of the afore-mentioned) by the oblique ascension of those houses from which the stars project the rays, as is before recited, and as may be seen in the former Canon. This Canon needs no other example, nevertheless you will meet with several in the sequel.

Canon XXIX.
To direct the Cardinal Signs to the Rays of the Quintile, Sesqui-quadrate, and Biquintile.

Beside the usual rays of the ✶, ☐, △, and ☌, I only suppose the quintile, sesqui-quadrate, and biquintile, to be powerful, as experience evinces from the symmetrical concerts of sound, from which the very excellent Kepler, in a most exquisite manner of resemblance, collects the rays of the stars in the heavens. Whatever may be the opinion of others, with regard to the semi-sextile, semi-quadrate, and several others, to which it seems quite absurd to assign any efficacy (with this one exception), I confess, that in the semi-quadrate's distance, sounds begin to arrive at a degree of harmony, but altogether imperfect; to this, therefore, some portion of efficacy may be attributed; and, on this principle, I think that neither the Sun nor Moon become the prorogators of life, except they be semi-quadrate distance from the horoscope, or half of their semi-diurnal arc above it. We may easily calculate the sesqui-quadrate ray to the cardinal signs, for it consists of the quarter of the world, and half of another quarter; or, of the semi-diurnal or nocturnal arc; and, also, of half of the same, or another, so that the stars have this ray to the *medium cœli*, and the east, in the mean distance between the west and *imum cœli;* to the *medium cœli* and west, in the mean distance from the *imum cœli* to the east; to the west and *imum cœli*, in the middle distance between the east and the *medium cœli*, to the *imum* and east; in the middle distance between the *medium cœli* and the west. For the calculation, divide the semi-diurnal arc into two equal parts; or, as occasion requires, the semi-nocturnal arc of the star, and this half part is the secondary distance from both the cardinal signs, as before mentioned.—In the example of the former Canon, the Sun forms the sesqui-quadrate to the west, and to the *imum cœli:* when it is the mean distance between the east and *medium cœli*, the Sun's semi-diurnal arc is 64.12, the half of which is 32.6; wherefore I subtract this secondary distance from the primary, which is betwixt it and the *medium cœli*, being 51.32, and there remains the arc of direction 19.26. But as this secondary distance, as well from the preceding as the succedent cardinal house, is the same, the Sun's primary distance from the east is 12.40. I subtract this from the secondary, and the remainder is the same arc of direction, 19.26. Likewise, half the same semi-diurnal arc consists of the triplicate horary times; wherefore, if we add the Sun's horary times to its distance from the twelfth house, which was the arc of direction of the *medium cœli* to the Sun's *, that is, 8° 44′, the Sun's horary times are 10° 42′; the sum is the arc of direction 19° 26′. You see, therefore, there are several ways of directing the angles to the aspects of the stars; but to calculate the rays quintile and biquintile with ease and exactness, we must understand the following Pentagonal figure,

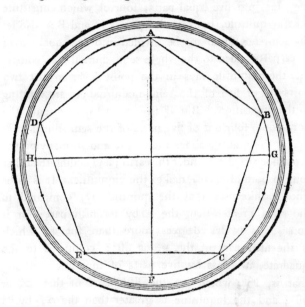

wherein the point A may represent any cardinal sign of the world, or any other significator to be directed to the quintile and biquintile: the points F, G, H, are the other three cardinal signs; B is the end of the quintile, C of the biquintile, D the point of another quintile, E of another biquintile, and F of the opposition; the four lines AG, CF, FH, HA, are the quadrates or quarters of the world, or arcs, which are effected by the stars in those quarters, and are semi-diurnal or semi-nocturnal, which may be various in quantity, according to the variety of the declination of the stars, and altitude of the pole. If the point A may be said to be the *medium cœli,* divide the semi-diurnal arc of the aspecting star into five equal parts, four of which constitute the ray quintile, both in the points D and B: also let the semi-nocturnal arc be divided into five equal parts; three parts added to the whole semi-diurnal arc, constitute the biquintile rays in the point EC; so that two parts out of five of the semi-nocturnal arc are wanting to the opposition. But if the point A represents the horoscope, four out of five parts of the semi-diurnal arc makes the quintile above the earth, and so many of the semi-nocturnal arc under the earth; and adding the other four to both of them, makes the biquintile. It is to be known, likewise, that the quintile ray, compared to the ✶, is greater than the ✶ by its fifth part; for it consists of twelve degrees more than the ✶, which is the fifth part of the ✶, or 60°; compared to the quadrate, it is less by five parts of the same quadrate, that is, 18°, which are the fifth part of that ◻, or 90°; and the biquintile is greater than the △, by its fifth part, viz. 24°, which are the fifth part of the trigon or 120°, but is less than the ☍ by five parts, that is, 36° of the ☍, viz. 180°, or three parts out of five of the ✶, that is, made at the ☍; from these it is inferred that there are two ways very easy to calculate the directions of these rays.

The first is, by adding the quintile's distance to the

PRIMUM MOBILE. 83

ascension of the aspecting star, if it precedes the cardinal sign that is directed; or by subtracting, if it follows; and from the sum or remainder, subtracting the cardinal ascension, for the remainder is the arc of direction required.

Let there be an example of the Quintile.

We have said, in the above given example, the Sun's oblique ascension is 296° 51', that is, to the latitude of the country; the semi-diurnal arc 64° 12', the fifth part of which is 12° 50'; which taken from the whole semi-diurnal arc, leaves four of the five parts of that semi-diurnal arc, viz. 51° 22'. I add these to the Sun's oblique ascension taken in the horoscope, as it precedes it; and I make the aggregate 348° 13', from which I subtract the horoscope's oblique ascension, and there remains the arc of direction 38° 40', viz. the quintile of Sol to the horoscope. Or I subtract 51° 22' from the Sun's right ascension, which is 271° 5', by reason it succeeds the *medium cœli*, and the remainder is 219° 43'; from these subtracting the right ascension of the *medium cœli*, which is 219° 33', leaves the arc of direction of the *medium cœli* to the Sun's quintile 0° 10'; or I subtract the quintile's secondary distance, which is 51° 22', from the Sun's primary distance from the *medium cœli*, which is 51° 32', and there remains the same arc of direction 0° 10'.

Of the biquintile, care must be taken that if we want to subtract the distance of this ray, which consists of eight parts out of ten of the whole diurnal or nocturnal arc, when to those rays we direct either the *medium* or *imum cœli;* instead of these five parts, we must take the whole semi-diurnal or nocturnal arc of the aspecting star of the other hemisphere; the other three of the same hemisphere in which the star remains; but of the biquintile, let us reject this method. The easier way, which also serves for all these rays, whenever the significators, as we call them, are found out of the cardinal signs, is this:

When you have found the arc of direction, either to the sextile, quartile, or opposition, by only adding or subtracting the proportional parts, by which the quintile, sesqui-quadrate, and biquintile, are greater or less than the other ray, we shall obtain the arc of direction; for, if you have the arc of direction to the *, and want the same to the quintile, add, if the quintile be subsequent, or subtract if it precedes the fifth part of the sextile to or from its arc of direction, and the remainder or aggregate is the arc of direction required. But, remember the * consists of the diurnal horary times, four times computed, if the aspecting star be above the earth; of the nocturnal, if below. Or if you have the arc of direction to the quartile, for the quintile add, if it succeed; or subtract, if the quintile precede the fifth part of the quadrate, to or from that quartile's arc of direction.

If you have the arc of direction to the trine, and want that of the sesqui-quadrate, add, if this follows, or subtract, if it precedes, the horary times of the aspecting star, by which the sesqui-quadrate is greater than the trine. When I say horary times, understand diurnal, if the aspecting star be above the earth, and nocturnal if below.

If you require the direction's arc to the biquintile, and have already the arc of direction to the trine, multiply four times the diurnal horary times of the aspecting star, if it be above the earth; the nocturnal, if under the earth; and, from the product, take two of the five parts, which add, if the biquintile succeeds the trine; but, if it precedes, subtract from the trine's arc of direction, and the remainder or sum is the arc of direction to the biquintile; but if you have the direction's arc to the opposition, take two of the five parts of the star's semi-diurnal arc, if it is above the earth; or semi-nocturnal, if below; and if the biquintile succeeds the opposition, add to the same direction's arc; but, if it precedes, subtract these two parts, and the remainder, or sum, is the arc of direction to the biquintile. As in the example of the former Canon, the arc of direction of the *medium cœli* to the Sun's sextile is 8° 44′, the Sun's diurnal horary times, as being above the Earth, are 10° 44′; four times computed makes the sextile's quantity 42° 48′, whose fifth part is 8° 34′; I therefore take 8° 34′ from the sextile's arc of direction, for the quintile to the *medium cœli*, because it precedes the sextile, and there remains the arc of direction to the Sun's quintile 0° 10′. The direction of the *imum cœli* to the Sun's sesqui-quadrate (as it follows the trine), is had by adding the Sun's diurnal horary times 10° 42′, to the arc of direction of the *medium cœli* to its ✳, which is the △ to the *imum cœli*, and the arc of direction becomes 19° 26′, as above.

Of the *imum cœli*, to the Sun's biquintile, by adding (as it succeeds the △), two of the fifth parts of the Sun's diurnal ✶, because it is above the Earth, which, as we have said, is 42° 48', whose fifth part 8° 34', doubled, makes 17° 8'; wherefore the arc of direction becomes 25° 52'.

Another way.—The arc of direction of the *medium cœli* to the Sun, or of the *imum cœli* to the Sun's ☌, is 51° 32'; from this I subtract (as the biquintile precedes) three parts out of five of the ✶ of the Sun diurnal, that is, 25° 40', and there remains the arc of direction 25° 52', as above.

The direction of the horoscope to the Sun's quintile is thus obtained:

We have already, in the former Canon, calculated the Sun's sextile to the horoscope, which was 30° 6'; to this I add (as the quintile succeeds the sextile) the fifth part of the Sun's sextile ray, which is 8° 34', and I make the horoscope's arc of direction to the quintile of the Sun 33° 40'.

Another method.—The Sun's semi-diurnal arc, which is the quadrate to the horoscope, is 64° 12' (that is, of the distance, not of direction), its fifth part is 12° 50', which is the Sun's secondary distance from the *medium cœli*, the primary is 51° 32'; from which, subtracting that of the secondary, leaves the arc of direction 38° 42' greater than the former by 2', by reason of the fractions that are to be met with in the different calculations.

We have said, that the horoscope's direction to the Sun's trine was 72° 56'; to this I add the Sun's horary times, 10° 42', and I make the horoscope's arc of direction, to the Sun's sesqui-quadrate, 83° 38'; or, I add the Sun's semi-diurnal arc, 64° 12', to the arc of direction of the *imum cœli*, to the Sun's sesqui-quadrate, which was, as we have said, 19° 26', and it produces the same arc of direction, 83° 38'.

And it is the same in all of them; so that by addition and subtraction only, the arc of direction of those rays may be calculated with the greatest exactness. But, if any one would provide himself with a Ptolemaic Planisphere, with the horary circles, crepuscules, the Zodiac's latitude, and all other things requisite, it would be of very great service towards foreseeing the aspects, before the calculation, both of this and the following Canons.

Canon XXX.

To direct any Significator, being placed about the Cusps of the Cardinal Houses, to the ☌ and ☍.

Understand this, as within 3° beyond, or on this side the cusp, the right ascension of the Prorogator, if he possesses the right circle; or the oblique, if the oblique, is to be taken to the polar elevation of the house in which it remains; which subtract from the right ascension of the occurrent, or the oblique taken to the same pole, preserving the latitude of both, and the remainder is the arc of direction required. In the opposition, the contrary latitude of the occurrent place is preserved; the difference in regard to preserving the latitude, between this Canon and XVII and XVIII, is, that the ☌ and ☍ are *there* taken in the Zodiac, but *here* in the world; *those* aspects in the same real longitude, but *these* in the horary circle: as in the example, Canon XVII, the right ascension of ♀, with latitude, is 261° 52′, from which, subtracting the right ascension of the Sun, which is 215° 58′, there remains the Sun's arc of direction to the ☌ of ♀ in the world 45° 54′.

Concerning the Sun constituted below the Earth, the things to be avoided shall be mentioned in a proper Canon, viz. XXXV. The significator, when found distant from the cusp of the house, is directed in the manner explained in Canon XIX, except only that the latitude of both should, as we have remarked, be preserved.

Canon XXXI.

To direct any Significator, when near the Cardinal Houses, to the ✶, □, or △.

If the significator has the same ascension exactly to minutes, as the angle, or the other houses, wherein he is found, then, as it is on the cusp, the directions to the sextile, quartile, and trine, are made like those of the angle, as before explained: but if it is not on the cusp, exact to the minutes, provided its distance be not more than 3° of the equator, add the ascension or descension of the significator to that of the angle, or house, so that the significator may be constituted on the cusp of the angle or house. According to this situation, by adding or subtracting 30° you will constitute the ascensions of the other houses as usual; and by subtracting the ascensions of the houses (from whence the star aspects the significator) from the ascension of that star, taken under the pole of the same house, you will have the arc of direction. As, for example, in Cardinal Gymnaseus, the Sun is in the ninth house, not 3° of the equator distant from the cusp, the oblique ascension of the Sun's opposite place under the pole of the third house, which is 18°, is 314° 0'. I want to direct the Sun to the sextile of Jupiter, which Jupiter has to the Sun from the cusp of the seventh, wherefore I subtract 60 from the oblique ascension of the third house, constituted in the Sun's opposition, and there remains the horoscope's oblique ascension 254° 0', that is, supposing that the Sun remains on the cusp of the ninth house, though, indeed, it is about 3° distance. Lastly, I subtract this oblique ascension of the horoscope 254° from the oblique ascension of Jupiter's opposite place, taken in the horoscope, which is 296° 52', and there remains the arc of direction, 42° 52'. For the subsequent square which Jupiter has to the Sun from the sixth house, I add to this arc of direction the duplicate nocturnal horary times of ♃, by reason that the sixth house is below the Earth : for the △ I add again the duplicate nocturnal horary times of ♃, &c.

Canon XXXII.

To direct any Significator, when found beyond the Cusp of the Cardinals and Houses, to the ✶, □, and △.

Find the horary times of the significator, or its semi-diurnal arc, if it be above the earth ; or semi-nocturnal arc, if below, and its distance from the cusp of the preceding or succeeding house, as you please. Find, also, the horary times, the semi-diurnal arc, or semi-nocturnal arc of the promittor, with this proviso :—If the promittor's ray, to which you direct the significator, projects from places above the earth, take the diurnal horary times, or semi-diurnal arc; and below the earth, the nocturnal horary times, or the semi-nocturnal arc; but that you will know from the houses; for the whole tenth house has all the twelfth and eighth houses for the sextile; the first and seventh, for a quartile; the second and sixth for the trine; and so of the rest.—*Query*, By the Golden Rule, if the horary times of the significator give its distance from the house, what will the distance of the promittor's horary times give? The fourth number that is produced, is the secondary distance of the promittor from the cusp of either the preceding or succeeding house, after the same manner as you have seen of the significator; and from this house, the ray is emitted by that promittor to the significator; wherefore, if that house precedes the promittor in both distances, primary and secondary, subtract the lesser from the greater. So, also, if it follows in both distances. But, finally, if in the one distance it precedes, and in the other it follows, so that the promittor, by the motion of the direction, has passed through its cusp, add both distances, and the remainder or sum is the arc of direction required. Let the example be in *Cardinal Salviatis:* I would direct the ☽ to the ☐ of ♃, which has this ray to the ☽ from the sixth house. The ☽'s horary times diurnal, are 19° 5'; distance from the *medium cœli*, 10° 24'. ♃'s horary times nocturnal is 14° 32', and distance from the seventh house 8° 59'. Now the oblique ascension of the ☍ of ♃ is 193° 1'; from which subtracting the oblique ascension of the horoscope, there remains the distance of Jupiter 8° 59'. But by the Golden Rule, there arises the secondary distance of ♃ from the west 7° 55', which, added to the primary, because ♃ in the nativity is above the west, and is placed below when the direction is complete, makes the arc of direction 16° 54'. To this direction, if the duplicate horary times nocturnal of ♃ be added, as he now lustrates the lower hemisphere, it makes the arc of direction to the △ of ♃ 45° 48'; but if you want the ☽'s direction to the ✶ of ♄, take the horary times diurnal of ♄, together with its primary distance from the twelfth house, the fourth emerging number is the secondary distance from the twelfth house; from which, subtracting the primary, because the distance from both is from the succedent house, the remainder is the arc of direction required. If you want the ☽'s direction to the △ of ♀, find the horary times nocturnal of ♀, as it is below the Earth; and its distance from the sixth house, by the oblique ascension of the opposite places at the twelfth house. The fourth number that is produced, is the secondary distance of ♀ from the sixth house; from which subtract the primary, which is less than the secondary, as the distance of both is from the succedent house, and the remainder is the arc of direction required. And observe, that the first number of the Golden Rule is always either the semi-diurnal arc, or the horary times of the significator; the second is the distance of the same from the nearest house.

Canon XXXIII.

To direct any Significator, wherever posited, to the Quintile, Sesqui-quadrate, or Biquintile.

The method is nearly the same as that explained in Canon XXIX, for when any direction is known, whether it be of the sextile, quartile, trine, or opposition, from only adding or subtracting the proportional part, whereby the rays of the quintile, sesqui-quadrate, and biquintile, either exceed or are less than the other rays, is produced the arc of direction. As, in the example of *Cardinal Salviatis*, the ☽'s arc of direction to the △ of ♃ is 45° 48'. If we add the nocturnal horary times of ♃ 14° 32', we make the ☽'s arc of direction to the sequi-quadrate of ♃ 60° 20'. But, if to the same arc of direction of the △ 45° 48', we add two of the five parts of ♃'s nocturnal ✶, which consists of his quadruplicate nocturnal horary times, that is, 58° 8', the two-fifth parts of these are 23° 16', we make the ☽'s arc of direction to the biquintile of ♃ 69° 4'. But, first of all, care must be taken, that if the rays are emitted from the superior places above the Earth, the proportional parts of the rays to be added or subtracted, should be taken by the diurnal horary times, or by the semi-diurnal arc of the aspecting star; but, if from the inferior places, or under the Earth, by the nocturnal, as you have seen in the given example. The second necessary caution is, that, to the adding or subtracting for the ray which is projected from the subterraneous places, we cannot make use of the ray which is emitted from those subterraneous places; or the contrary, because their transit is from one quantity of the horary times to another; from one hemisphere to the other; from the semi-diurnal to the semi-nocturnal arc, or the contrary, from which a true proportion cannot be had; but it is necessary, that, for the ray which is projected from the subterraneous places, we add or subtract the proportional part to or from the ray which is found above the Earth, and likewise under the Earth; as in the example of *Cardinal Salviatis*, the direction of the quintile of ♃ to the ☽ cannot be taken by subtraction from the direction of the quartile, as the ☐ falls below the Earth, the quintile above. Wherefore, in such cases as these, let the distances of the rays of the ✶, ☐, and △, be taken in the same hemisphere in which the significator remains, if they fall upon that same hemisphere; but if they fall in the other, in which the opposition of the significator falls, they must be taken in the other, as in the example of *Salviatis*, for the quintile of Jupiter to the Moon. I first take the quantity of ♃'s diurnal ✶; that is, from the diurnal horary times, which are 15° 28', four times computed, and the ✶ becomes 61° 52'; the fifth part of these are 12° 22', and, added to 61° 52', they make the quantity of the ray quintile 74° 14', and are the secondary distance of ♃ from the ☽. The oblique ascension of ♃'s opposition to the pole of the ☽, is 190° 6'; this subtracted from the oblique ascension of the ☽'s opposition, which is 265° 33', leaves the primary distance of ♃ from the ☽ 75° 17', which being greater than that of the ray by 1° 3', this quintile ray had preceded, and ♃ had this ray to the ☽ in the nativity. In the example of *Cardinal Gymnaseus*, the ✶ of ♃ to the Sun falls above the Earth, the quintile below; for which reason we cannot add to the ✶'s arc of direction the quintile's excess above the ray. But I direct the Sun to the quartile of ♃, and from that direction I subtract the fifth part of the nocturnal quadrate or semi-nocturnal arc of ♃, thus:

The Sun's direction to the □ of ♃ is thus obtained: From the Sun's semi-diurnal arc $7^h 18'$, is given its distance from the *medium cœli* 33° 31'; wherefore from ♃'s semi-nocturnal arc $7^h 33' = 113° 24'$, you have his secondary distance from the west 34° 40'; the oblique ascension of ♃'s opposition is 312° 33'; from which, subtracting the oblique ascension of the horoscope, there remains the primary distance of ♃ from the west 61° 28'; but because ♃ is above the west, and posited below, by the direction I add both his distances together, and make the arc of direction of ♃'s □ to the Sun 96° 8'; the semi-nocturnal arc of ♃ is 66° 36', whose fifth part is 13° 19'; which I subtract from the quadrate's arc of direction 96° 8', and there remains the Sun's arc of direction to the quintile of ♃ 82° 49'. There is not any difficulty in the Canon, if due attention be paid to the rays, whether they are projected from places above the Earth, or below, which cases seldom happen.

Canon XXXIV.

To direct the Significators to their own Rays.

The Sun and Moon, only by reason that they possess the virtue both of the significator and promittor, if directed to their own rays, have remarkable effects, but the houses are entirely excluded from their own rays; the arc of direction of each luminary's proper sextile is that which arises from its horary times, four times computed; of the quintile, with the addition of the fifth part of that sextile; the quartile's arc of direction is either the semi-diurnal or nocturnal arc; and so of the rest. If, however, the significator in these rays passes not from the upper to the lower hemisphere, or the contrary, as we have said, then we must calculate in the manner laid down in Canon XXXII, as if the Sun in the *primum mobile* was another promittor; and we shall know when it happens that the significator passes to the other hemisphere; by the oblique ascensions from which will appear the significator's distance from the horizon, which distance, if it be less, and the ray greater, that ray falls on the other hemisphere: if the distance be greater, the ray less, it falls on the same. As in *Cardinal Gymnascus*, the Sun's proper sextile is, indeed, a proof of itself, that it falls above the Earth, that is, above the west, because the Sun is above the cusp of the 9th house; yet, if we inquire by calculation, the Sun's horary times are 18° 15′, which, four times computed, makes the ✳ ray 73°; but the Sun's distance from the west is 75° 56′, which is greater, and the ✳ ray less; and, therefore, the Sun's ✳ ray falls upon the same hemisphere, and its arc of direction will be from the diurnal horary times, four times computed, 73°; but the Sun's proper quartile falls below the Earth, and is to be calculated as in Canon XXXII, as if the Sun was another promittor. Other examples follow; and remember, that if the Sun is below the Earth, he must likewise be directed to the proper rays, in the manner shewn in Canon XXXVI.

Canon XXXV.

To direct any Significator whatever to the Parallels.

I call a parallel in the world, that distance which two stars have in an equal proportion from the same angle, the one remaining beyond, the other within; as if one possesses the cusp of the 11th, and the other the 9th, then they are equally distant from the *medium cœli*, or meridian; and if one is found in the twelfth, the other in the second, they are equally distant from the ascendant, or horizon. But it is to be observed, that in this aspect it not only happens that an equal proportionate distance is formed from one of the angles, but likewise in some manner from every one of them; as a star in the ninth is equidistant from the *medium cœli*, as another star in the 11th; and these two stars are at an equal distance from the *imum cœli*, and from the east and west horizon. This will be evident, from the calculation, and should be taken as a proof of the virtue and efficacy of this aspect, and likewise for the ease of calculation. From hence it is inferred, that the calculation of this aspect may be made several ways, of which the easiest is by the distance from the *medium cœli*, whether these two stars form a parallel to the meridian or horizon, that is, whether both are found above the Earth, or below it: I mean when the direction is finished; for it matters not where they remain in the nativity. If both are found above, when they have this parallel, take the significator, and promittor's right distance, which they have in the nativity, from the *medium cœli*, and this distance I call the primary. Then say, by the *(Mundane Proportion.)* Rule of Three, if the horary times, or semi-diurnal arc of the significator, give his distance from the *medium cœli*, what distance will the promittor's horary times give? When you have found that, proceed according to Canon XIX. But if they form this aspect, while they are both below the Earth, take the distances from the *imum cœli* in the same manner, and the distances from the horoscope may be taken by the oblique ascension. If one be above the Earth, and the other posited below, or the contrary, take the distance of one from the *medium cœli*, and the other from the *imum cœli*, or make use of the opposite place of one. Examples follow.

Hitherto in this Canon, mention has been made of the direction to the parallels in the world, with the supposition that the significators remain immoveable in the horary circle of position. But because, in the nativity, the virtue both of the significator and promittor is impressed in the *primum mobile*, and this agreeable to the opinion of all professors, therefore both their virtues are conveyed, by the *primum mobile*, from east to west; consequently it may sometimes happen, that the significator and promittor are posited in an equal proportionate distance from the same angle, that is, in a mundane parallel of the same kind, of which, in this Canon, we give the calculation; and how great the active virtue of this application is, will be seen in the examples following: but it may happen that, by direction, even the significator and promittor, both may be posited above the Earth, or both below; or the one above, the other below, though in the nativity they are different. If both are posited above the Earth, take the semi-diurnal arc, and the significator's primary distance from the *medium cœli*, and the semi-diurnal arc of the promittor, with his distance, in right ascension from the significator, subtracting the lesser from the greater; then add their semi-diurnal arcs together, and say, as that sum is to the semi-diurnal arc of the promittor, so is the promittor's distance from the significator to the promittor's secondary distance from the *medium cœli*; use this distance, as in Canon XIX. You may likewise make use of the promittor's place, as significator, together with its semi-diurnal arc, right distance, &c. called a converse direction. If both are below the Earth, use the semi nocturnal arcs and distances from the *imum cœli*, in like manner. Lastly, if one be above, and the other below the Earth, take its opposite place, and use the semi-diurnal arc of that above the Earth, and the other's opposite place. Examples in Henry IV, King of France: Cardinals Pius and Gymnascus.

Rapt Canon

Canon XXXVI.

To direct the Sun, when below the Earth, to the Aspects in the World.

As the situation of the immobility, or position of the Sun, constituted below the Earth, is not the horary circle after the manner of others, but either the crepusculines parallel to the horizon, if the ☉ is in the crepusculines, or that which is made in the proportional distances from the obscure arc, as has been mentioned before, then doubtless the Sun receives the promittor's aspect in the world, when the promittor is proportionally distant from a Cardinal, or other house, as the Sun's distance is in the afore-mentioned places after the direction is finished, where his distance is different from his primary one in the nativity, as has been remarked ; for the Sun changes successively his secondary distance ; wherefore, the calculations of the Sun's directions to the aspects in the world, are attended with somewhat more difficulty. If the Sun is in the crepuscules, first calculate the Sun's direction to the promittor's ray, whether it be sextile, quartile, or trine, in the manner of other significators, that is, from the proportional distances from the angles, and other houses, by the horary times, &c. as hath been said above, which arc of direction may be called a fictitious one. Secondly, you may know what degree of the Zodiac the Sun at that time hath arrived at, by taking his polar elevation, in the usual manner, and in the same place the oblique ascension ; and by adding thereto the false arc of direction above taken, for this sum of the oblique ascension, will give the degree of the Zodiac, at which the Sun arrives in its revolution; for it is of very little, or no consequence, in case you do not know its true place in this calculation. Thirdly, with the Sun's primary distance from the horizon, see what crepuscular parallel it possesses, and in the same, take his secondary distance under the degree to which the supposed feigned direction shall come; then say, fourthly, As the ☉'s nocturnal horary times is to his secondary distance from the horizon, so is the promittor's horary times to his secondary distance from the angle or other determinate house, to be applied as usual, and you will have the true arc of direction. Let the example be in Cardinal Odoardus Farnese; I want to direct the ☉ to the △ of ♃ in the world, which he has to the Sun in an equal proportional distance from the cusp of the fifth, as the Sun is distant from the east, the Sun's horary times nocturnal 19° 17'; his primary distance from the horoscope 20° 57', ♃'s horary times 11° 51', to the pole of the eleventh house 18°, the oblique ascension of ♃'s opposition is 242° 38'; by subtracting from this the oblique ascension of the eleventh house, there remains ♃'s distance from the fifth house, 34° 3'. By the Rule of Three, you have ♃'s secondary distance 12° 59', which, subtracted from the primary, as both distances are from the preceding house, leaves the arc of direction 21° 4', which arc is necessary, in order to know the degree which the Sun may arrive at.

I require the Sun's polar elevation. If its duplicate nocturnal times gives the polar difference between the first and second houses 11°, the Sun's primary distance from the horoscope, 20° 57', will give 6° nearly, and there remains the Sun's polar elevation 38°, to which the Sun's oblique ascension is 284° 35'. To this I add the arc of direction 21° 4', and I make the sum 305° 39', answering in the same table to 15° 20' of ♑. In the tables of crepuscules for the pole 44°, I look for the Sun's primary distance from the horoscope, under 25° of ♐, and I find the ☉ in the crepusculine circle 13° 28';

under 15° 0' of ♑, I take the Sun's secondary distance 20° 46', always keeping the proportional part; wherefore again, by proportion, I say, As the Sun's horary times 19° 7', is to his secondary distance from the horoscope 20° 46', so is Jupiter's horary times, 11° 51' to ♃'s secondary distance from the fifth, 12° 52', which, being subtracted from the primary, leaves the true arc of direction, 21° 11'. To equate this, proceed as directed in Canon XVI, and it gives 18 years, at which time he was made a Cardinal (vide the Geniture). If the Sun is found in the obscure nocturnal place, first calculate the false direction, whether it be to the sextile, quartile, or trine ray, as we said in the first part of this Canon; secondly, find the degree of the ecliptic to which the Sun arrives by this direction; thirdly, let it be required, if the Sun's obscure arc gives his primary distance from the 4th, what secondary distance of the same will the obscure arc of that degree of the ecliptic give, at which the Sun arrives by the aforesaid direction; and when this secondary distance of ☉ from the *imum cœli* is known, if the ☉ be in the third or fourth house, use this distance; but if it be in the second or fifth house, subtract the Sun's duplicate nocturnal horary times from this distance, and the remainder will be the Sun's secondary distance from the third or fifth house; that is, when the direction is finished: then again say, As the Sun's nocturnal horary times is to his secondary distance from the determinate house, so is the promittor's horary times to its distance from that house from which it projects its proposed ray to the other house, from which you have taken the Sun's secondary distance, &c.: you must finish as usual. Let the example be in Cardinal Zachia: in this I want to calculate the Sun's direction to the ✶ of ☿, in the world, which ☿ has to the ☉, in a proportional distance from the third house, as the Sun is from the fifth; the Sun's horary times nocturnal are 14° 26', the oblique ascension of the Sun's opposition under the pole 18° of the eleventh house is 189° 7', from which subtract the oblique ascension of the eleventh, which is 175° 22', and there remains the Sun's distance from the fifth house, 13° 45'. Mercury's horary times nocturnal is 16°; his oblique ascension, under the pole of the third house, is 354° 13', wherefore there remains his primary distance from the third 58° 51'. I therefore say, if the Sun's horary times, 14° 26', give his distance from the fifth house, viz. 13° 45', what distance will ☿'s horary times 16° 0' give from third? Answer, the secondary distance of ☿ is 15° 15', which, subtracted from the primary, leaves the false arc of direction 43° 36', which is necessary to know the degree of the ecliptic, at which the Sun may arrive in its revolution. The Sun's pole, taken as usual is 25°; the oblique ascension of the same in the place of his opposition is 189° 35'; by adding to this the feigned arc of direction, the sum is 233 11', answering in the same table to 17° 30' of ♏, so that the Sun must remain in 17° 30' of ♉. Now it remains to know what is the Sun's distance from the *imum cœli*, or fifth house under 17° 30' of ♉, according to the proportional parts of the Sun's obscure arc, and also of 17° 30'

PRIMUM MOBILE.

of ♉. The semi-nocturnal arc of the ☉ is 5ʰ 46′, the arc of the whole crepusculine 1ʰ 44′; the Sun's obscure arc is, by subtraction, 4ʰ 2′.

	h. m.
The semi-nocturnal arc of 17° 30′ of ♉ is	4 50
The arc of the whole crepusculine . . .	2 4
The obscure arc of ♉, 17° 30′	2 46

The Sun's right ascension is 8°, from which subtract the right ascension of the *imum cœli*, gives the ☉'s primary distance therefrom 42° 38′. Now say, if the Sun's obscure arc 4ʰ 2′ gives his primary distance from the *imum cœli* 42° 38′, what will be the distance of the obscure arc of ♉ 17° 30′, which is 2ʰ 46′ ? And there arises the secondary distance 29° 15′; from which I subtract the ☉'s duplicate horary times 28° 52′, for the fourth house, and there remains the ☉'s distance from the fifth 0° 23′. Lastly, I demand, if the ☉'s horary times 14° 26′ give his distance from the 5th, 0° 23′, what will the horary times of ☿, 16° 0′, give? Answer, ☿'s secondary distance from the third, 0° 26′; which being subtracted from the primary distance of the same, 58° 51′, there remains the true arc of direction 58° 25′: more examples you will see afterwards in their places. To the other rays, quintile, sesqui-quadrate, and biquintile, after you have calculated the false arc of direction to the sextile, quartile, or trine, add or subtract the proportional parts, as we have said above, then see what degree the Sun has arrived at, and in that his secondary distance from the angles and houses; and what distance he hath, the promittor always should be at the same distance. See also, what I have said elsewhere in an example given for illustration. To this Canon pertains the mode of directing the Sun to the proper rays in the world, for his place is to be taken under the *primum mobile*, as if it was another promittor different from the Sun, always remaining immoveable under the same polar elevation; wherefore let all be done as has been said. The Sun's virtue is impressed on the *primum mobile*, under the determinate degree of the ecliptic, and in mundo to a determinate polar elevation, and in either place their virtue continues immoveable; but that which is impressed in the *primum mobile*, is moved round the world with the same *primum mobile*, and is separated from the mundane impression; and this remaining immoveable, under its polar elevation, is moved to the more eastern parts under the *primum mobile*, and so arrives at the rays of the other virtue impressed under the *primum mobile*; this, in a direct motion, is the same as the promittor; in a converse, as a significator; on the contrary, the other, &c.; the reasons of which distinction you may see in the Celestial Philosophy.

Canon XXXVII.

To direct any Significator whatever, in a converse Motion, to all the Aspects made in the World.

If you have rightly understood all the Canons in this third part, this, likewise, before you will be found very easy; for it contains nothing more than what we have said in this third part, with this difference only, that in a contrary manner, not the promittor, but the significator, remaining immoveable under the *primum mobile*, is carried to the place of position of the promittor, or to their rays, which continue immoveable in a mundane situation; therefore the rules given, concerning the significator, are to be understood of the promittor; and, on the contrary, those given relative to the promittor, are to be understood of the significator; for which reason, there is an alteration in the order of numbers of the Golden Rule; so that, in the first place, the horary times of the promittor are to be taken; and, in the second, its distance from the angles or houses; in the third, the horary times of the significator; and the fourth number will be the secondary distance of that significator, which is to be compared with the primary distance of the same from the cardinals or houses, in the manner before explained, relating to the promittor in Canon XIX. There are more examples afterwards, together with their effects. The angles are not directed in a converse motion, for they have none to the preceding places.

Canon XXXVIII.

To direct the Significator to the West, with the Addition and Subtraction of the Parts which is formed from the interjacent Rays or Stars, according to the Precepts of Ptolemy.

By the oblique descensions or the ascensions of the opposite places to the horizon of the country, direct the significator to the west, not omitting his latitude, if it has any; meanwhile, you must consider what stars or mundane rays are intercepted between the significator and the west, which you will know from the direction of the stars or rays to the west; for those that arrived first, that is, by a less arc of direction than that of the significator to the west, are interposited; but those that follow by a greater arc of direction are not interjacent, and you must observe their arc of direction, whether of the stars or rays to the west. Then of every one of the planets, which either lie between or interpose the rays, take the conditionary arc, the horary times to the hemisphere, wherein the stars, and not the rays, may be; for it is thus, the nocturnal from the night, and diurnal from the day, as Ptolemy informs us. Lastly, say, by the Golden Rule, if the whole conditionary arc of a star give its horary times, what will a star or rays arc of direction to the west give? Multiply the second and third, and divide by the first; add the result, if treating of the fortunate; but if of the unfortunate, subtract it from the significator's arc of direction to the west, and it will give the arc of direction, augmented or diminished, according to Ptolemy, which is be equated in the usual manner. Suppose the example be in *Cardinal Dominic Gymnascus,* the Sun's arc of direction to the west is 75° 56'; ♃ is interjacent, whose semi-diurnal arc is 113° 24'; horary times 18° 53', his arc of direction to the west is 61° 28'. I then require if the whole diurnal arc of ♃, 226° 48', give his horary times 18° 53',

PRIMUM MOBILE. 107

how many will the arc of direction 61° 28' give? The answer is 5° 7'.† Venus interposes the Sextile; the right ascension of ♀ is 160° 46'; which, subtracted from the right ascension of the *medium cœli*, makes the distance of ♀ from thence 0° 19'; which, subtracted from the duplicate horary times of ♀ 33° 14', there remains the arc of direction of ♀ to the ✶ of the west 32° 55'. If, therefore, the whole diurnal arc of ♀, which is 199° 36', gives the horary times 16° 37', how many will the arc of direction 32° 55' give? and I receive for answer, 2° 45'. Venus likewise interposes the quintile. I compute the four horary times of ♀, and they make 66° 28', the fifth part of which is 13° 28'; I subtract this from the ✶'s arc of direction, and there remains the arc of direction of the quintile of ♀ to the west 19° 27', from which, in the fourth place, are had 1° 38', all which make 9° 24' of the fortunate to be added; so that the Sun's arc of direction to the west is augmented to 85° 20'. Mars interposes the □, whose arc of direction, by the right ascensions of the *medium cœli*, is 7° 57'; if, therefore, the whole diurnal arc of Mars, which is 189° 48', gives his horary times 15° 15', the direction's arc 7° 57' will give 0° 40'. Saturn interposes the sesqui-quadrate; his distance from the *imum cœli* is 18° 13', which I subtract from his duplicate horary times, which are 35° 24', and there remains his distance from the third house, 17° 11'; to this I add his horary times,

---

† If you divide the arc of direction to the west by 12, it gives the proportional part required.

and I make the arc of direction of the sesqui-quadrate of ♄ to the west 34° 53′. If, therefore, the whole nocturnal arc of ♄ 212° 14′ gives his horary times 17° 42′, the arc of direction 34° 53′ will give 2° 54, which, added to ♂'s 0° 40′, make 3° 34′ to be subtracted from the Sun's arc of direction, 85° 20′, and there remains the true arc of direction 81° 46′, calculated according to Ptolemy's method, which shews the years the native has lived, as you may see afterwards in its proper place. That you may not look upon what we have said as a dream, and therefore to be rejected, see the example of Urban VIII. In the Celestial Philosophy, page 277, you may likewise do the same in the example of Leonora Ursina, Duchess of Sfortia. But how largely and differently authors have spoken of this direction of the significator to the west, putting various constructions on the words of Ptolemy, is known to every one. See Cardan in his Commentaries, Maginus in his *Primum Mobile*, and the Use of Legal Astrology in Physic, c. viii. where he delivers the sentiments of Naibod. Argoll censures wholly this doctrine of Ptolemy's, of directing the moderators of Life to the west, as vain and useless. But I say, it is worthy of remark, and altogether conformable to truth; because, then the rays and intermediate stars of the malign only lessen the arc of direction to the west, and do not destroy life; when, by a right direction, the moderator of life does not remain at the same time with the malignant planet; for should this happen, they kill, without any manner of doubt, as in *Salviatis*, and several other examples.

PART IV.

OF

Secondary Directions, Progressions, Ingresses, and Transits.

HAVING already calculated and obtained the number of years of the primary directions of the significators to their promittors, and likewise taken the lords of the Terms, all which Ptolemy, in the last chapter of the fourth book, calls the General Arbiters of Times; for this reason, because they preordain the general times of their effects, which, as its motion is slow, and its perseverance long, discovers its effects after a very long time; that is, after months and years. In order that we may know, in this extent of time, on what particular month and day the effects appear, Ptolemy proposes these motions for observation, wherein, when the majority of the causes agree together, then, doubtless, the effect is accomplished, or most clearly manifests itself: whence we ought to conclude, that though, with our greatest care and exact calculation, we have obtained the true time, not only to the year, but also month and day of the primary direction, we cannot argue from thence, that the effect has happened on that very day, and therefore it matters not, though the primary direction has been even exceeded, or not quite exactly accounted to a few minutes, as notwithstanding the particular times of their effects, may depend upon other motions of the causes now proposed; for which reason the times of these subsequent motions of the causes demand our greatest attention; and we must not insist upon the first places which present themselves, but inquire further, till we find where proof may be had, viz. by the method we are now going to speak of.

Canon XXXIX.
OF SECONDARY DIRECTION.

Under this name, I understand the motion of the celestial causes which are made on the days succeeding the nativity, according as they are marked in the Ephemeris; for the aspects to the luminaries and angles, which happen on those days, have their effects from every day to every year; so that the first day may be referred to the first year, as a measure to the mensurate; the second to the second, &c. for which reason we must observe, when the luminaries are posited in any aspect of the stars; for if with the fortunes, they conduce to happiness and good health; if with the unfortunate, and from an hostile ray or parallel of declination, they portend misery and distress in those years which depend on those days these aspects happen on. But, without doubt, these effects are remarkable, if at that time there are primary directions of the same kind and nature; and, moreover, from such motions originate the climactical, or, more properly, critical years; for, on the days the ☽ is posited in the ☌, □, or ☍, to and with the place of the nativity, she makes the years which depend on those days obnoxious to dangers and infirmities. But, if at that time any unfortunate primary direction of the vital prorogator is powerful, life may be said to be in danger, and, particularly, if in the secondary direction, the Moon is afflicted by the malignant planets. But, if the Sun is so too, the danger is still greater. Lastly, if the primary direction is unfortunate, when the ingress and transit agree, death is inevitable. See the examples in the Exposition of the Nativities.

Canon XL.
OF PROGRESSIONS.

That progressions, or, if we should say, equal processes, taken as usual, according to the general opinion and custom hitherto received, are fictious, impossible, and contrary to nature, has been sufficiently proved in my Celestial Philosophy. The method which you are to take as natural, we now explain and prove in every one of the future examples. Know, therefore, that progressions are derived from embolismical lunations succeeding the nativity, every one of which are formed in the space of twenty-nine days nearly, in which time the Moon separates from her ☌, with the Sun forming the □ and ☍, and returns to a □ and ☌ again, in which circuit she passes over almost thirteen signs, and the Sun one sign.

Progressions, if we may give our judgment, originate from these motions of the luminaries; for the first lunation succeeding the nativity, or the ☽'s circuit, bounds the progression of the first year of the native; the second, the progression of the second year; the third, of the third, &c. in such a manner, however, that the first part of the ☽'s circuit may measure or bound the first part of the year; the middle, the middle; the last, the last, &c.

To calculate the progressions, and know with ease where they will arrive at; so many embolismical lunations succeeding the nativity, must be computed, as there are years which have elapsed of the age of the native, by always placing the Moon in that appearance and distance from the Sun she is at in the nativity. Lastly, for every month to the Moon's place, there must be added 32° 30′, which are the twelfth part of one lunation; but if you desire to obtain a ready calculation of the progressions for several years, take notice that the ☽ does not finish the twelve lunations in one whole year, but in eleven days less; having, therefore, the Moon's distance from the Sun in the nativity, look for this eleventh day before the end of the first year after the nativity; and when you have found it, then the progression of twelve years are completed; in like manner, twenty-two days before the end of the second year after the nativity, the progression of twenty-four years are completed, &c. Thence proceed from every lunation to every year of the native's age, and from every one of the signs with 32° 30′ of the ☽'s motion to every month; and whenever the luminaries are well affected, as well in the progressions as towards the places of the favourable planets of the nativity, they induce to happiness; and on the contrary, &c. See examples in every one of the nativities following.

Canon XLI.
OF INGRESSES.

Of these we have said some are active, some passive. ACTIVE ingresses are the familiarities of active stars, acquired by an universal daily motion, with the places of the primary and secondary directions and processes of the significators. PASSIVE are the familiarities of the universal prorogators in the whole world with the active stars of the secondary directions and processes. Under the name of ACTIVE stars, we mean whatever hath the quality of acting, and are usually posited in the promittor's place, as ♄, ♃, ♂, ♀, ☿ ; and the ☉ and ☽ also, when they assume the nature of any of the afore-mentioned; and such ingresses, whether of the benign to the places of the motions of the significators, or of any of the significators to the places of the motions of the benign; that is, both active and passive are good, but of the malign, in the same manner, are hurtful, as will be observed in the following examples.

Canon XLII.
OF TRANSITS.

Some of these, also, are active, some passive; the active are the familiarities of active stars acquired by an universal daily motion with the prorogators of the nativity; that is, with their immoveable places. Passive Transits are the familiarities of any of the significators in the world with the active stars of the nativity; that is, with their immoveable places, according to their immobility, of which we have frequently mentioned;

R

so that in this, ingresses differ from transits; that ingresses respect the places of the moveable motions; but transits, the fixed places of the nativity. But the most of all to be observed, are the lunations in the daily motions, whether it be ☌, ☐, or ☍ of the ☽, with the ☉ upon the obnoxious places; for when the subject of the direction is on the progress to happiness, if the lunations are good, by reason of the aspects of fortunate stars, they greatly conduce to the procuring of happiness in their effects; but if, on the contrary, we are speaking of the directions and process to the unfortunate planets, and those lunations are unfortunate, on account of the hostile rays there of the malignant stars, the native must be supposed to be in very great danger; and, doubtless, there is great reason to fear it, from the unhappy event of the things signified. Hence it is evident, that promotions to dignity very frequently happen in lunations wherein the luminaries are surrounded by the benefics. On the contrary, tribulations, diseases, murders, &c. in lunations wherein the luminaries are besieged by the unfavourable planets: and this is found never to fail.

And this is the true doctrine of Ptolemy, and the whole of this most noble science.

But let us begin our observations on the examples which we have subjoined to verify things, and likewise to elucidate the Canons.

THIRTY
Remarkable Nativities,

TO PROVE THE

TRUTH OF THINGS BY EXAMPLE,

AND ILLUSTRATE THE

METHOD

OF

Computation by the Canons.

TO THE READER.

There is nothing by which man ever arrived at a more perfect knowledge of the secrets of nature, than by the immediate effects of things, that is, by the experience which the understanding discovers to us; for from these, it is evident, that they who first directed their studies to philosophy, have opened a way to discover secrets replete with wonder.

And, indeed, reason, for its excellence, is better than example; as is the immortal soul, whose work it is, than that of corporeal sense: yet, in a consequential order, this has the precedence, and is, as it were, the door and way to that understanding, to which there is not the least access, unless transmitted through the senses. Further, whatever, by the light of reason, the mind of man may either comprehend or invent, if experience does not make it plain, is justly and deservedly condemned and rejected as false. Of the power of the Stars, and their manner of acting upon those inferior elementary and compound bodies, beginning from the first causes, properties, passions, motions, and other active qualities, being guided by reason in all and each of them, from the axioms of the most eminent men in physic and mathematics, I have sufficiently treated in my Celestial Philosophy; and from thence, by way of theory, I have transferred hither a few theses the most concise. But, as there are some who refuse to follow reason and the most enlightened authors for their guides, I was unwilling to make any distinction between this part of philosophy and experience; that they who will listen to reason and the understanding, might, by the help of the senses, and, to use the expression, with their hands, attain to and comprehend the method I have taken; for which reason, it seemed good to me, in this place, to subjoin thirty Nativities of the most famous men, truly worthy of admiration; and, that no one might condemn them, either as false or selected, in preference to any casually taken, to suit my purpose, I have extracted them from the most approved authors, and such only, wherein not the horoscope, which may, with a small variation of time, be very easily adapted to the aspects of the stars, but the luminaries become the moderators of life; which, as they always continue in the same place in the Zodiac, notwithstanding the times of the nativities are remote, I thought proper to dispose these with the calculations of the aspects and directions, in the most convenient order.

Now, therefore, my very courteous reader, if you look for any power in, or true and natural knowledge from, the stars, in any of these examples, when, from the natural effects contained in them, you find any calculations for directions more agreeable to time and nature, be so kind as to publish them, and point out my errors; and, by so doing, you will oblige me greatly, as, in every thing, I desire nothing but plain and simple truth; but if, after all, you cannot find any, confess, ingenuously, that my opinion concerning this Celestial Science is right, my mode of calculation true, and the method universal; and hesitate no longer in confirming it to be so. But, in these examples, it is to be observed:—

1. That the luminaries preside over subjected things, not only by that one motion of direction, which is made in the Zodiac according to the succession of the signs, agreeable to the method usually followed by all professors, but by both, viz. the right and converse.

2. That the same familiarities, by the same method of calculating, may be found in more of the like examples, when alledged as proofs, is the greatest evidence of the truth of things; for it might be argued, that they happened to agree only in one example.

3. That my directions are conformable to the nature of things; as, for example, I do not take the dignities from the horoscope, but from the Sun and *medium cœli*, according to Ptolemy and others.

4. I have not taken remarkable effects from the fixed stars, as many do (and, truly, without foundation), but from the erratics; though the fixed stars do specify and afford some little assistance to the power of the erratics.

5. In all these examples, the measure I have found for the arc of direction corresponds with the years of the age.

6. I have not varied the time of the nativities to make the directions agree with my calculations; but if, in any example, I have made a little alteration, it is very small, and scarce makes any difference in the arc of direction of the luminaries, whether direct or converse, except only in the mundane parallels. However, from this

small alteration it may be inferred, that either on that account the time is reduced to the true one, or, at least, that the directions of the parallels in the world were not far distant, and might, notwithstanding, have been of very good use, though there were no change of time in the nativity; for every direction causes an alteration in bodies; but the full effect plainly appears, by means of the powerful directions which arrive first, and the subsequent assist more or less, according to the proximity of the application, or their strength and power are greater or less: but no credit is to be given to the time of those nativities, in which authors have adopted the horoscope for the giver of life, where either of the luminaries ought to have been taken; for we may reasonably conclude, that, when the said authors have not found their directions of that luminary to which, undoubtedly, belonged the power of life, to agree with the effects, they have made a considerable alteration in the given time of the nativity, in order that they might bring down the horoscope to any aspect of the planets. I can affirm what I have said to be true, for in my youth I saw several nativities, which were afterwards published by the authors, wherein was a visible alteration in the time, and the reason why was, that they might answer the above end.

7. In these examples you will plainly see, that I have always taken the moderator of life by the rules of Ptolemy; as in the day, first the Sun, if he is found in an aphetical place, then the Moon, &c.; but in the night, first the Moon, &c.

8. You are to observe, that if either of the luminaries, being the significator of life, is found in a nativity, with an hostile ray in the zodiac, by the application of any malignant planet strong in power, the same is weak, for its virtues are but small, as a prorogator in the zodiac, but stronger through the other motions and aspects, for then the moderation in the zodiac seems to be, in a manner, separated; and in the same

manner ought we to reason in the other motions; for if, lastly, according to all the motions, and every species of aspect, the significator of life is aspected by the rays of the unfortunate planets, the native, according to Ptolemy, will not survive, especially if the fortunate afford no assistance, &c. yet each direction must always be consulted and calculated, agreeably to the two kinds of familiarities.

9. You may know that those nativities are stronger, when either of the luminaries become the significator of life, by reason of the duplicate motion of the prorogation, which does not happen when the horoscope of the country is the giver of life, for it only performs in a right motion, and not converse.

10. You are not to observe what is generally alledged by professors, respecting the satellites of the luminaries for dignities; viz. that the satellites are those planets which are found within 30° on either side towards

the luminaries; but that a satellite is any kind of aspect of the stars to the luminaries of what kind soever; which, if it be made by application, its power extends inwardly over the whole orb of light of the aspecting planet, and the more so, as the proximity is greater, but by separation it is not so. This doctrine may be seen in several chapters of Ptolemy; for, an aspecting star influences the significator, and disposes him to produce effects co-natural to him, by a subsequent direction. But a star of no aspect does not predispose the significator, and produces very little or no effect of its nature by a subsequent direction; this is the true doctrine of the stars.

11. That in these examples, as to the time of death, I have observed the most powerful directions of them all, and afterwards I give a reason why the antecedents that are past are not anaretical; from which it is evident, that the directions, whereof I now give the calculations, were the true anaretic causes.

12. There is no truth in what is commonly alledged by some ; viz. that as I invented the mundane aspects, it is no wonder if any aspect may agree with the times of the effects in those examples, as well the familiarities in mundo among the stars as to the angles; but I afterwards rejected the aspects in the zodiac, and also the antiscions to the angles. I do not direct the significators to the cusps of the houses, nor to the ☋, ☊, or to the fixed stars, as having of themselves a power to kill. I do not direct the planets ♄, ♃, ♂, ♀, ☿, as if they were significators, which is the practice of several professors. Maginus has described the rays in the equator; others, besides the rays, which the ingenious Kepler thought to be efficacious, add the semi-sextile and sesquiquadrate. Wherefore, if you carefully observe, you will doubtless perceive I have produced less aspects than other authors.

13. If you are desirous to see of what importance the secondary directions are, to discern the particular times of effects, and

also the progressions, I have calculated the ingresses and transits, both active and passive ; but the equal processes, according to the usual and general way, how idle and empty in effect they are, I will leave to yourself to consider, as I would not spend time to no purpose to calculate them.

14. The revolution, as taught by some, I have not seen, though in reality they may possess some virtue, but only according to the constitution of the stars to the places of the prorogators of the nativity, and their places of direction, but no farther, as Ptolemy was of opinion, and briefly expresses himself in his Chapter of Life. "Those " who are afflicted, both in the places and " conclusions of the years, by the revolution " of the stars infecting the principal places, " have reason to expect certain death ;" therefore, let any one, if he pleases, observe the return of the years, but at the same time, let him not place so great a value on them, as some authors usually do ; who, from the constitution of the stars, judge of

the Sun's return in the same manner as of the nativity; so that they are not afraid to dissent from the same, nor even from the directions.

15. And note, that when I speak of dignities and promotions, I am to be understood in a natural way, as I have made mention of in the Celestial Philosophy, and in such a manner, that men may endeavour to render themselves capable and worthy of mental accomplishments, as well as of the other virtues, and not by any means that those who are at liberty to act as they please should be compelled to, and, as it were, pushed upon, advancement: for I am wholly of opinion, that every man is the author of his own fortune, next, however, to the divine decree, according to that of the prophet,

"*In manibus tuis sortes meæ.*"
"My lot is in thine hand."

Lastly, if, in the calculations of the directions, you find any difference of minutes from the time of the effects (this, however, I am certain, will always be very small), remember, first, that the places of the stars are not perfectly known to us; and then in the producing of effects, several motions of the stars concur to prevent a true calculation; as the secondary directions, the process, ingress, transit, lunation, &c. which may cause the effect either to precede or follow the true calculation.

THIRTY
Remarkable Nativities.

I SHALL begin, by drawing my examples from the most principal families in Europe; and in them, by way of conciseness, only regard important accidents.

EXAMPLE I.

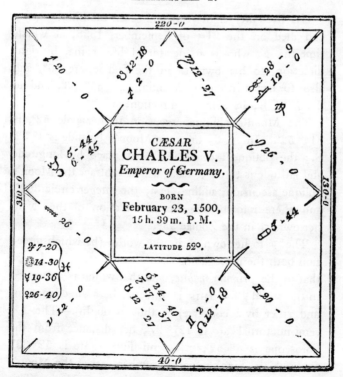

PRIMUM MOBILE.

	LATITUDES.				DECLINATIONS.		
♄	..	2°	0'	S.	15°	13'	N.
♃	..	0	50	S.	9	37	S.
♂	..	0	53	N.	19	52	N.
☉	..	0	0		6	8	S.
♀	..	1	3	S.	2	13	S.
☿	..	3	0	N.	1	51	S.
☽	..	2	4	S.	25	24	S.

HE lived fifty-eight years and seven months, nearly; and died on the 21st of September, 1558, at which time the ☽, who is moderator of life, came, by right direction, to her own □ in the Zodiac, arc 55°, and also to her own □ in Mundo, arc 55° 33', and to the ☍ of ♄, by converse direction, arc 52° 58'.

The Moon's oblique ascension to her pole 52°, is 314° 52'. In ♈ 6° 45'; the Moon's latitude is 4° 32' S.; the oblique ascension of that place by longitude and latitude is 9° 52'; from which subtract the Moon's oblique ascension, adding, first, the integer circle 360°, and there remains the arc of direction of the ☽ to her own □ in the Zodiac 55°.

The ☽ to her own □ in the world (by which direction both the prorogatory virtues of life are injured, viz. that in the *primum mobile,* and that which is impressed in the world; for THIS is directed by a direct motion, and THAT by a converse) is thus wrought:—The ☽'s semi-nocturnal arc is 127° 27', her distance from the horoscope is 4° 52', ☽'s semi-diurnal arc is 52° 33', from which, for the fourth number, arises the Moon's secondary distance from the *medium cœli* 2° 0': This subtracted from the primary, which is 57° 33′, there remains the arc of direction 55° 33′.

To the ☍ of ♄, by converse motion, the distance of ♄ from the *imum cœli* is 5° 43′, for his right ascension is 45° 43′; the pole's elevation of the fifth and eleventh is 24°, the semi-nocturnal arc of ♄ is 69° 37′, the third part thereof 23° 13′, which gives the pole's elevation of ♄ nearly 6°; to this pole the oblique ascension of the opposite place of ♄ is 227° 21′, and the ☽'s oblique ascension there is 280° 19′; from which subtracting that of the opposition of ♄, leaves the arc of direction 52° 58′. For the equation, to take the years, I add this arc 52° 58′ to the ☉'s right ascension, which is 345° 44′, and I make the sum 38° 42′, answering to 11° 10′ of ♉, at which the sun, from the day and hour of the nativity, arrives in 58 days, which denotes so many years; but it must be observed, that the converse directions did not wait for the other two by a right motion, as by it the ☽ in the nativity, applied to the □ of the infortunes in the world, and to the sesqui-quadrate of ♂ in the zodiac; so that the significator of life appeared stronger and more fortunate by a converse motion: for though the ☽ was favoured by the ✶ of ♃ in the zodiac, the infortunes prevailed, as being more numerous and in the angles.

In the 41st year of his age, when, after a series of successes, *Fortune* turned her back upon him; he suffered a very great loss of his fleet and army, by a tempest near the coast of Africa: the ☽ arrived at the parallel of ♂ in the world, whilst both, by a converse motion of the *primum mobile*, were in rapt motion round the world, for they happened to be posited in equally proportional distances from the horoscope. The ☽'s semi-diurnal arc is 52° 33′, the semi-diurnal arc of ♂'s ☊ is 62° 27′, and their sum is 115° 0′; therefore, as the sum of the semi-diurnal arcs 115° 0′ is to the ☽'s semi-diurnal arc 52° 33′, so is the difference between ♂'s ☊ and the ☽ in right ascension 45° 25′ (for the right ascension of ♂'s ☊ is 232° 3′, and the right ascension of the ☽ 277° 28′), to the ☽'s secondary distance from the *medium cœli* 20° 45′, which, subtracted from the primary, which is 57° 28′, leaves the arc of direction 36° 43′, which, being equated in the usual way, gives 41 years.

In his 19th year, when he was chosen emperor, the ☽ had arrived at the cusp of the twelfth, and ♀ at the second; therefore the *medium cœli* was directed to the ✶ of the ☽ and △ of ♀, and they were both in parallel by rapt motion: the ☽ also came to the ✶ of ♀ in zodiac, near 26° ♑, and to the quintile in the world by converse motion. But the most important was, the ☉ to parallel of ♃ in the zodiac, near 25° of ♈, where he acquires the same declination as ♃; the ☉'s crepuscular arc is $1^h 58'$, his semi-nocturnal arc $6^h 32'$, from which subtract the crepusculine arc, and his obscure arc is $4^h 34'$. The crepusculine arc of ♈ 25° is $2^h 18'$, its semi-nocturnal arc is $5^h 9'$, and the obscure arc is $2^h 51'$. The ☉'s distance from the *imum cœli* is 54° 16′; wherefore, as the ☉'s obscure arc $4^h 34'$ is to his distance 54° 16′, so is the obscure arc of 25 ♈ $2^h 51'$ to its secondary distance 32° 22′; from which, subtracting the primary distance of ♈ 25°, there remains the arc of direction 17° 31′, which being equated, gives 19 years. For 58 years and 7 months nearly, I thus calculate the secondary directions. To the day and hour of the nativity I add 58 days for the same number of years, and 14 hours for the 7 months, and I come to the 22d day of April of the same year 1500, with 5^h 39′ P. M., and in the secondary directions the planets are in the following position:

	☉	♄	♃	♂	♀	☿	☽	☊
Deg. of Long.	♉ 11.36	♉ 24.11	♓ 20.28	♊ 29.19	♊ 8.4	♉ 5.45	♓ 4.0	♊ 9.8
Lat.		S. 1.46	S. 1. 2	N. 0.38	S. 0.22	S. 1.23	S. 5.0	

When the ☽ was in the 4th degree of ♓, lat. 5° South, by which she had the declination 14° 44′; the same with ♄, as well there as in the nativity; and lastly, on the day of death, wherein ♂ was in the 4th degree of ♍, in ☍, (that is partile) to this place of the ☽. The ☉, in the secondary direction, on the 22d day of April, was in 12° of ♉, in the parallel of ♄'s declination there both from the nativity and at death. The ☉, on the day of death, from the ☍, entered the place of the direction of the ☽'s □ in the zodiac; and, two days before he died, there happened to be a lunation of the ☽'s □ with the ☉ in those obnoxious places. On the day of his death, the Moon was in the last degree of ♑, with South latitude, whereby she was posited in the same parallel of declination ♂ was in, on the 22d day of April, of the secondary direction; therefore, there was a mutual permutation of aspect between the Moon and Mars, viz. an active and passive ingress to these motions on the day of death; and is an admirable proof of the calculation being exactly true. The places of the planets, on the day he died, which was the 21st of September 1558, are as follow:

	☉	☽	♄	♃	♂	♀	☿	☊
Deg. of Lon.	♎ 7.31	♑ 29.29	♉ 24.31	♒ 2. 4	♍ 4 28	♌ 29.25	♎ 17.23	♈ 19.20
Lat.		S. 4.55	S. 2.34	S. 0.51	N. 0.24	0. 0	N. 0.42	

The manner I look for the process for the same year is thus: For full 48 years, 48 embolismic lunations are finished, in four years following the nativity, yet less than that by 44 days, that is, 11 × 4, for we have said in its Canon, that the Moon finisheth 12 embolismic lunations in 11 days less than a whole year; wherefore, from the 23d February, 1504, subtracting 44 days, we go back to the 10th January, when the Moon, from the 22d degree of ♏, is posited in the same distance from the Sun which she hath in the nativity, viz. of 68°; and then the process is finished for full 48 years; then, for the other ten years, passing over the other 10 embolismic lunations, I come to the 31st of October of the same year, 1504, when the Moon was in 10 degrees of ♍, and the Sun in 18 degrees of ♏. That we may preserve their distance from each other at the nativity for the six remaining months, and 27 days, i. e. to the day of his death, I add to this place of the Moon six signs and 15 degrees for the six months, and 29° 30' for the 27 days, and I come to 24° 30' of ♈, wherein the Moon is posited on the 18th of November. In the progressions, the planets are thus posited:

	☉	☽	♄	♃	♂	♀	☿	☋
Deg. of Lon.	♐	♈	♌	♌	♐	♐	♐	♓
	6.3	24.30	3.26	16.15	14.15	13.40	22.44	10.39
Lat.		N.	N. 0.11	N. 0.40	S. 0.2	N. 0.9	S. 0.40	

The Sun was in six degrees of ♐, which ♂ entered by a quadrate ray, on the day of death: the Moon had passed the place of her direction in the zodiac; but when she was arrived at 25 degrees of ♈, she struck upon, by ingress, (on the day of death) the parallel of ♂'s declination, and entered on the fatal day from the □; from the 24th degree of ♑, this place of her progression; the Moon also applied in the progression to the □ of ♄. The most noble satellite in this Nativity is to the Moon the conditionary luminary, from the ✶ of ♃, and from the quintile of ☿. To the *medium cœli,* from ♃ and the Sun the △, from ♀ the biquintile. To the ☉, from ♃ and ☿ by presence, from ♄ and ♂ the Sextile.

It is presumed that the following incidents of the life of this extraordinary man will not be unacceptable to the intelligent reader, as they may serve to illustrate the effects of Celestial Influx, by comparing the effects with the cause which produced them. At the age of 14, he had the government of the Netherlands given him; at 16 he was crowned King of Spain; at 19 he was elected Emperor, and crowned the following year at *Aix la Chapelle.* He had great wars with Francis the First King of France, whom he took prisoner at the battle of Pavie, in the year 1525, and sent him to Madrid; he likewise seized Rome, and besieged the Pope in his castle there, and annexed the Dutchy of Milan to his house for ever. In 1532, at a diet then held at Ratisbon, the Protestant confession of faith was exhibited, and publicly read before him; some years after which he entered into wars with the Protestants, and took John Frederick, Elector of Saxony, prisoner in 1545; and thereupon transferred the Electoral dignity from him to Maurice, Duke of Saxony. He also caused Philip, Landgrave of Hesse, to be put into custody; but, in the end, concluded the Peace of Passaw, in the year 1552; three years after which, he abdicated the government, and retired to a cloister, in St. Justus's monastery in Spain, where he died in 1558. He married Isabel, the daughter of Emanuel, King of Portugal, by whom he had issue, one son and two daughters; besides whom he had one natural daughter, named Margaret, by Mademoiselle de Plumbes, which daughter was married to Alexander de Medicis, Duke of Urbin; and, after his decease, to Octavia Farnesse, Duke of Parma. He had also a natural son by Mademoiselle de Blomberg, viz. the renowned Don John of Austria.

EXAMPLE II.

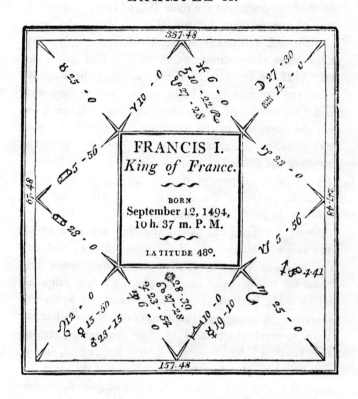

FRANCIS I. *King of France.*

BORN
September 12, 1494,
10 h. 37 m. P. M.

LATITUDE 48°.

	LATITUDES.			DECLINATIONS.		
♄	2°	10′	S.	9°	43′	S.
♂	0	24	N.	14	12	N.
☿	2	0	S.	9	22	S.
☽	2	30	N.	10	2	S.

THIS King, in a stout engagement with a large body of the enemy, at the river Po, in Italy, suffered a very great overthrow, his general and valiant armies being all slain, and he himself wounded and taken prisoner by the soldiers of the Emperor Charles V. This was in the year 1525, on the 24th of February, when he was 30 years and five months old; at which time the Sun, who is the significator of glory, liberty, and power, came, by a right direction, to the mundane parallel of ♄, and also to the parallel declination of ♂ ; and, by a converse motion, was posited as near as possible to the Moon's ☍, and mundane parallel of ♄.

To the parallel of the declination of Mars, the calculation is as follows; and it corresponds with the time of the direction, when the Sun arrives at 6° of ♏, where he obtains the declination 13° 34′, and the declination of Mars 14° 12′, for this reason, either because the true place of Mars is wanting a few minutes, which made the declination of Mars lesser ; or, as the luminaries, by reason of the magnitude of their bodies, begin to touch at a parallel of their declination, before they arrive at it by the centre of their bodies ; or, lastly, that they have already reached the times of the other directions : be it as it will, the Sun was conjoined, as near as could be, to the declination of ♂ ; it might be, likewise, that the secondary directions and powerful ingresses may have made the effect appear a little before the exact application of the primary direction.

Of the Sun.

The semi-nocturnal arc is	5ʰ	57'
Crepusculine arc	1	50
Obscure arc	4	7
Right ascension	178°	46'
Distance from the *imum cœli*	20	58

Of the 6th degree of ♏.

The semi-nocturnal arc is	7ʰ	2'
Crepusculine arc	1	50
Obscure arc	5	12
Right ascension	213°	40'
Primary distance from the *imum cœli*	55	52
wherefore, as ☉'s obscure arc	4ʰ	7'
is to his dist. from the 4th	20°	58'
so is the obscure arc of ♏ 6°	5ʰ	12'
to its secondary distance	26°	29'

which being subtracted from the primary, leaves the arc of direction 29° 23'.

The Sun's direction to the parallel of ♄ in *Mundo*, by direct motion is thus calculated.

As the ☉'s semi-nocturnal arc, 5ʰ 57', is to its distance from the *imum cœli*, 26° 29' (which the Sun requires after the direction is finished, at which time, as we have said, he lustrates the sixth degree of Scorpio), so is ♄ 's semi-diurnal arc, 5ʰ 16', to his secondary distance from the *medium cœli* 23° 47', which added to the primary (because ♄ passes from the ascendant part of heaven to the descendant), which is 4° 56', give the arc of direction 28° 43'; to equate which I add to it the ☉'s right ascension, and it makes 207° 29′ = 29° 30′ ♎, to which the ☉, from the day and hour of nativity, arrives in 31 days, answering to so many years.

The next is the ☉ to the parallel of ♄ in *Mundo,* converse direction.

Thus wrought, as ♄'s semi-diurnal arc, 5^h 16′, is to his distance from the *medium cœli* 4° 56′, so is the ☉'s semi-nocturnal arc 5^h 57′ to the ☉'s secondary distance from the 4th, 5° 35′, which, added to the primary 20° 58′, makes the arc of direction 26° 33′, so that this direction had preceded two years and some months before.

It is easy to calculate the ☉'s converse direction to the ☍ of the ☽, whereby he applied also to the ☌ of ♂ : the ☽'s declination is 10° 2′, answering to ♓ 4° in the ecliptic, whose horary times, 13° 7′, doubled, are 26° 14′, the ☽'s right ascension is 328° 50′, which subtracted from the right ascension of the *medium cœli,* leaves the ☽'s distance 8° 58′: the polar elevation of the 9th house is 21°; therefore, As the double horary times of ☽, 26° 14′, is to the polar elevation of the 9th house 21° 0′, so is the ☽'s distance from *medium cœli* 8° 58′ to the ☽'s pole 7° 0′, under which the oblique ascension of the ☽'s ☍ is 147° 36′, that of the ☉ 178° 42′, from which subtracting that of the ☽, leaves the arc of direction 31° 6′, so that the ☉ and ☽ were as nearly opposite as possible.

I look for the secondary directions thus : To the day and hour of the nativity I add 30 days and 10 hours, for the 30 years and 5 months, and I come to the 12th of October, with 20^h 26′ P. M. when the ☉ was in ♎

29°, in exact parallel of ♄'s declination, who was in ♓ 7°, with latitude 2° 10' South, ♂ had arrived at ♍ 11°, to wit, the opposition of the *medium cœli* of the nativity, and the ☽ in ♈ 8 degrees. On the 22d of February, 1525, there happened a remarkable new ☽, in ♓ 13°, in which the three superiors, by an exact calculation, had the same declination, and, for this reason, were in parallel, and the luminaries applied to their declination nearly. These aspects of the stars usually are the causes of very grievous wars, and this new ☽ was celebrated upon ♄ of his nativity, and then ♄ applied to the ☍ of the ☉ of the nativity, and place of the ☽'s direction. This new Moon likewise happened in the ☍ of ♂ in the progressions, and, by the ingress of ♂ from ♎ 22°, had its morning station nearly above the place of the secondary direction of the ☉, and in the ☽'s declination.

On the 24th of February, the ☽ was found in the same 9° of ♈, in its secondary direction, under the parallel of ♂; in the same place the ☽ also was in the parallel of ♃, but could be of no service, as not being conjoined to the places as well of the radix as the directions: yet she delivered from a more grievous calamity, which, from the constitution of the nativity, was denoted to be extremely unfortunate; for the ☽, the conditionary luminary, was in the parallel declination of ♄, and in his mundane parallel; but, what is worse, is ♄ being in the centre of the supreme cardinal house, or *medium cœli*, and the ☽ cadent in the ninth, from which ♄ was very strongly elevated above it, and, moreover, as the unfortunate directions were, as has been observed, at that time powerful, ♃ afforded but small assistance.

He died in the year 1547, in the month of April, from the ☽'s direction, the significator of life, to the ☍ of ☿, followed by the parallel declination of ♄, for ☿ was of the nature of ♄, on account of the parallel of declination, and by reason of the sign ♎, and had something of ♂, because of the sextile. The oblique ascension of ☿ to the pole of the ☽ 7°, is 198° 4′, from which, subtracting the ☽'s oblique ascension there taken, 147° 36′, there remains the arc of direction 50° 28′, which, for the equation, I add to the ☉'s right ascension, and I make the sum 229° 14′ = 21° 20′ of ♏, at which the ☉, from the day and hour of the nativity, arrives in 52 days 16 hours, which denotes 52 years 8 months. By converse direction, the ☽ had descended to the ☉'s ☐ :

As the ☉'s semi-nocturnal arc . . . 5ʰ 57′
is to the ☉'s dist. from the *imum cœli* . 20° 58
so is the ☽'s semi-nocturnal arc . . . 5ʰ 15
to the ☽'s secondary dist. from the west 18° 30

The oblique ascension of the ☽'s opposition in the horoscope is 137° 30′, from which, subtracting the horoscope's oblique ascension, there remains the ☽'s primary distance from the west 69° 42′; the secondary subtracted from this, leaves the arc of direction 51° 12′, greater by 44′ than that taken above, which makes but little difference.

You will ask, why the ☌ of ♄ with the ☽ was not the cause of his death. I answer, because there the ☽ was in a contrary latitude, and happened in the terms of a benefic: also the ☍ of ♂ to the ☽, by a converse direction, did not kill*, as the ☽ applied to the parallel of ♃ in the world by the same converse motion. But this nativity, with respect to life, certainly was not very strong, by reason of the unfortunate state of the ☽, the significator of life.

The causes of the antipathy between these two princes were the ascendants in signs and places opposite to degrees and minutes; ♄ of Francis upon the ☉ of Charles; ♂ of Charles in □ to the ☽ of Francis; the ☽ of Charles in the sesqui-quadrate of ♂ of Francis; ♄ in the opposite cardinals; ♂ angular in the one, cadent in the other, alternately in the □, &c.

Francis the First was crowned King of France in 1515, and, in the same year, lost the Duchy of Milan, but overthrew the Swiss at the battle of Marignan. He was taken prisoner by the Emperor Charles the Fifth, at the battle of Pavia, in the year 1525, and, being set at liberty, began the war again, but was wholly beaten out of Italy. Francis had likewise wars with Henry the Eighth, King of England, who took Boulogne from him in 1544. He was married twice; his first wife was Claudia, daughter of his predecessor Lewis the Twelfth; and, his second, Eleanor, daughter of Philip the First, King of Spain, by whom he had issue one son and two daughters, viz. Henry the Second, who succeeded him in the throne of France; Magdalen, who was afterwards married to James the Fifth, King of Scotland; and Margaret, married to Charles, Duke of Alencon; and, after his death, to Henry the Second, King of Navarre.

---

* Ptolemy says, there is only one converse direction able to kill, viz. *Apheta ad Occasu.*

EXAMPLE III.

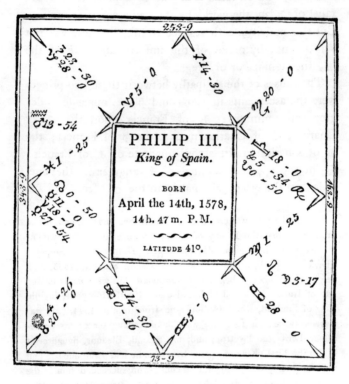

	LATITUDES.				DECLINATIONS.		
♄	..	0°	6'	N.	23°	15'	S.
♃	..	1	35	N.	0	43	S.
♂	..	1	39	S.	18	17	S.
☉	..	0	0		19	13	N.
♀	..	1	13	S.	9	40	N.
☿	..	3	0	S.	1	37	N.
☽	..	4	14	N.	23	40	N.

PRIMUM MOBILE. 147

HE died on the 31st of March, 1621, aged 42 years 11 months. He was, for the first time, in 1614, seized with a flow of humours from the head, which lasted without any intermission, together with a weak state of health.

The horoscope, significator of life, in the 43d year of his age arrived at the □ of ♄ by our method, whereof the calculation is as follows:

The right ascension of the *medium cœli* is 253° 0′, the right ascension of ♄ 295° 23′; from which there remains the arc of direction of the *medium cœli* to ♄ 42° 14′, from which place ♄ projects the □ to the horoscope.

For the equation, I add this arc of direction to the ☉'s right ascension 32° 9′, and I make the sum 74° 23′, answering to 15° 40′ of ♊, which the ☉ from the day of the nativity arrives at in 43 days, which denote so many years of life. For the secondary directions, I add 42 days for so many years, 22 hours for 11 months, and 28′ for 7 days; therefore, the secondary directions are made on the 27th of May, 1578, with 13^h 15′, P. M.

	☉	☽	♄	♃	♂	♀	☿	☊
Deg. of Lon.	♊ 15.40	♓ 12.0	♑ 22.50	♎ 1.50	♓ 15 0	21.0	28.0	♓ 28.37
Lat.		S. 1.25	N. 0.14		S. 2.18			

PRIMUM MOBILE.

The ☉ is found in the parallel of the declination of ♄, and in the □ of ♂ and □ of the ☽ in ☌ with ♂, by long. and lat. And to the hour, P. M. 13ʰ 15′, the 27th of May, is posited in the horoscope ♈ 5° 45′, and in the *medium cœli* 3 of ♑. The progressions for 43 years happen on October the 5th, 1581, whilst the ☽ had 21° ♑; but we must subtract 24°, in order that the ☽ may be posited in ♐ 27°; the rest as follow:

Deg. of Lon	☉	☽	♄	♃	♂	♀	☿	☊
	♎	♐	♒	♑	♎	♏	♎	♑
	20.0	27.19	22.19	10.20	28.15	10.0	3.40	23.42

The ☉ was conjoined to ♂, the ☽ to the □ of ☿; the former had arrived at the □ of ♄ of the nativity, and the latter to its parallel. On the day of death, the stars were posited thus:

Deg. of Lon	☉	☽	♄	♃	♂	♀	☿	☊
	♈	♋	♋	♉	♏	♓		♐
	10.58	19.3	0.42	21.16	22.6	13.9	18.53	10.53

The ☉, on the day he died, was posited upon ☿ of the nativity, for ☿ was malefic by reason of the sign and mundane parallel of ♂; ☽ opposite to ♄ of the nativity, and secondary direction; ♄ in the □ (of the secondary direction) of the horoscope, that is, from the *imum cœli;* for in the *medium cœli* are, as we have said, ♑ 3°; and, when the horoscope is significator of life, such rays, when directed to it, are very powerful. Lastly, there is a remarkable new Moon in ♈ 3° before his death, and, afterwards, the quadrant of the ☉ being upon the secondary direction of the horoscope, and the ☽ in its □, and ☿ with ☉ with the ray □ of ♄ to the horoscope; but it was expected that the ☽ would arrive at the ☍ of ♄, of the nativity and secondary direction. An eclipse of the ☽ preceded the year 1620, in 24° of ♐; the ☽ remaining between the ☍ of ♂ and ♄ in the *medium cœli;* the sign ♐ respects Spain and the men, the *medium cœli* royal dignities; all this is agreeable to the sentiments of Ptolemy: and, also, another eclipse of the ☉ in 14° of ♊, that is, in the □ of the king's ascendant; and, lastly, in the revolution, the ☉ was with ♂ and the ☽ in their □ and parallel of declination, and ♄ in the □ of the ascendant of the nativity.

In the year 1614, on the 2d of June, in the 36th year of his age, he was taken ill of a violent flow of humours from the head, at which time the ☽ arrived at the sesqui-quadrate of ♂ in the zodiac near ♉, and parallel of the declination of ☿, and, by converse motion, the ☽ to the □ of ☿, when she was separated from the sesqui-quadrate of ♂; the quintile of ♀ followed, which is injured by the □ of ♄, the ascendant to the ☌ of ♀.

As any one will find, if he pleases to calculate these directions.

By secondary directions, on the 36 days succeeding the nativity, the ☉ was conjoined to ♀, and entered the parallel of the declination of ♄, with ☍ of the ☽, followed by the □ of ♂ to both, in which parallel the ☉ continued almost without interruption, but was not the significator of life.

A disorder in the head is chiefly denoted from the parallel of the ☽'s declination with ♄ in the nativity and mundane parallel with ☿, who is also found in the mundane parallel of ♂.

This king came to the crown of Spain in 1598, at the age of 20 years; and, in 1610, he expelled 900,000 Moors and Jews out of Spain. He was married to Margaret, daughter of Charles, Archduke of Austria, by whom he had eight children, three of which died infants.

EXAMPLE IV.

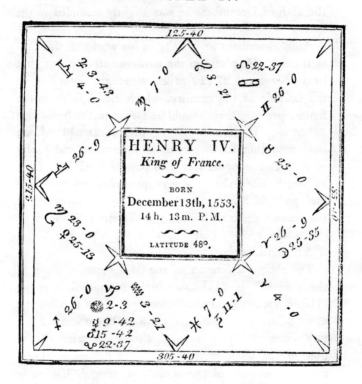

LATITUDES.			DECLINATIONS.		
♄	1° 55′	S.	9° 13′	S.
♃	1 26	N.		
♂	0 8	S.	22 42	S.
☉	0 0		23 31	S.
♀	2 12	N		
☾	5 0	S	5 16	N.

IN the year 1610, on the 14th of May, 4ʰ 48′ P. M. he received a wound of which he died. In 1594, on the 15th of December, he was slightly wounded in the face.

Argol describes this nativity in his works on the Critical Days: He places in the *medium cæli* 3° 21′ ♌, but in the horoscope 27° 20′ of ♎, although, according to the latitude of the country, which he explains in the figure, page 48, there should be placed in the horoscope 26° 9′ ♎. He likewise places the ☽ 21° 14′ of ♈; but, according to the common Ephemeris and Tables of moveable seconds, the ☽ is posited in 25° 35′ of ♈, in which place she is a very powerful significator of life, and which is manifestly proved by an agreement of the time of death with the ☽'s direction to the □ of ♄ in the zodiac, near 11° 1′ of ♊, when the ☽ has 3° 21′ south latitude.

The oblique ascension of the ☽'s opposite place to the pole 48°, is 211° 25′, which, subtracted from the oblique ascension of the horoscope, there remains the ☉'s distance from the west 4° 15′. The nocturnal horary times of the ☽ are 14° 2′, the elevation of the pole of the sixth house is 37°; the difference, therefore, of the pole of the sixth and seventh houses is 11°; I say, if the duplicate nocturnal horary times of the ☽ 28°, gives the polar difference of the houses 11°, what will the ☽'s distance from the west 4° 15′ give? Facit 2°, which, being subtracted from the pole of the seventh house, there remains the ☽'s pole 46°, under which the oblique ascension of the ☽'s ☍ is 210° 59′, and the oblique ascension of ♐ 11° 1', in north latitude 3° 2 ı', is 270° 37', from which, subtracting the former, leaves the arc of direction 59° 38', which, being equated, points out 56 years and 6 months nearly.

By converse direction the ☽ and ♄, by the rapt motion of the *primum mobile*, happened to be posited in equal proportional distances from the *imum cœli*, called a rapt parallel, calculated thus:

The ☽'s semi-nocturnal arc is 84^h 6' or 5^h 37'
Saturn's semi-nocturnal arc 6 41
The ☽'s right ascension . . . . . . 25° 33
Her distance from the *imum cœli* . . 79 53
Saturn's right ascension 343 14
Distance in right ascension from the ☽ . 42 19
Then, as the sum of the semi-noct. arcs . 12^h 18
is to the ☽'s semi-nocturnal arc . . . 5 37
so is the distance in right ascension . . 42° 19
to the ☽'s secondary dist. from the 4th . 19 19

which, being subtracted from the primary, leaves the arc of direction 60° 34', one degree subsequent to the other direction.

Argol tells us, King Henry escaped, with danger, by a wound he received in his under lip, which struck out some of his teeth, in the year 1594, on the 15th of December, when he was exactly 41 years of age; at which time the ☽, in a right motion, arrived at the □ of ♄ in the world, which is thus wrought:

As the ☽'s semi-nocturnal arc . . . . 5^h 37'
is to her distance from the west . . . . 4° 15
so is the semi-nocturnal arc of ♄ . . . 6^h 41
to the secondary distance of ♄ from the 4th 5° 3

which, added to his primary, $= 37°\,34'$, makes the arc of direction $42°\,37'$, which being equated, as usual, gives 40 years; therefore, the true direction had preceded some time before.

There was likewise, a little before that, the ☽ $=$ to the rapt parallel of ♂, being equi-distant from the *imum cœli*. The ☽'s semi-nocturnal arc is $5^h\,37'$, the semi-nocturnal arc of ♂ $7^h\,50'$, their sum $13^h\,27'$, the right ascension of ♂ $287°\,5'$, his distance in right ascension from the ☽ $98°\,28'$; hence you have her secondary distance $41°\,7'$, which, subtracted from her primary, which is $79°\,53'$, leaves the arc of direction $38°\,46'$.

These directions of ♄ and ♂ to the ☽ were not mortal, as she continued, by right direction, within the rays of ♃, and in his terms, and, also, in a parallel of the declination of ♀. On the 15th of December, 1594, ♂ was in $23°$ ♏, in ☍ of the ☽'s place of direction, and the ☽ in $4°$ of ♒, with latitude south $5°$; nearly in the parallel of ♂'s radical place.

The secondary directions to the 56th year, together with the 4 months and 20 days, fall on February 8, 1554, almost in the meridian.—The places of the planets were as follow:

	☉	☽	♄	♃	♂	♀	☿	☋
Deg. of Lon.	♒ 29.44	♉ 18.14	♓ 17.19	♎ 1.55	♓ 1.16	♒ 4.47	♒ 16.26	♋ 18.36
Lat.			S. 1.42	N. 1.52	S. 0. 2	N. 0.16	N. 1.26	

Where the ☉ was conjoined to ♂ by longitude and latitude, about the beginning of the sign ♓, ♂ was also there, and not far from ♄, who surrounded the ☉'s place on the day he received the wound, and which place the ☉ entered by a □ ray, in which he was afflicted by ♄ in an angle; and the ☽, on the 8th of February, was in 18° of ♉, in latitude 4° 20′ south, by which she gained the declination 14° 20′; ♄ had this same declination, and likewise was in □ to this same place of the ☽, on the day he got the wound; at which time the ☽ was in 7° of ♒, in □ of ☿, which received the nature of ♂ from the parallel of declination; and, also, ♄'s □ in the world.

Places of the Progressions of the Planets, the 7th of July, 1558.

	☉	☽	♄	♃	♂	♀	☿	☊
Deg. of Lon.	♋	♈	♉	♒	♋	♊	♌	♈
	24.0	11.34	22.51	8.33	16.19	10.11	15 ℞	23.21

The progressions to the end of the 56th year, depend on the 24th of June, 1558, when the ☽ was posited in 6° of ♏; for the 4 months and 24 days, we advance five signs and 6°, and come to the 7th of July; the ☉ was then separated from ♂, denoting a conspiracy to have preceded; ♄ was in 23° of ♉; the ☉ entered this place exactly on the day he was wounded, ♂ in 17° of ♋, whose declination the ☽ had on the same day.

But it was six days before the famous full Moon, the ☉ being 17° of ♉, and the ☽ 17° of ♏, which, applied to □ of ♄, and the ☽, having 4° latitude, was in exact parallel of the declination of ♄ and ♂. You see, therefore, that the many agreements with the places of the secondary directions and progressions from the day he received the wound, together with the preceding lunation, are agreeable to what Ptolemy says in the last chapter of Book IV; from which we are likewise taught, always to observe those lunations wherein the luminaries are afflicted by inimical rays; and, particularly, if the places in which those rays are unfortunate, either by ingress or transit, and afflict the prorogators of the nativity, or, rather, if their aspects with them be hostile, as we shall find in the following examples.

Henry the Fourth was called the Great King of France and Navarre. In his 15th year he was head of the Protestants in France. At 19 he was invited to the French Court at Paris, to be present at the massacre of the Protestants, and in the same year, upon the death of his mother, he took upon himself the title of King of Navarre. He thrice extorted peace from the King's party; and, by the battle of Courtray in 1581 (Henry III. being then living), dissolved the league entered into by the Pope, the King of Spain, and the Guisian Faction, against the Protestants. Henry was crowned King of France in 1594, and was assassinated in Paris by Francis Ravillac, on May 4th, 1610. He was married twice, but divorced his first wife and married Mary de Medicis, daughter of Francis the Great Duke of Tuscany, by whom he had four children, two sons and two daughters.

EXAMPLE V.

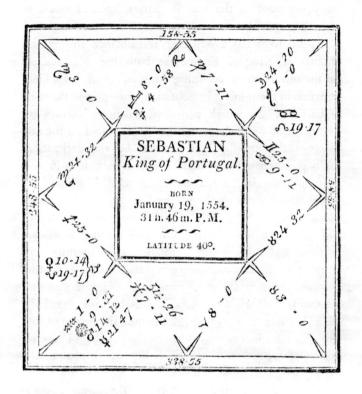

LATITUDES.				DECLINATIONS.		
♄ . .	1°	43′	S.	7°	47′	S.
♃ . .	1	44	N.			
♂ . .	0	4	S.	16	42	S.
☉ . .	0	0				
♀ . .	1	10	N.			
☿ . .	1	48	N.			
☽ . .	2	51	N.	16	12	N.

IN the year 1578, on the 4th of August, he was mortally wounded in the war in Africa, aged 24 years, 6 months, and 11 days.

This nativity has a very near resemblance to that of Francis I, King of France; in both, the ☽ is posited in the ninth house, declining from an ☍ of ♂, which remains in the third. In Sebastian, the ☽ has the declination of ♂, which constitution denotes journies for the cause of war. In both, the ☽ is injured by the aspects of the malefics. In Francis, by the declination of ♄; in Sebastian, by that of ♂; in both ♄ is in the sign ♓, angular in the mundane parallel of the ☽, above which he is elevated. In Francis, from the *medium cœli;* in Sebastian, from the *imum cœli;* in both, the ☽ is the conditionary luminary; which being so unhappily affected, denoted calamities in journies; in both ♃ is unfortunate, succeeding the rays of ♄ to the *medium cœli;* in Francis cadent in the sign ♍; in Sebastian ℞; where to the good things by him signified, he added sorrows; in both, ☿ assumes the nature of the enemies; for in Francis, he is in the parallel of declination of ♄, and ✶ of ♂; in Sebastian, in the mundane parallel of ♄, which is elevated above it from the fourth house; in the other from the *medium cœli;* which constitution infers the fixed obstinacy of his mind and tendency to perform things that are difficult, nay, even impossible.

Argol, in this nativity, omitting the ☽, to whom the right of hyleg belongs, directed (when the numbers of his calculation did not agree), the ascendant to the ☐

of ♄, which ray contains signs of the smallest ascensions, as are ♑, ♒, and ♓; the place also of the direction is in the terms of ♀, and the antiscion of ♀ succedent, according to common opinion, and doubtless they were strong and sufficient grounds for this opinion; but as we have fully demonstrated in the Celestial Philosophy, the rays of the stars taken to the angles in the zodiac, are altogether as nothing; and in this nativity the ☽ becomes a very powerful significator of life; who, at the time of this King's accident, came by direction to 21° of ♍, with latitude 4° 23′ north, where it was afflicted by the parallel declination of ♄ 7° 47′, which is thus calculated.

The ☽'s declination 16° 12′, answers to ♌ 15° 40′, whose horary times, 17° 22′, doubled, are 34° 44′; the polar elevation of the ninth house is 16°, the ☽'s right ascension 147° 29′; from hence arises her distance from the *medium cœli* 11° 26′, and her polar elevation 5°; under which the oblique ascension of the ☽'s ☍ is 328° 56′; the oblique ascension of ♓ 21°, with latitude 4° 23′ South, is 354° 9′, from which subtracting the former, leaves the arc of direction 25° 13′, which being equated, as usual, produces 25 years.

By converse motion, the ☽ was separated from the ✶ of ♃, and applied to the sesqui-quadrate of ♄; but the hyleg, by a converse motion, was weak, owing to the ☍ of ☿ and ♂, to which the ☽, by a converse motion, applied nearly.

When ♃ arrived at the *medium cœli*, he undertook he friendly office of restoring Prince Muly to his father's kingdoms.

But you will ask, why the ☍ of ♄ to the ☽ did not destroy life? I answer, from several causes: the King, at that time, was preserved; first, the ☽ in the ☍ had gained much latitude, whereby she was far distant from the diametrical point; second, the direction happened in the terms of ♀; third, the mundane △ of the same was succedent; fourth, after the mundane parallel of ♃ had preceded by a right motion, he applied by a converse motion; but in ♍ 21°, none of the friendly rays assisted, but there is the beginning of the terms of ♂. All these remarks are taken from Ptolemy, in the Chapter of Life.

The Secondary Directions are made on the 13th of February, 1554, at 2 Hours 26 Minutes, P. M.

	☉	☽	♄	♃	♂	♀	☿	☊
Deg. of Lon.	♓ 4.50	♋ 21.20	♓ 18.0	♎ 1.26	♓ 5.10	♒ 11.1	♒ 13.30	♋ 18.20

The Progressions on the 14th of January, 1556.

	☉	☽	♄	♃	♂	♀	☿	☊
Deg. of Lon.	♒ 3.55	♒ 27.13	♈ 8.7	♏ 29.26	♒ 27.34	♒ 10.14	♑ 8.47	♊ 11.16

PRIMUM MOBILE. 161

The following was the Position of the Planets on the unfortunate Day.

	☉	☽	♄	♃	♂	♀	☿	☊
Deg. of Lon.	♌ 21.7	♍ 7.25	♑ 18.12	♎ 10.58	♈ 26.0	♍ 14.25	♌ 10.23	♓ 25.0

For the secondary directions I add to the hour of the nativity 24 days, 12 hours, 40 minutes; and I come to the 13th of February, 1554, 2ʰ 26′, P. M. in which the ☉ was conjoined in longitude and latitude with ♂, exactly in 5° of ♓, without the least assistance of the friendly rays; but the ☽ was, on the day of his accident, in the ☍ of the ☉, applying to the parallel of the declination of ♄ of these motions; the ☽, on the same 13th of February, was in 21° of ♋, to which, on the unhappy day, ♄ from the ☍, and ♂ in the □, were mischievously disposed; therefore, from the active and passive ingress, the ☽ continued unhappily situated, and was also on the unfortunate day, with the declination of ♄ of the nativity, and of his direction; and hath the same almost with that of ♂, from 26° of ♈, with latitude 4° south. The progressions for 24 years are finished on the 29th of December, 1555, when the ☽ is there posited in 2° of ♌; for the other six months I add six signs and a half, and I come to the 13th of January, 1556, when the ☽ was found in 17° of ♒, that is, when the ♂ with the ☉ has passed 15°, as the ☍ of the ☉ had passed so many in the nativity, and the ☽ is posited in 28° of ♒; on the 14th of January, the ☽

Z

was in partile ☌ with ♂, and both in the ☍ of the ☽ of the nativity, to whose ☍ the ☉ applied on the fatal day. The ☉, in the progressions, was between the ✶, and quintile, together with the parallel of declination of ♃, who, during the war, favoured by his △ this place of the ☉. There had also preceded in the progressions a ☌ with the ☉ and ♀ ; and ♃, by transit from a △, aspected the ☉ of the nativity ; hence it is evident, that the affairs of the King, together with his army, were successful, as he with his troops had seized upon the kingdoms of others; but the stars threatened life, which when extinguished, every thing fell equally with it.

The four following nativities, as they have the ☉ in the crepusculums, the significator of life, and the calculations of the directions belonging to the same Canons, I was unwilling to separate, but have explained them, one after another: as they bear testimony to the truth of my opinions concerning the crepuscules, it was likewise my desire to have them all ready at hand, for every one who wishes to have a proof of it.

EXAMPLE VI.

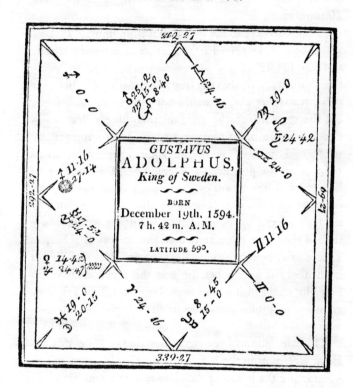

LATITUDES.

♄ . . 0° 29′ N.
♃ . . 0 47 S.
♂ . . 0 14 N.

ON the 16th of October, 1632, 3^h 17', P.M. he was mortally wounded in an engagement, aged 37 years 10 months.

In this nativity, to the given matutine hours, 7^h 28', there ought to be placed 20° 30' of ♎ in the *medium cœli*, and not 15° 42' of ♎, according to the Argoline position; others assert, that the true hours are 7^h 42': however it be, it matters not, as we do not direct the horoscope, but the ☉, who, at the time of this king's death, was directed, by a right motion, to the ☌ of ♃, the □ of ♂, and the ☍ of ♄ in the zodiac, within the terms of ♂; but the presence of ♃ could be of no service as being alone, the enemies numerous; then the ☉, by converse motion, was directed to the ☌ of ♂ and □ of ♄, followed by the parallel of ♄ in the world, where indeed there is a concurrence of the □ of ♃; but, as I have said, being alone against several, he could not influence, and even when he was the giver of true valour, he changed it to rashness, because afflicted by the enemies, as Ptolemy tells us in his chapter on the Nature of the Mind.

The calculation of the right direction. The ☉'s oblique ascension in the horoscope is 313° 15', from which subtracting the horoscope's oblique ascension, there remains the ☉'s primary distance from the horoscope 20° 48', the oblique ascension of 25° ♒ the place of the rays of ♄ and ♂ is 350° 21', from which subtracting the ☉'s oblique ascension, there remains the arc of direction, 37° 36', calculated in the horoscope; but as the ☉ is in the morning crepuscule, I enter the table of crepuscules to the pole 59°, with 28° ♐, and the ☉'s distance 28° 48', which is his primary; and I find the ☉ remaining in the crepusculine circle of depression 8°, opposite to this crepusculine circle under ♒, 25°; after taking the proportional part, I obtain 16° 33', which I call the secondary distance, and subtract it from the primary; there then remains the ortive difference, 4° 15', but as the secondary distance is less than the primary, the difference therefore must be added to the arc of direction, taken in the horoscope, and the true arc of direction is then 41° 21'; this arc I add to the ☉'s right ascension, which is 266° 59', and the sum is 308° 20', answering to 5° 56' of ♒, at which the ☉, from the day of the nativity, arrives in 38 days, which denotes so many years. The calculation of the ☉'s converse direction to ♂ is thus: The 11th house is elevated 31°, its oblique ascension is 232° 27'; to the same pole the oblique ascension of ♂ is 244° 33'; the distance therefore of ♂ from the 11th house is 12° 6': the 12th house is elevated 49°, its oblique ascension is 262° 27'; the oblique ascension of ♂ to the pole of the 12th, is 255° 51'; therefore the distance of ♂ from the 12th house is 6° 36'; those distances of ♂, added together, make 18° 42', the space of the house of ♂ above the earth: the difference of the polar elevation of the 11th and 12th houses is 18°, from which arises the polar elevation of ♂ 43° nearly; the oblique ascension of ♂ to this pole 43°, is 251° 16'; the ☉'s oblique ascension there is 290° 52'; from which there remains the arc of direction 39° 36', less than the preceding by

1° 45′, so that from the ☌ with ♂ the ☉ began to be separated.

The direction of the ☉ to the ☐ of ♄ *in mundo*, by converse motion is calculated as follows: the oblique ascension of the ☍ of ♄ is 351° 16′, to the pole 59° (that is, in the horoscope); the right ascension of ♄ is 327° 11′, which, subtracted from the former, leaves the ascensional difference of ♄ 24° 5′, and the semi-diurnal arc of ♄ becomes 114° 5′: the distance of ♄ from the West is 58° 49′, the ☉'s declination is 23° 30′, ascensional difference 46° 23′, semi-diurnal arc 43° 37′; and the ☉'s right ascension is 266° 59′, from which his primary distance from the *medium cœli* is 64° 32′. I now require, if the semi-diurnal arc of ♄ 114° 5′, gives his distance from the West 58° 49′, what distance from the *medium cœli* will the ☉'s semi-diurnal arc 43° 37′ give? and by the logarithms the ☉'s secondary distance from the *medium cœli* is 22° 29′, which subtracted from the primary, leaves the arc of direction 42° 3′ of the ☉ to ☐ of ♄. But if we add this secondary distance of the ☉ 22° 29′ to his primary from the horoscope, we make the ☉'s arc of direction to the mundane parallel of ♄ 43° 17′; therefore the directions followed very near one after the other. But as I declare myself sincerely ingenuous, and desire nothing but the bare truth of every thing, observe, gentle Reader, that I have inserted this example in my Celestial Philosophy, page 252, and have there remarked, that from Tycho's calculation, one degree is to be added to the ☉'s place; for as Argol has placed a matutine hour, that is, from midnight, in the middle of this figure, I thought it belonged to the night following the 19th day, for, among several reasons, midnight is the end of the preceding, and the beginning of the following day; but if $7^h\ 28'$ be from midnight, it certainly preceded the 19 days; and I afterwards found, from the ☽'s place, that that matutine hour belonged to the night preceding the 19th day, therefore the ☉'s place seems to have been rightly calculated.

For the secondary directions, I add to the hour of the nativity 37 days 20 hours, for so many years and 10 months, and I come to the 25th of January 1595, with the hour from meridian $17^h\ 42'$: the ☉ was in ♒ 6°, and the ☽ in ♌ 6°, who by a sesqui-quadrate ray and parallel of declination assumed the nature of ♂, with whom she had these aspects while remaining in partile ☍ of the ☉, and infected the ☉ also with the same evil qualities; the ☉ too was in parallel of ♂ in the radix, and likewise at setting ♄ and ♂ entered a parallel exactly to this place of the ☉; and ☽ at the time of the accident entered the exact parallel of ♂ by these motions on the 25th of January. The progressions for full 38 years were made on the 13th of January 1598, whilst the ☽ was in ♈ 16°; but there is a deficiency of two months and four days, for the ☉ at his death was in ♎ 23°, but in the nativity ♐ 27°, wherefore, from this place of the ☽ in ♈ 16°, I subtract 65° for the two months and four degrees, to denote so many days, so that the ☽ is posited in ♒ 7°, that is, on the 8th of January 1598, when the ☉ was in ♑ 18° upon ☿ of the nativity; and it is to be observed, that ☿ in the nati vity takes upon him an inimical nature, because not conjoined with the benefics, but, on the contrary, in the house of ♄; the in ☽ the exaltation of ♄, ✱, and also mundane parallel of ♂; and applied to the parallel of ♂ in the nativity, and also set with ♄ and ♂ on the day of the accident, ♂ in the progressions from 28° of ♊ was found in ☍ to the ☉ of the nativity On the 13th of October, 1632, three days before the accident, there was celebrated a new ☽ in 20° of ♎, in □ of ☿ of the nativity, and □ of the ☉'s progression.

But it appears that ☿ contributed not a little to the accident which befel the King, who is reported to have gone, merely out of curiosity, to reconnoitre the enemy, and was by them wounded mortally.

Secondary Directions.

	☉	☽	♄	♃	♂	♀	☿	☊
Deg. of Lon.	♒	♌	♌	♓	♐	♓	♑	♉
	6.0	6.0	22.40	1.55	21.29	16.50	13.10	6.37

Progressions.

	☉	☽	♄	♃	♂	♀	☿	☊
Deg. of Lon.	♑	♒	♎	♊	♊	♒	♑	♓
	18.0	7.0	4.28	6.40	28.9	28.22	8.0	9.30

Places of the Stars at the Time of the Accident.

Deg. of Lon.	☉	☽	♄	♃	♂	♀	☿	☋
	♎	♐	♏	♉	♏	♏	♎	♈
	23.35	0.15	27.11	24.29	25.48	0.31	23.44 R.	27.5

Gustavus Adolphus was crowned King of Sweden in the year 1617. In 1613 he made peace with the Danes; and, with the Russians, the year he was crowned. He had wars with the Poles, and reduced all Liffland in 1625. In 1630, he made an expedition into Germany, and was slain at the battle of Lutzen. Gustavus married Mary Eleanor, daughter of John Sigismund, Elector of Brandenburg, and left issue only one daughter, the Princess Christina, who, under the regency of her mother, carried on the war in Germany.

EXAMPLE VII.

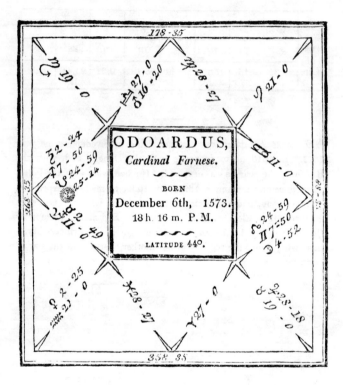

LATITUDES.			DECLINATIONS.		
♄	1° 46′	N.			
♃	1 18	S.	18° 35′	N.	
♂	1 5	N.	5 26	S.	
☉	0 0				
♀	1 41	S.			
☿	1 56	S.			
☽	1 43	S.			

HE was elected Cardinal in March 1591, being 17 years and 3 months old: a catarrh put an end to his life on the 21st of February, 1626, in the 52d year, 2 months and 7 days of his age.

Argol directs the ascendant to the antiscion of ♄; whereas the significator of life belongs entirely to the ☉, which he omits, because the numbers of his calculation do not agree. And as my method is perfectly right, insomuch, that not only in these examples, wherein the ☉ is in the crepuscules, but also in others, wherein the ☉ is found in the obscure space, my calculations agree wonderfully with the times. Doubtless, these examples of deceased persons ought to be received; and that no one may look upon this new opinion concerning the crepuscules as ridiculous, and not to be depended upon, there are several people who can vouch for its truth.

The ☉ then, in the 53d year, arrived at the □ of ♄ in the zodiac; the ☉'s oblique ascension in the horoscope is 289° 32'; the oblique ascension of the quadrate of ♄ is 344° 50'; from which, subtracting the former, leaves the arc of direction 55° 18', calculated in the horoscope; I subtract the horoscope's oblique ascension from the oblique ascension of the ☉, and there remains the ☉'s primary distance from the horoscope 20° 57', which I look for in the Tables of the Crepuscules to the pole's elevation 44°, but, as I do not find it, I take the nearest, which is 20° 14', to the crepusculine circle of depression 13°; to the solar degree 25° of ♐; and, to the same circle, under 2° ♓, I take the secondary distance 18° 20′; I subtract this from the primary found in the Tables, which is 20° 14′ (for it is of little or no consequence, as we have said in its Canon, if we do not take the exact distance of the ☉ 20° 57′), and there remains the ortive difference 1° 54′; but as the secondary distance is less than the primary, I add the ortive difference to the arc of direction 55° 18′, and I make the true arc of direction 57° 12′.

By converse motion, whilst the ☉ and ♂ were carried away by the rapt motion of the *primum mobile*, they happened to be posited in the mundane parallel alternately, that is, in an equal proportional distance from the *medium cœli*; the ☉'s semi-diurnal arc is $4^h 21′$; the semi-diurnal arc of ♂ is $5^h 38′$ (for the declination of ♂ is 5° 26′, answering to 14° of ♎ in the ecliptic). I add these semi-diurnal arcs together, and I make the sum $9^h 59′$, which I put in the first place; in the second, the semi-diurnal arc of ♂ $5^h 38′$; in the third, the right distance which is between ♂ and the ☉, the right ascension of ♂ is 195° 27′, but, of the ☉, 264° 48′; therefore, there remains their alternate right distance 69° 21′; and, in the fourth place is produced the secondary distance of ♂ from the *medium cœli* 39° 8′, which I add to the primary, because ♂ is in the ascendant part of heaven, and when the direction is finished is in the descendant, and the arc of direction is 56° (for the primary distance of ♂ from the *medium cœli* is 16° 52′). For the equation, I add this arc to the ☉'s right ascension, which is 264° 48′, and the sum is 320° 48′, answering to ♒ 18° 20′, at which the ☉ from the day and hour of the nativity ar-

PRIMUM MOBILE. 173

rives in 52 days and 2 hours. The right direction to
the □ of ♄ was succedent; if, however, the place of
♄ be true, which was succeeded by a □ of ☽ in the
zodiac, which, in the nativity, was in the ☍ to ♄, and
the disease in its proper and natural signification was denoted to be mortal from the violence of the catarrh,
which was so great, that it caused a suffocation. For the
secondary directions, I add to the hours of the nativity
52 days, 4 hours, 30 minutes; for the 52 years, 2 months
and a quarter, and I come to the 28th of January, 1574,
a little before noon; the ☉ applied there to the exact
parallel of ♂; also, the ☉ was conjoined to ☿ ℞,
who, being in 3.50 south latitude, was in the same parallel of declination with ♄, and so, by reason of the
signs and aspects, assumed the nature of ♄. But it
deserves admiration, to find, that on the day he took to
his bed, the ☉ was found in ☌ with ☿ ℞, and nearly
in the same degrees of that sign, both being in the
parallel of ♂, in which parallel ♂ entered the ☉'s
place of these motions; and, on the day preceding the
sickness, there happened a full ☽ also near to these
places; the ☽, by her motion, was in ♉ 1°, with
3° 53' south latitude, whereby she had the declination
of 18° 14'; this declination ♄ entered at his sickness
and death; on the day his disorder began, the ☽ was
in ♍ 7°, in a □ of ♄ by these motions. You see,
therefore, a mutual commutation of the active and
passive ingresses. Lastly, on the day he died, the ☉
arrived at ♓ 3° by primary direction, under a □ of ♄
of the nativity, and ♂ to 7° in ♉; whence both in
the quadrate and parallel he maligned the ☉'s place of

these motions of the secondary direction; but, when ☿ communicates any kind of aspect to the significator of life, if endued with the nature of the malefics, he assists towards a defluxion of humours, and, more particularly, if he participates with ♄.

Hear what Ptolemy says in the Chapter of Diseases incident to the Body: "But ☿ (says he) is a help to "the inveteracy of disorders, as he increases the frigi- "dity of ♄, when reconciled to him, and with a more "constant motion stimulates the phlegm and heap "of humours, in particular, about the breast, belly, "and throat, &c."

The progressions for 48 years are finished on the 24th of October, 1577, when the ☽ remains in ♈ 21°, for its distance there from the ☍ of the ☉ is 20°, as in the nativity, for 52 years are finished on the 20th of February, 1578, whilst she was in ♌ 22°; for the two remaining months the ☽ goes over 65°, and is posited in ♎ 27°. Lastly, for the other 7 days she goes 8°, and is posited in 5° of ♏; the ☉ was then in ♓ 17°, to which, from the opposition, ♄ entered at the time of his sickness and death; and ♂ in the parallel, and nearly in the ☍, entered the ☽'s place of the progression ♏ 5°.

In his 18th year, when the native was created a Cardinal, the ☉, by right direction, had arrived at a △ of ♃ in the world, which we have calculated in Canon XXXVI, to which we refer you; the *medium cæli* likewise came to the △ of ♀; for the oblique ascension of the second house, which is elevated 33°, is 298° 35'; the oblique ascension of ♀ in the same place is 318° 8', from which, subtracting the former, leaves the arc of direction 19° 28′; so that *this* preceded, and *that* succeeded.

Secondary Directions to the Time of his Death, January 28, 1574.

	☉	☽	♄	♃	♂	♀	☿	☊
Deg of Lon.	♒	♉	♐	♉	♏	♈	♒	♊
	18.48	1.0	7.14	27.12	11.55	2.57	19.10 R.	22.21

Progression on the 25th of February, 1556.

	☉	☽	♄	♃	♂	♀	☿	☊
Deg. of Lon.	♓	♏	♑	♎	♑	♒	♈	♈
	17.0	5 0	21.10	9.30	10.36	27.14	6.14	3.30

On the Day of the Sickness, 12th of February, 1626, the Stars were posited thus:

	☉	☽	♄	♃	♂	♀	☿	☊
Deg. of Lon.	♒	♍	♍	♏	♉	♒	♒	♍
	24.1	7.37	13.48 R.	1.0	11.32	2.59	22.29 R.	5.20

176   PRIMUM MOBILE.

EXAMPLE VIII.

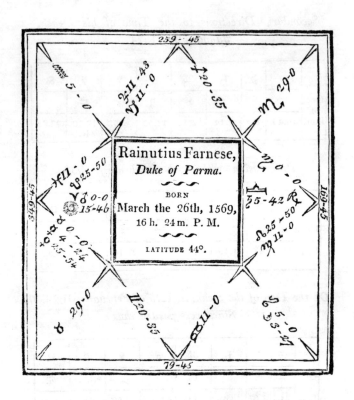

LATITUDES.   DECLINATION.

♄ .. 2° 35′ N.   0° 6′ N.
♃ .. 0 42 N.
♂ .. 0   9 S.

HE died the 5th of March, 1622, of a dropsy, aged 52 years and 11 months. The ☉ is, doubtless, the significator of life in this nativity; but Argol not finding, in his numbers, any direction of the ☉ for 53 years, directs the ascendant to a △ of ♄, which is in signs of the longest ascension, and the place of the direction is the beginning of the terms of ♃, so that this direction has not the least deadly appearance. According to our method the ☉ arrives by right direction to a □ of ♂ in the zodiac; the ☉'s oblique ascension in the horoscope is 8° 28′, from which, subtracting the horoscope's oblique ascension, there remains the ☉'s distance from the horoscope, 18° 43′; the oblique ascension of ♋ 0.0 is 65° 10′, from which, subtracting the ☉'s oblique ascension, leaves the arc of direction calculated in the horoscope 56° 42′. In the Table of Crepuscules I look for this distance of the ☉ 18° 43′, under the pole's elevation 44°, to the degree of the ☉ in ♈ 16°, and I take the proportional part between the distance 18° 32′, which is to ♈ 10° to the crepusculine circle 13°, and the distance 19° 1′ which is to 20° ♈, *i. e.* for 6°, for the ☉ is in ♈ 16°; and the difference is 29′, from which, for the 6°, 17′ are due to be added to 18° 32′, and I make 18° 49′. But the ☉'s distance is 18° 43′; this I reject, and take 18° 49′, for it matters not, as we have said in the Canons. To the same crepusculine circle 13° under ♋ 0.0, I take the 24° 45′, which are the secondary distance, and greater than the primary by 5° 56′, which are therefore to be subtracted from the arc of direction above found, and there remains the true arc of direction 50° 46′, which, for the equation, I add to the ☉'s right ascension 14° 31′, and I make the sum 65° 17′ answering to ♊ 7°, which the ☉ from the hour of the nativity reaches in 53 days, which measures so many years. At the same time, the ☉, by a converse motion, came to the sesqui-quadrate of ♄ *in mundo*. The oblique ascension of the opposite place of ♄ is 6° 19′, from which, subtracting the horoscope's oblique ascension, there remains the distance of ♄ from the west 16° 34′; but, as the horary times of ♄ are 15°, it is evident that ♄ was posited about the middle of the seventh house, distant from the middle 1° 34′; therefore, the ☉, as he has nearly the same horary times as ♄, is posited in his sesqui-quadrate before he arrives at the cusp of the twelfth house 1° 34′; the ☉'s horary times 16°, doubled, make 32°, to which I add the ☉'s distance from the east 18° 43′, and I make the sum 50° 43′, from which, subtracting 1° 34′, there remains the arc of direction 49° 9′, so that this direction had preceded a year, in case the place of ♄ be true. But there happened also to be a sesqui-quadrate of ♄ to the ☽ *in mundo*, by a converse motion. There had likewise preceded a parallel of ♃ to the ☉ in the world, whilst both were moved together by the motion of the *primum mobile;* but, as ♃ is unfortunate, and the ☽ in the sixth house in the sesqui-quadrate of the ☉, the significator of life, they denoted a dropsy, and, according to Ptolemy, a bad state of the lungs. I take the secondary directions to the 52d year complete, together with the 11 months, from the 18th of May, 1569, with the meridional hours 14ʰ 24′; the ☽ was in ♋ 12°, who

PRIMUM MOBILE. 179

was separated from the ☍ of ♃. On the day he died, which was the 5th of March, ♄ was found upon the place of the ☽; and, again, on the same day, the ☽ entered a □ of ♄ of these motions; the ☉ arrived at ♊ 7°: there was a full ☽ before he died, that is, on the 26th of February, 1622, the ☉ being in 8° of ♓, and the ☽ in ♍ 8°, in □ to the place of the ☉'s secondary direction; and, at the full ☽, the luminaries were in the parallel of ♂: on the day he died, ♄ entered the parallel of ♊ 7°, the place of the ☉'s secondary direction.

The progressions are made on the 6th of July, 1573; the ☉ was in ♋ 23°. On the day he died, ♂ entered, from the □, this place of the ☉; the ☽ in □ of ♂ near ♎ 11°, to which ♄, on the day of his death, was in □.

The secondary directions were as follow:

	☉	☽	♄	♃	♂	♀	☿	☊
Deg. of Lon.	♊ 7.0	♋ 12.0	♎ 3.27	♑ 10.21	♉ 11.32	♋ 22.21	♉ 15.26	♍ 23.10

The places of the progressions are these:

	☉	☽	♄	♃	♂	♀	☿	☊
Deg. of Lon.	♋ 23.0	♎ 11.0	♏ 20.10	♉ 29.33	♋ 11.15	♋ 20.3	♋ 4.0	♋ 3.16

On the day he died, the planets were in the following places:

	☉	☽	♄	♃	♂	♀	☿	☋
Deg. of Lon.	♓ 15.0	♐ 28.0	♋ 14.6	♊ 16.54	♈ 21.15	♉ 1.6	♓ 15.39	♏ 23.13

Observe the unfortunate disposition of ♃ in all these places to signify a dropsy.

EXAMPLE IX.

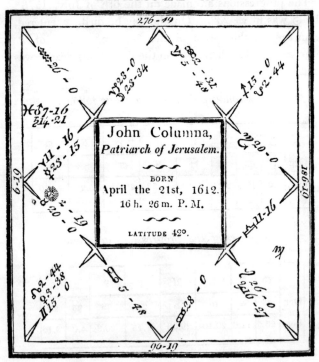

	LATITUDES.			DECLINATIONS.	
♄ . .	1°	7′	S.	7° 14′	S.
♃ . .	0	50	N.	16 34	N.
♂ . .	0	41	S.	9 30	S.
☉ . .	0	0			
♀ . .	1	2	N		
☿ . .	1	55	S.	7 18	N.
☽ . .	3	53	S.		

HE died the 14th of April, 1637, of an apoplectic fit. In June, 1626, he was much troubled with violent pains in the head.

In this nativity, Argol directs the ascendant to the □ of ♃ for the time of his death, as if it happened that ♃ was an anareta; whereas the significator of life is entirely proper to the ☉, who is in the angle of the east, and the benefics can by no means be anaretas. Indeed, it is true, if they are unfavourably mixed together with the destroyers of life, they can distinguish the kind, nature, and cause of death. But, from their nature, the benefics use their power rather to save than destroy, even from the ray □ and ☍, as we find it in Ptolemy, in the Chapter of Life; the ☉, therefore, the significator of life, arrives at a □ of ♂ in the zodiac in 25 years, and, by converse motion, was elevated above the horizon to the mundane parallel of ☿; the ☉'s oblique ascension is 18° 52′, from which, subtracting the horoscope's oblique ascension, there remains the ☉'s primary distance from the east 12° 33′; the oblique ascension of the □ of ♂ is 44° 37′, from which, subtracting the ☉'s oblique ascension, leaves the arc of direction 25° 45', calculated in the horoscope. In the Table of Crepuscules, for latitude 42°, I look for the ☉'s distance, and, in the crepusculine circle 9° to 0° of ♉, I find 12° 54'; to 10° of ♉, I find 13° 21'; the difference is 27'. I take the proportional part for 2° and one-third, and I make the primary distance 13°; then, in the same crepusculine circle 9°, under ♊ 7°, by taking the proportional part, &c., I obtain the secondary distance 14° 45'; the ortive difference is 1° 45'. But as the secondary distance is greater than the primary, the difference, therefore, must be subtracted from the arc of direction 25° 45'; therefore the true arc of direction is 24°, which, for the equation, added to the ☉'s right ascension 30° 7', makes the sum 54° 7', answering to ♉ 26° 26', to which the ☉, from the day and hour of the nativity, arrives in 25 days, which signifies so many years of age. The ☉ is, by a converse motion, posited in a mundane parallel of ☿, whose declination is 7° 17', answering to 18° 30' of the ecliptic; its horary times nocturnal are 13° 54'; its distance from the east 9° 20'; and its oblique ascension in the horoscope is 15° 39'. The diurnal horary times of the ☉ (for he is posited above the earth) are 16° 53', wherefrom, in the fourth place, is produced the ☉'s secondary distance 11° 20', which, added to the primary, makes the arc of direction 23° 53'.

But it is very evident, that ☿ possesses an anaretic power; even from the nature of the effect, which is apoplexy; for ☿ is in exact parallel of ♄'s declination, applying to the declination of ♂; he is likewise in the mundane parallel of ♄; and, as he has his □ to the

☽, denotes a very grievous disorder in the head, especially when found in the centre of the horoscope, and western angle. The ☉ was likewise joined, by a converse motion, to ♄, whose declination is reduced to ♓ 11° 40′ in the ecliptic, and the diurnal horary times become 13° 55′, which, doubled, is 27° 50′; the pole of the twelfth house is 31°, the oblique ascension of ♄ in the horoscope is 352° 34′, and there remains his distance from the east 13° 45′; from which, in the fourth place, are produced 5°, to be subtracted from the pole of the country, and there remains the polar elevation of ♄ 37°, under which his oblique ascension is 351° 28′: the ☉'s oblique ascension there is 20° 41′, from which, subtracting the former, leaves the arc of direction 29° 13′, so that the ☉ was only 4° distant from ♄; therefore, from these four examples of the ☉, constituted in the crepuscules, it is sufficiently and plainly proved how well the calculations by the crepusculine circles agree. But I proposed this method by reasoning upon, and also observing, the accidents in these examples, as I never could persuade myself to neglect the true significator of life. It it usual, with some, to answer this method of proceeding, by saying, that there is no occasion to be so rigorously exact in the judgment of nativities, and that a malign influence to the horoscope may kill, if it has not the primary signification of life. But, from such reasoning, the order and method which Ptolemy lays down for the election of a prorogator are quite absurd; unless life be at the disposal of a sole primary significator only, and a very powerful reason convinces us it is so. For either one prorogator only, that is, if more powerful with respect to the rest, denotes life; or else one, with others competent, as colleagues; but this last cannot be admitted, as it would create a confusion which could not be cleared up, and Ptolemy never taught it should be so. They say, that life primarily regards the principal prorogator; and, secondly, the ascendant; so that, in the occourses to the malefics, it may kill; but it is quite the reverse, for if a prorogator, who, from its powerful and dignified place, is entitled to the signification of life, can, by his influencing power, support that life, no other of inferior virtue can put an end to it. Again, they say, the reason why those nativities are stronger, wherein several concur, to signify life, is because the significators of life being numerous, there is a proportional increase of strength to prolong life. But it is quite otherwise, for, from several significators, the aspects of the destroyers are multiplied by the different and numerous directions; therefore, any person having several significators of life, would be lower in station and shorter lived; in truth, they direct the horoscope to the malefics, purely that it may kill; though the luminaries at that time happily signify life, and are strong, owing to the aspects of the favourable planets with which they continue in direction; one, therefore, only signifies life, elected, according to Ptolemy's method, &c. But let us look for the other motions in the nativity now before us.

The secondary directions are made May 16, 1612, at 16 hours nearly, when the ☽ was in ♐ 24° in □ of

♂, ☿ in the □ of ♂'s radical place, and that of the deadly direction. At his illness, the ☽ was posited in □ to this place; and, on the day he died, was found there with the ☌ of ☿ in □ of ♂ of these motions, for ♂ was in ♓ 25°, and ☽ in ♐ 25° on the day of death, and ☿ in ♓ 26°. On the 9th of April, which preceded his death, there was celebrated a full ☽, the ☉ being in ♈ 20°, upon ☿ of the nativity, and the ☽ opposite: and, at his death, the ☉ exactly transited this place of ☿, maligned by the □ of ♄, who, in his transit, was found to remain upon the ☊, and in the □ of ☿'s radical place.

The progressions to the end of the 25th year, are made on the 29th of April, 1614, the ☽ being in ♒ 0°; but 7° must be subtracted, for his death happened 7 days before the ☉'s return to the natal place, and the ☽ was posited in 23° of ♑ upon her proper place of the nativity, in the □ of ☿, where ♄ was found at death; the ☽, at his illness, entered the ☍ of ♂ of the progressions, where it was in 29° of ♓, and, at his death, she was posited in its □, and ☿ was found exactly in the same place on the day he died; the ☉, on the same day, was posited in the □ of the ☽ of the progressions, and parallel of ♂'s radical place; and it is truly admirable to see how well these agree. You are to observe, likewise, that the ingresses and transits, both active and passive, agree; aspecting the lunations in the places, which are the cause of the effect, according to the true sense of Ptolemy.

PRIMUM MOBILE.

Secondary Direction Places of the Stars.

	☉	☽	♄	♃	♂	♀	☿	☊
Deg. of Lon.	♉ 26.0	♐ 24.0	♓ 16.52	♌ 17.50	♓ 25.17	♋ 2.39	♊ 10.1	♊ 1.48

The Progressions of the Stars are those:

	☉	☽	♄	♃	♂	♀	☿	☊
Deg. of Lon.	♉ 8.20	♑ 23.0	♈ 7.50	♎ 19.36	♓ 28.57	♉ 24.19	♉ 28.52	♉ 24.6

Places of the Planets, at the Time of Death, on the 14th of April, 1637, 3ʰ Night.

	☉	☽	♄	♃	♂	♀	☿	☊
Deg. of Lon.	♈ 24.48	♐ 27.0	♑ 25.7	♍ 7.20	♉ 14.31	♈ 1.34	♓ 27.0	♑ 29.0

EXAMPLE X.

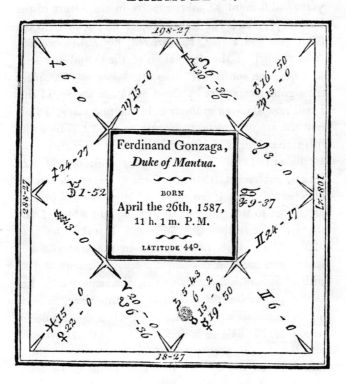

LATITUDES.				DECLINATIONS.		
♄	. .	2°	2' S.	11°	34'	N.
♃	. .	0	11 S.			
♂	. .	2	34 N.	7	35	N.
☉	. .	0	0	13	34	N.
♀	. .	0	40 N.			
☿	. .	0	50 N.			
☽	. .	4	59 N.	13	34½	S.

HE died in the month of October, 1626, aged 39 years and 6 months: as the ☽ is in the centre of the horoscope, she is the significator of life, which, in the 39th year and a half, had arrived, by right direction, to a parallel of the declination of the ☉ and ♄; and, as a question sometimes arises, to know at what place the significator arrives by direction in the zodiac, of this I will now shew an example: In the first place, I thus find the arc of direction adequate to the 39 years and a half; the ☉ in $39^d\ 12^h$, arrives at ♊ 14°, whose right ascension is 72° 38'; the ☉'s right ascension is 33° 42', which, subtracted from the former, leaves the arc of direction for the given years 38° 56'; the ☽'s oblique ascension to the pole 44°, is 290° 48', to which I add the arc of direction 38° 56', and I make the sum 329° 44', at which the ☽ arrives in the said year. I find this in the table of oblique ascensions about ♒ 16°, with 3° 50' north latitude, that is, the same the ☽ has in that place; but the declination of this place, according to longitude and latitude, is 12° 50'; the ☉'s declination is 13° 34'; ♄'s declination is 11° 34'; therefore the ☽, in that place, obtained a mean declination between the ☉ and ♄. But, as the ☉ was conjoined to ♄, and in the mundane parallel of ♂, he was endowed with their deadly qualities; from which ♃ being alone, in his ✶, could not relieve him. By a converse direction the ☽ applied to a mundane parallel with the ☉ and ♄, whilst all were carried away by the motion of the *primum mobile*. But if ♎ 26° 45' are posited in the *medium cœli*, this ray, by a true calculation, exactly agrees, for the ☽'s semi-diurnal arc is 4ʰ 44′; semi-diurnal arc of the ☉'s opposition is 5ʰ 6′; which, added together, make the sum 9ʰ 50′; the ☽'s right ascension is 271° 58′; her primary distance from the *medium cœli* (26° 45′ of ♎ being posited there, whose right ascension is 204° 48′) is 67° 10′; the right ascension of the ☉'s ☍ is 213° 42′; and the right distance between the ☽ and ☍ of the ☉, becomes 58° 16′: therefore, if that sum, 9ʰ 50′, gives the ☽'s semi-diurnal arc 4ʰ 44′, the right difference 58° 16′, will give 28° 3′, which, subtracted from the ☽'s primary distance from the *medium cœli*, leaves the arc of direction 39° 7′: she likewise applied to the mundane parallel of ♂; and lastly, to the ☍ of ☿, which direction may easily be calculated.

For the secondary direction, I add to the hours of the nativity 39 days 12 hours, for the same number of years and 6 months, and I come to the 5th of June, 1587, nearly in the meridian, in which the places of the planets were as under:

	☉	☽	♄	♃	♂	♀	☿	☋
Deg. of Lon.	♊	♎	♉	♋	♍	♈	♊	♎
	15.43	14.24	10.45	16.38	24.25	28.55	10R40	4.31
Lat.		S. 4.20	S. 2. 9	S. 0. 5	N. 1. 5	S. 2 10	S. 2.24	

The ☽ under the ☉'s rays and the ☉ with ☿ ℞ in the parallel of ♃'s declination; but ♃ was adverse to the sign of the luminaries: in October, 1624, in which the native died, there was a full ☉ in ♎ 12°, with ☿ retrograde in ☌ with ♂ and parallel of ♄, and the secondary direction in the parallel of ♂, and to the nativity in the parallel of ♀ and ♂.

The progressions are made on the 6th of July, 1590, or on the following day, because the day is not known when the native died, yet the planets were nearly as follow:

	☉	☽	♄	♃	♂	♀	☿	☋
Deg. of Lon.	♋ 14.33	♍ 17.42	♊ 21.33	♎ 9.33	♋ 13.28	♉ 29.36	♌ 8.37	♌ 4 46
Lat.		N. 3.25	S. 1.36	N. 1.32	N. 0. 3	N. 3.11	N. 1.22	

The ☉ was with ♂, the ☽ in the □ of ♄; in the month he died, ♄ was upon this place of the ☽, and ♂ in the □ of the ☽'s place, and the lunations in an hostile ray to this place of ♂, and also of the ☉.

PRIMUM MOBILE. 191

EXAMPLE XI.

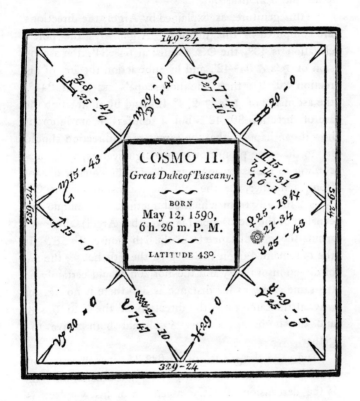

LATITUDES.

♄ . . 1° 39' S.

♂ . . 0   4 N.

☿ . . 4   8 S.

☽ . . 2 25 N.

HE died in the month of February 1621, being 30 years and 9 months old.

In this geniture, as explained by Argol, the directions are computed in this manner. Argol says the pole's elevation is 43°, the ☉'s ascension 64° 34', the ascension of ♄'s ☌ 94° 42', and by subtraction the arc of direction 30° 8'; then the horoscope's ascension 244°, the ascension of ♄'s ☍ 274° 42', and by subtraction the arc of direction 30° 42': but I confess I am ignorant how it can happen, that the same arc of direction should fall to the same promittor of two significators, who, according to the ascensions, are 3° of the equator distant from each other, for the oblique ascension of the ☉'s ☍ is 246° 58', from which subtracting the oblique ascension of the horoscope (as given by Argol) there remains the ☉'s distance from the 7th house 2° 58'. If the ☉ remained upon the cusp of the 7th house, the arc of direction of the ☉ and the horizon would certainly be the same; but as his distance is 3°, there is no reason why, at the same time, the direction of the ☉ to ♄'s ☌ and the horoscope to his ☍ should both arrive together.

And as to the ☉'s ascension 64° 34', it is uncertain in what manner that was taken; for ♄'s ascension 94° 42' is the descension, for the ascension of his ☍ place is 274° 42', from which take 180°, there remains the descension of ♄ 94° 42'. But the oblique ascension of the ☉'s ☍ is 246° 58', from which subtract 180°, and it gives his descension 66° 58'; therefore the calculations of Argol are unintelligible.

In this nativity there should ascend ♏ 15° 43′; and the ☉ becomes altogether a powerful significator of life, and was first directed to the ☌ of ♂, but as the △ of ♃ followed about the beginning of ♃'s terms, the native was preserved; then he came to the ☌ of ♄, whose latitude was 1° 39′ south, and passed through, by a latitudinal distance, according to the doctrine of Ptolemy, " When the moderator and occourse have not the same latitude."

The place of the direction was likewise in the terms of ♀, and the ☉ at that time was in □ of ♃ *in mundo* from the *medium cœli*, all which profited the more, as the ☉ in the nativity was conjoined to ♀ in her house, and within the terms and mundane △ of ♃; therefore he escaped the ☉, also to the ☌ of ♄, yet, I think, not without a great detriment to his health, and that ♂ having descended below the horizon, and in an equal proportional distance which the ☉ hath from the 7th house, the ☉ entered into its mundane parallel at the time of his death, being found within the orbs of ♂ in the zodiac.

Also, the ☉, by converse motion, came to the parallel of ♄ *in mundo*, having passed by ☿, who was found under the same parallel of the enemies, and the ☽ in the □ of ♂, whereby a complaint in the head was pre-noted, without doubt the more grievous, as the ☽ in the nativity was in the mundane □ of ☉. The calculation of the ☉ to the mundane parallel of ♂ direct direction:

As the semi-diurnal arc of the ☉ . . . . 7ʰ 12′
To his distance from the 7th house . . . 7° 34

So is the semi-nocturnal arc of ♂ . . . 4ʰ 34'
To his secondary dist. from the 7th house . 4° 41
The oblique ascension of ♂'s ☍ . . . 265 34

Whence his prim. dist. from the 7th house is 26 9 which being added to his secondary distance is 30° 50' for the arc of direction, and being equated as usual, produces 31 years, almost.

By converse motion the ☉ came to the parallel of ♄ *in mundo,* thus calculated:

As the semi-diurnal arc of ♄ . . . . . . 7ʰ 24'
To his distance from the 7th house . . . 34° 55
So is the semi-nocturnal arc of the ☉ . . 4ʰ 48
To his secondary distance . . . . . . 22° 89
The oblique ascension of the ☉'s ☍ is . . 246 58

Whence his primary dist. from the West is 7 33 which, as he is above the earth, and posited below, must be added to the secondary, and makes the arc of direction 30° 12'. From this example we are taught carefully to observe the places of the occourses, for, if the fortunes assist, they preserve, and more particularly in their terms, as it happened in the preceding directions.

For the secondary directions, I add to the hour and day of the nativity 30 days for so many years, and 18 hours for 9 months, and I come to the 12th of June, 1590, nearly, in the meridian, in which the places of the planets are these:

Deg. of Lon.	☉	☽	♄	♃	♂	♀	☿	☊
	♊	♎	♊	♎	♎	♉	♉	♌
	20.40	16.45	18.12	8.10	26.45	16.57	24.18	6.6
Lat.		N. 4.36	S. 1.35	N. 1.42	N. 0. 5	S. 1.55	N. 0.24	

Where you see the ☉ is between ♄ and ♂ ; ☿ conjoined to ♂, and both unassisted by any of the benefics. In February, 1621, the lunations happened in the meridian angles of the nativity, in the ☉'s □ with the parallel of ♂. The progressions for full 30 years, depend on the 14th of October, 1592: For the 9 months I add 9 or 10 signs, and come to the 4th or 5th of November; for we are not certain of the day he died: this is certain, that on the 4th of the said month there happened a new ☽ in 11° ♏. To the middle of February, 1621, ♂ was found in 11° ♏.

EXAMPLE XII.

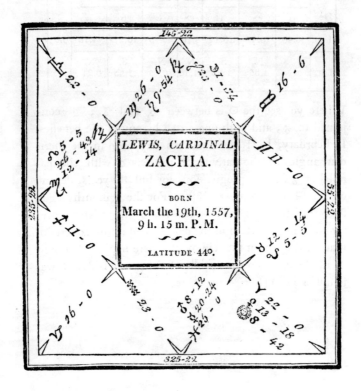

LATITUDES.				DECLINATIONS.			
♄	. .	2°	13′	N.	9°	56	N.
♃	. .	1	55	N.	13	45	S.
♂	. .	0	13	S.	8	43	S.
☉	. .	0	0		3	28	N.
♀	. .	1	0	S.	4	21	N.
☿	. .	2	34	S.	6	9	S.
☽	. .	5	0	S.	15	0	N.

HE was made a Cardinal in 1626, on the 19th of January, aged 68 years and 10 months; and died on the 30th of August, 1637.

For which effect, Argol directs the horoscope to the □ of the ☉; whereas, the one is not aphæta, nor the other anareta; for the ☉ is conjoined to ♀, and in her declination, to which the ☽ applies by a fortunate △ ray, she also makes application to the □ and declination of ♃, being constituted in his terms; so that to the ☉ she transmits none but fortunate qualities. We, therefore, in imitation of Ptolemy, make the ☽ hyleg, who is past her first dichotome, in her increase, approaching nearest to the fulness of light, constituted in the ninth house, and between benefic rays.

She, in 70 years and 5 months, which the native lived, arrived at the parallel declination of ♂, that of ♄ succeeding near 18° of ♎, without the assistance of the benefics. I first look for the arc of direction, which is due for 70 years and 5 months: the ☉, in 70 days and 10 hours from the birth, comes to ♊ 17°, whose right ascension is 75° 52'; from which subtract the ☉'s right ascension, 8°, and there remains 67° 52', the arc of direction. The ☽'s declination, 15°, answers to 19° 35' of ♌ in the ecliptic, whose horary times are 17° 30', her right ascension is 122° 40'; this, subtracted from the right ascension of the *medium cœli*, gives her distance from the 10th, 22° 42'; the pole of the ninth house is 18°, which produces the ☽'s pole 12°, under which the oblique ascension of her ♉ is 305° 57', to which I add the arc of direction 67° 52', and the sum is 13° 49′, which in the same table of oblique ascension is near 18° of ♈, with latitude 1° 28′ north, which the ☽ obtains there ; so that she passed ♎ 18°, with 1° 28′ south latitude, the declination of which place is 8° 26′; but the declination of ♂ is 8° 43′ ; but the luminaries, as I have mentioned in another place, do not wait for a true and intimate declination, by reason of the magnitude of their bodies.

By converse motion the ☽ came to the *mundane* □ of ♂, and ♄ thus computed, the declination of ♂ is 8° 43′, answering to 7° 40′ ♓ in the ecliptic, whose nocturnal horary times are 16° 25′ ; the right ascension of ♂ is 339° 56′ ; his distance from the *imum cœli* 14° 34′ ; the ☽'s declination 15°, answers to 19° 35′ ♌, whose horary times are 17° 30′, which gives her secondary distance from the 7th house 15° 34′; the oblique ascension of the ☽'s ☍ under the pole of the horoscope is 317° 38′, from which subtracting the oblique ascension of the horoscope, there remains the ☽'s primary distance from the seventh house 82° 16′ ; from which subtracting the secondary 15° 34′, leaves the arc of direction 66° 42′, near 1° less than that above taken ; the ☽ had also, about two years before, arrived at the □ of ♄ by converse motion ; but as she, in the nativity, was very fortunate and strong, these directions waited for the approach of the direct directions.

This example also teaches us, what the sentiments of Ptolemy were concerning a violent death : when in a peremptory place both the enemies meet together, it is to be understood, that in the nativity the violence is sometimes first pre-ordained from the unfortunate position of the aphæta; at other times quite the contrary. But because the direct direction happened to be in the terms of ☿, the sickness was attended with a delirium and lethargy, so that you may perceive this to have been the true cause of the native's death.

It may be asked, why did not the multiplicity of evil aspects, as the ☌ of ♄, the ☍ of ♂, and their preceding parellels, kill? I answer, because the ☽ was in a different and distant latitude from that of the malefics, and had the declination of ♀ and the ☉; and was supported by the ✶ of ♃, both in the zodiac and in the world, in the terms of ♀; the ☽ was likewise fortunate, and strong to resist. Lastly, there was the parallel of ☿, who is of the nature of ♃, on account of the sign and mundane △ of ♃ and parallel of ♀; so that ☿ was entirely propitious. For which reason, he was the author of the dignities in the native, as we have calculated in Canon 36, and shall hereafter add; for neither the ☉ nor *medium cœli* had any aspect with ♃ in the 59th year, nor with ♀, who being combust, could not effect any thing, except only predispose the ☉, by being present with her. The secondary directions to the time of death are thus calculated. For the 70 years I add 70 days; and for the 5 months 10 hours, to the day and hour of the nativity; and I come to the 28th of May, 1567, with 19^h 13′, P. M. at which time these were the places of the planets:—

	☉	☽	♄	♃	♂	♀	☿	☊
Deg. of	[illegible]	♒	♍	♎	♉	♋	♋	♏
Lon.	16.30	26.0	8.5[illegible]	28℞5	3 0	9. 0	1℞15	1.24
Lat.		N. 4.32	2. 4	N. 1.50	S. 0.20	N. 1. 6	S. 1.54	

The ☽ had the same declination as ♄, and both malefic in the nativity, the ☽ had likewise, by direction, the same declination; this place of the ☽'s ☍, ☿ entered on the day he died, and ♂, too, not far distant; the ☉ in ♊ 17°, which ♄ entered from a parallel declination on the day he died; and on the contrary, the ☉, on the day he died, entered the place of ♄ of these motions.

The Places of the Planets on the day of his death, the 30th of August, 1637.

	☉	☽	♄	♃	♂	♀	☿	☊
Deg. of	♍	♑	♑	♎	♌	♍	♌	♑
Lon	7.3	10.44	19.23	7.16	16.33	20.42	28.33	24.30

On the 19th of August there was celebrated a new ☽ in ♌ 27°, when she was in 3° south latitude, nearly, whereby she obtained the declination of the malefics, and near the ☍ of the ☽'s place of the secondary direction. We look for the progressions to the day of death, as follows: For 60 years I come to the

20th of March, 1572, but I go 55 days back, viz. to the 24th of January, when the ☽ is in ♊ 8°; afterwards I advance 10 embolismical lunations, and come to the 14th of November, by positing the ☽ in ♓ 27°. For the 5 months the ☽ goes over 5 signs and 12°, so that she is posited in ♍ 9° upon the malefics of the nativity.

Planets Places in the Progressions.

Deg. of Lon.	☉	☽	♄	♃	♂	♀	☿	☊
	♐	♍	♏	♈	♒	♎	♏	♋
	15.0	9.0	21.14	21.10	1.0	28.50	27.0	15.0

Mars was, therefore, in ☍ to the ☽ of the nativity; ♄ on the day he died was in the parallel of the ☉'s progression; and on the 13th day, which was that of his sickness, there was a □ of the ☽ with the ☉; the latter continued in ♌ 21°, in the □ of ♄'s progression from ♉ 21°; and ♂ was found upon the ☽ of the nativity, and ♄ in the □ of the place of the ☽'s right direction. In 59 years the ☉ came to the ✳ of ☿, not only in the world, according to the calculations in Canon XXXVI, but also to his ✳ in the zodiac.

Of the ☉.

Right ascension	8°	0′
Distance from the *imum cœli* . . .	42	38
Semi-nocturnal arc	5ʰ	47
Crepusculine arc subtracted	1	44
Remains the obscure arc	4	3

Of ♉ 21°.

Right ascension	48° 33'
Distance *ab imum cœli*	83 11
Semi-nocturnal arc	4ʰ 47
Crepusculine arc	2 7
Remains obscure arc	2 40

Hence the secondary distance is 28° 4', which subtracted from the primary, leaves the arc of direction 55° 7'. The secondary directions to 58 years, 9 months, and 20 days, are made on the 17th of May, 1567, with hours P. M. 4ʰ 33', in which the planets were as under:

	☉	☽	♄	♃	♂	♀	☿	☋
Deg. of Lon.	♊ 5.30	♎ 2. 0	♍ 8.30	♎ 28R.50	♈ 23.8	♊ 26.24	♋ 0.14	♏ 1.56
Lat.		S. 2.30	N. 2. 5	N. 1.51	S. 0.19	N. 0.44		

The ☉ is in exact biquintile of ♃ and △ of the ☽. On the 18th and 19th of January, 1626, the luminaries were in an alternate △ ray to these places, and ♃ was in the same sign and degree, viz. ♎ 29°, with the biquintile to the place of the ☉'s secondary direction. On the 12th of January, 1626, there was a full ●, the ☉ in ♑ 22°, the ☽ in ♋ 22°, in favourable rays to ☿ and the place of the ☉'s direction, and ✶ of ♃ of the progressions, and the ☉ in the quintile of ♃'s radical place. The progressions are made on the 19th of December, 1571, in the following position:

	☉	☽	♄	♃	♂	♀	☿	☊
Deg. of Lon.	♑ 8.0	♒ 23.0	♏ 13.14	♓ 18.10	♎ 3.20	♑ 9.0	♐ 20.0	♌ 3.0

The ☉ was joined with ♀, and between the quintile and ✶ of ♃, in the parallel of ☿; on the 19th of January, 1626, ♀ was upon this place of the ☉, ♃ was separated from the ✶ and applied to the quintile of the ☉'s place of the progressions, which things are well worth observing.

EXAMPLE XIII.

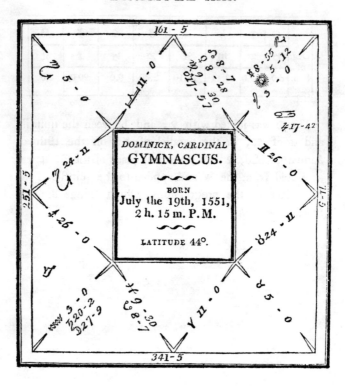

LATITUDES.				DECLINATIONS.		
♄	1° 14'	S.		16° 2'	S.
♃	0 0			22 21	N.
♂	0 17	N.		5 3	N.
☉	0 0			19 2	N.
♀	1 42	N.		10 0	N.
☿	4 0	S.		14 12	N.
☽	0 57	N.		11 37	S.

WHEN he was 52 years and 10 months old, he was created a Cardinal, on the 9th of June, 1604. His death happened on the 12th of March, 1639, aged 87 years, 7 months, and 20 days.

Argol directs the horoscope to the ☽ ; but the moderator of life altogether pertains to the ☉, who, according to our calculation, came to a parallel of ♄'s declination near 13°, with some minutes, of the sign ♏ : the ☉ does not reach the cusp of the 9th house, but his distance therefrom is 2°: the polar elevation of the 9th house is 18°, therefore the ☉'s polar elevation will be near 17°, to which the oblique ascension of the ☉'s ♂ is 313° 37'; the oblique ascension 13° of ♉ is 35° 35', from which subtracting that of the ☉, leaves the arc of direction 81° 58', which, for the equation, add to the ☉'s right ascension, which is 127° 34', and the sum is 209° 32', answering to 1° 40' of ♏, to which the ☉, from the day of birth, arrives in 88 days, so that the ☉ had not yet exactly reached the declination of ♄ ; but as, by reason of the magnitude of his body, he did not, by his centre, gain that declination, yet a part of his body entered it.

By converse direction, the ☉ was in a mundane parallel with ♄ under the earth whilst both advanced by the motion of the *primum mobile*, which is calculated thus : The ☉'s semi-nocturnal arc is $4^h\ 42'$; the semi-nocturnal arc of ♄ is $7^h\ 4'$, which I have taken with 13° 47' of ♏ in the ecliptic, or with ♒ 16° 13', which is the declination of ♄ ; I add these arcs together, and they make 11^h 46'. The right ascension of ♄ is 322° 52'; this I reject from the ☉'s right ascension, in order that I may have their right difference below the earth, and the remainder is 164° 44'. I now say,

As the sum of the semi-nocturnal arcs . 11^h 46'
is to the semi-nocturnal arc of ♄ . .   7   4
so is the right ascen. diff. of ♄ from ☉   164° 44
to ♄'s secondary distance from 4th . .   99   10

The primary distance of ♄ from the *imum cœli* is 18° 13'; which, subtracted from the secondary, gives the arc of direction 80° 57', less by 1° than that above taken: this parallel precedes, and the other succeeds. Lastly, the ☉, by converse direction, applied very closely to a □ of the ☽, whose declination is 13° 23', which, reduced to the ecliptic = ♒ 24° 30', whose semi-nocturnal arc is 6^h 55'. The ☉'s semi-nocturnal arc is 4^h 42'; the oblique ascension of his ☋ 327° 1'; his primary distance from the west is 75° 56': the ☽'s right ascension is 329° 3'; her distance from the *imum cœli* is 12° 2'. Then

As the ☽'s semi-diurnal arc . . . . 6^h 55'
is to her distance from the *imum cœli* . 12°   2
so is the ☉'s semi-nocturnal arc . . . 4^h 42
to his secondary distance from the west 8°   11

But the ☉'s primary distance from the west is 75° 56', for the oblique ascension of the ☉'s ☋ is 327° 1'; therefore the primary distance added to the secondary, makes the arc of direction 84° 7'. Now the ☽ was besieged between ♄ and the mundane parallel of ♂, who was elevated above her from *medium cœli*, and co-ascended nearly with ♄, and continued in his house, terms, and triplicity, so that she was afflicted with the nature of the malefics. To the same time the ☉'s direction to the west agrees, with the addition and subtraction of the degrees formed from the interjacent stars and rays, a calculation whereof is given as an example in Canon XXXVIII. The secondary directions are made on the 14th of October, 1551, with the hours 17° 35′, P. M. at which time the planets were posited thus:

	☉	☽	♄	♃	♂	♀	☿	☋
Deg. of Lon.	♏ 1.0	♉ 7. 0	♎ 15.24	♌ 2. 7	♏ 16.33	♐ 17.20	♏ 19.10	♏ 3.27
Lat.		S. 4.30	S. 1.14	N. 0.10	S. 0. 1	S. 3. 0	S. 2.35	

The progressions depend on the 19th of August, 1558, with the planets posited thus:

	☉	☽	♄	♃	♂	♀	☿	☋
Deg. of Lon.	♍ 5.13	♏ 18.0	♉ 25. 4	♎ 3.18	♌ 13.50	♋ 22.0	♌ 21.30	♈ 21.4
Lat.		S. 2.16	S. 2.23	S. 0.52	N. 0.16	S. 1.40	N. 1. 7	

He died on the 12th of March, 1639, 10 hours, P.M. under this calculation of the planets:

Deg. of Lon.	☉ ♓ 22 13	☽ ♈ 25. 0	♄ ♒ 14.13	♃ ♐ 5.46	♂ ♉ 6. 8	♀ ♓ 28. 0	☿ ♒ 23.40	☊ ♐ 23.16
Lat.		S. 0.11	S. 0.51	N. 0.56	N. 0.22	S. 1.23	N. 0.10	

On the 4th of the same month there was a new ☽, near the ☍ of ♂ of the nativity, and ♂ was in ♉ 1° in ☍ to the ☉'s secondary direction: ♂, on the day he died, reached the place of the ☽'s secondary direction, and □ of the ☉'s radical place: the ☉, by the secondary direction, had gained the declination of the ☽ of the nativity, and the ☽ to the □ of the ☉, with the same declination. The ☉ by progression had nearly the same declination with the ☽ in the nativity: the ☽, by progression, was between the rays of the enemies, and under the parallel of both the unfavourable planets, to which, on the day of his death, ♄ and ☿ being conjoined by a quadrate ray, transmitted their mischievous qualities; and, which is worth observing, that the luminaries, with ♄ anareta, were, in the nativity, in fixed signs, and in them also they were constantly found in the secondary directions, in the progressions, and on the day he died, as were likewise ☿ and ♂.

In his 52d year and 10 months, the ☉ was directed to his own ✶, the *medium cœli* to his quintile; the calculations of which are easy. The secondary directions are made on the 9th of September, with near

22ʰ 30′, P. M. at which time the planets were as under:

Deg. of Lon.	☉	☽	♄	♃	♂	♀	☿	☊
	♍	♒	♎	♋	♐	♏	♍	♍
	26.20	6.0	16.6	27.56	21.52	10.25	22.10	5.18

The ☉ was in ✶ to ♃ and in ☌ with ☿, free from the enemies. The progressions were thus, and are made on the 27th of October, 1555, whilst the ☽ was in ♈ 5°.

Deg. of Lon.	☉	☽	♄	♃	♂	♀	☿	☊
	♏	♈	♈	♏	♐	♏	♏	♊
	13.15	5.0	7.17	13.50	26.4	0.0	8.20	15.27

The ☉ was in ☌ with ♃ and ☿, free from the enemies, near the △ of ♃ in the nativity.

On the day of election, which was the 9th of June, 1604, the planets were as under:

Deg. of Lon.	☉	☽	♄	♃	♂	♀	☿	☊
	♊	♏	♐	♐	♎	♋	♋	♏
	18.20	17.14	11.46	19.18	12.25	28.28	2.6	5.22

There preceded a new ☽ in 7° of ♊, under the ✶ of the ☉ of the nativity, and parallel of ♃, in which pa-

F f

rallel the ☉ was on the day he was elected; and the ☽ in a △ of ♃ of the nativity, and in ☌ in the progression. Hence is plainly evinced the great power the secondary directions and progressions have, together with the active and passive ingresses, to the places which the luminaries by these motions arrive at.

EXAMPLE XIV.

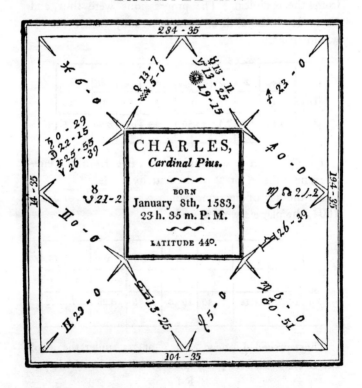

LATITUDES.

♄	. . 2°	1′	S.
♃	. . 1	37	S.
♂	. . 3	27	N.
♀	. . 1	16	S.
☿	. . 1	8	S.
☽	. . 2	25	N.

IN the 19th year and a half of his age he was elected a Cardinal, on the 9th of June, 1604; and in the 56th year and a half he died of the gout and consumption, June the 1st, 1641, to which time Argol directs the ascendant to a □ of ♄, though he is in the shortest ascensions, and the ☉, not the horoscope, becomes a powerful significator of life, as he is found in the supreme angle, and the rays taken in the zodiac to the angles are altogether as nothing, as we have in another place demonstrated.

The ☉, therefore, is the significator of life, and in 56 years and a half he comes, by right direction, to the mundane parallel of ♂, followed very closely by a parallel of ♄'s declination, and, by converse motion, to the parallel of ♂. The ☉'s semi-diurnal arc is 4ʰ 28′, his right ascension is 290° 51′, from which, subtracting the right ascension of the *medium cœli*, there remains the ☉'s distance 6° 16′. The semi-nocturnal arc of ♂ is 5ʰ 3′, and is taken from ♌ 21° 30′, to which the declination of ♂ 14° 25′ is reduced; whence the secondary distance of ♂ from the *imum cœli* is 7° 5′, and added to the primary, which is 49° 35′, (for the right ascension of ♂ is 154° 10′), makes the arc of direction 56° 40′, which, equated as usual, is 56 years and a half. The ☉'s polar elevation is near 5°, under which his oblique ascension is 292° 54′; to which, if we add the arc of direction 56° 40′, the sum is 349° 34′, which, in the table, is equal to ♓ 18° 10′, whose declination is 4° 42′, and that of ♄ 1° 40′; so that the ☉ applies, within 3°, to a parallel of ♄'s declination.

The ☉, by converse direction to a mundane parallel of ♂, is thus computed:

As the semi-nocturnal arc of ♂ . . . 5ʰ 3′
is to his distance from the *imum cœli* . . 49° 35
so is the ☉'s semi-diurnal arc 4ʰ 28
to his secondary distance from *medium cœli* 43° 51
which, added to his primary, makes . . . 50 7
for the arc of direction; so that it had preceded near seven years before.

Also, by converse motion, the ☉ had passed the sesqui-quadrate of ♄ in his 49th year. The semi-diurnal arc of ♄ is 5ʰ 54′, distance from the East 11° 46′, the ☉'s semi-diurnal arc is 4ʰ 28′; whence arises his secondary distance 8° 54′, which, added to the primary, makes the arc of direction of ☉ to the □ of ♄, by converse motion, 15° 10′; to which I add the ☉'s triplicate horary times, which are 11° 9′, and it makes the arc of direction of the ☉ to the sesqui-quadrate of ♄, 48° 37′.

The secondary directions are made on the 6th of March 11ʰ, P. M. 1585, at which time the planets are posited in the following manner:

PRIMUM MOBILE.

	☉	☽	♄	♃	♂	♀	☿	☊
Deg. of Lon.	♓ 15.50	♉ 17.30	♈ 6. 1	♉ 3.35	♌ 15.7 R	♈ 21.40	♓ 24.0 R	♏ 17.59
Lat.		0. 2	S. 1.47	S. 1.10	N. 4.0		N. 3.54	

The progressions are made on the 3d of August, 1589, for then 56 and a half embolismical lunations are finished, at which time the planets were thus posited:

	☉	☽	♄	♃	♂	♀	☿	☊
Deg. of Lon.	♌ 10.37	♉ 13.22	♊ 12.0	♍ 18.9	♏ 14.17	♌ 12.20	♍ 8. 9	♌ 22.40
Lat.		S. 5. 0	S. 2. 1	N. 1. 1	S. 1. 7	N. 0.57	S. 0.50	

On the 1st of June, 1641, the day of his death, the planets were thus posited:

	☉	☽	♄	♃	♂	♀	☿	☊
Deg. of Lon.	♊ 11.5	♓ 22.48	♓ 11.46	♒ 12.1	♋ 13.14	♋ 21.1	♉ 17.32	♏ 10.27
Lat.		N. 3.53	S. 1.37	S. 0.40	N. 1.13	N. 2.21	S. 2.34	

In which it is worthy of admiration, that the ☉, on the

day he died, was posited upon ♄ of the progression, and ♄ on the same day upon the ☉ of the secondary direction, the ☽ upon ☿ of the secondary direction, who had the declination of ♄, and the ☽ likewise gained the declination of ♄. In the secondary direction, the ☽ being likewise in □ of ♂, and in his declination. In the progression, the ☉ was in □, and declination of ♂, and the ☽ in the ☍ of ♂. On the day of death, ♂ transited the ☍ of the ☉ of the nativity; and there was a □ of the ☽ with the ☉ the preceding day, viz. the 31st of May, the ☽ continuing in ♓ 10°, and the ☉ in ♊ 10°, obnoxious places. You see, Reader, what a multiplicity both of the active and passive agreements happened; they are altogether wonderful. At 19 years and 5 months, the time of his being made a Cardinal, the ☉ was in the mundane parallel with ♀, whilst both were carried by the rapt motion of the *primum mobile;* the ☉ likewise came to the declination of ♀ : the calculation of this latter is easy. The declination of ♀ is 18° 9′, equal to ♒ 9° 20′ in the ecliptic, whose oblique ascension to the ☉'s pole 5° is 313° 24′, from which, subtracting the ☉'s oblique ascension, there remains the arc of direction 20° 30′, which, for the equation, add to the ☉'s right ascension, which is 290° 51′, and it makes 311° 21′, answering to 8° 54′ of ♒, to which the ☉, from the day and hour of birth, arrives in 19 days and one-third nearly.

The Sun's direction to the mundane parallel of ♀ is as follows:

The declination of ♀ is 18° 9′, equal to ♒ 9° in the ecliptic, whose semi-diurnal arc is 4^h 47′, the right ascension of ♀ is 315° 58′: therefore, the right difference between the ☉ and ♀ is 25° 7′. I then say,

As the sum of the ☉ and ♀'s semi-diurnal arcs 9ʰ 15′
is to the ☉'s semi-diurnal arc 4 38
so is the right difference of the ☉ and ♀ 25° 7
to the ☉'s secondary distance . . . 12   8

which, added to the primary, makes the arc of direction 18° 24′; therefore, it had preceded two years, in which the native had shewn himself deserving the honours conferred upon him. But as the ☉ continued, by right direction, in ♒ 9° 20′, he applied to the quintile of ♃ in the zodiac; at the same time the *medium cœli* had reached the quintile of ♃, whose declination is 8° 33′; ascensional difference 8° 21′: the semi-diurnal arc is 98.21; the fifth part of the same arc is 19° 40′, which should be the distance of ♃ from the horoscope when posited in the quintile to the *medium cœli*. The oblique ascension of ♃ in the horoscope is 16° 16′; from which, subtracting the horoscope's oblique ascension, there remains his primary distance under the horizon 1° 41′; this, added to the secondary 19° 40′, makes the arc of direction 21° 21′.

Lastly, the ☉ applied to a ✶ of ♃ *in mundo;* for,
As the ☉'s semi-diurnal arc . . . . 4ʰ 28′
is to its distance from *medium cœli* . . 6° 16
so is ♃'s semi-diurnal arc 6ʰ 33
to his secondary distance from 12th house 9° 12
The oblique ascension of the 12th house is 344 35
The oblique ascension of ♃ to the pole of
   the 12th house 33°, is 19 1

therefore, the primary distance of ♃ from the twelfth

house is 34° 26′, from which, subtracting the secondary distance, leaves the arc of direction 25° 14′, whereby it appears evident that the ☉ and *medium cœli* were, at that time, found between several aspects of the friendly planets. The secondary directions are made on the 28th of January, 1585, with 9ʰ 35′ P. M., under the following sidereal constitution :

	☉	☽	♄	♃	♂	♀	☿	☊
Deg. of Lon.	♒ 8.40	♑ 18.8	♈ 2.0	♈ 27.38	♌ 28.40R	♓ 6.13	♒ 16.0	♏ 20.0
Lat.		N. 4.14	S. 15.7	S. 1.32	N. 4. 0	S. 1.17	S. 2.0	

The progressions for 19 years and 5 months fall on the 5th of August, 1586, the ☽ being in ♈ 15°; and the rest as under :

	☉	☽	♄	♃	♂	♀	☿	☊
Deg. of Lon.	♌. 12 1	♈ 15.0	♉ 2.46	♋ 4.19	♋ 6.50	♍ 2.41	♌ 4.33	♎ 20.36

On the 9th of June, 1604, the day of election, the planets were found in this position :

	☉	☽	♄	♃	♂	♀	☿	☊
Deg. of Lon.	♊ 18.20	♏ 17.14	♐ 11.46	♐ 19.18	♎ 12.25	♋ 28.28	♋ 2.6	♏ 5.22

Where you see the ☉ in △ to his place of the secondary direction, and in ✶ to his progression, applying to the ✶ of ♃ of his secondary directions, and in parallel of ♃'s declination of the progression. Jupiter, on the day of his election, entered in △ to the ☉'s progression, and, also, both the malefics ♄ from the △, and ♂ from the ✶; there preceded a new ☽ in 7° of ♊ in exact △ of the ☉'s secondary direction, and ✶ to his progression.

This cannot but be convincing.

EXAMPLE XV.

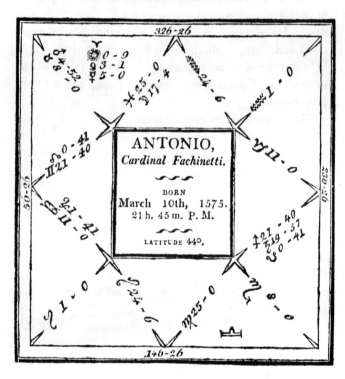

LATITUDES.

♄ . . 1° 30′ N.
♃ . . 0   4 N.
♂ . . 0   4 N.
♀ . . 1 20 S.
☿ . . 3   5 N.
☽ . . 4 48 S.

WE are told, by Argol, that this Cardinal had a dangerous illness in the 7th year of his age, owing (as he says) to the direction of the horoscope to the ☍ of ♄; but we say, it was from the ☉'s direction to the ☽ by converse motion: for the ☽'s pole is 16°, to which her oblique ascension is 352° 48'; this subtracted from the ☉'s oblique ascension 0° 7', leaves the arc of direction 7° 19'; for the ☽ was in the □ to ♄, by which means she assumed his nature. The ☉, also, by a right direction, afterwards fell upon the mundane sesqui-quadrate of ♄, whence a long sickness was the consequence, which was of the longer duration from ♄ being in the western angle; for thus we have the true causes from the real significator of life.

At the age of 16, he was elected Cardinal; from the ☉'s direction to the quintile of ♃ in the zodiac, the ☉'s duplicate horary times are 30°, his oblique ascension to the pole 18° of the eleventh house is 0° 7', and his distance from the same house is 3° 41'; the pole of the twelfth house is 33°; the difference then of the poles of the eleventh and twelfth houses is 15°; therefore, the ☉'s pole becomes 20°, to which his oblique ascension is 8°; the quintile of ♃ falls in 19° 41' of ♈, whose oblique ascension there is 15° 20', from which, subtract the ☉'s oblique ascension, and there remains the arc of direction 15° 12'; which, being equated, denotes 16 years. This direction is differently calculated in Canon XIX.

He died in May, 1606, and, according to Argol, from the ☽'s direction to ♂; but it was impossible for the

☽ to be hyleg, as she was under the ☉'s rays, going to the occultation; and as the nativity was diurnal, the first place belongs to the ☉, who remained in the eleventh house, and came to the ☌ of ♂, where the sesqui-quadrate of ♄ in the zodiac exactly coincided, and, by a converse motion, the ☉ came to the mundane parallel of the ☽, whilst both were carried away by the rapt motion of the *primum mobile*. The oblique ascension of ♂ to the pole 20°, is 27° 38', from which, subtracting that of the ☉, makes the arc of direction 27° 31', which, added to the ☉'s right ascension, makes 27° 39', answering to ♈ 29° 45', at which the ☉ arrives in near 31 days; and, as ♂ was in north latitude after the ☌, it followed his parallel of declination. The calculation of the ☉'s parallel with the ☽ is thus computed: the ☉'s semi-diurnal arc is 6^h, and that of the ☽ 5^h 23', for her declination answers in the ecliptic to near 5° 30' of ♓. I add these semi-diurnal arcs together, and the sum is 11^h 23'; the ☽'s right ascension is 349° 48', that of the ☉'s 0° 8'; from this of the ☉ I subtract the ☽'s, and their distance, in right ascension, is 10° 20' : Now say, as the sum of the arcs 11^h 23' is to the semi-diurnal arc of ☉ 6^h, so is their distance, in right ascension, 10° 20', to the ☉'s secondary distance from the *medium cœli* 5° 27'; his primary is 33° 42'; from which, taking the secondary, there remains the arc of direction 28° 15'.

The ☉ also applied very closely to the mundane □ of ♄, by converse motion.

The secondary directions for 31 years and 2 months are made on the 11th of April, 1575, with near 2 hours, P. M., the planets remaining in the following manner :

	☉	☽	♄	♃	♂	♀	☿	☊
Deg. of Lon.	♉	♉	♐	♋	♉	♉	♉	♉
	1. 0	9.19	19.16	4.35	26.14	11.36	29.39	29.14
Lat.		S. 1.48	N. 1.48	0.0	N. 0.8	S. 0.30	N. 1.47	

The progressions are made on the 15th of September, 1577 ; whilst the ☽ was in the last decanate of ♏, and the stars were disposed in the manner following :

	☉	☽	♄	♃	♂	♀	☿	☊
Deg. of Lon.	♎	♏	♑	♍	♍	♌	♍	♈
	2.10	22.0	5.30	24.40	20.40	16.40	28.0	12.8

To the middle of May, 1606, the time the native died, there was a □ of the luminaries, with this construction of the stars :

	☉	☽	♄	♃	♂	♀	☿	☊
Deg. of Lon.	♉	♌	♑	♓	♐	♉	I	♍
	24.0	24.0	7.40	0.0	8.0 R	18.20 R	12.0	28.2

The ingresses of the luminaries were the ☽ in □ to the place of ♂ and ☿ in ☌ in the secondary directions ; ♄ in □ of the ☉'s progression, who was there in the □ of ♄, and the ☉, by progression, came to the ☍ of his place in the nativity, with a □ of ♄, as we have said, and was, in the return of the year, in the same □ ray to the place of the ☉ unfortunate.

EXAMPLE XVI.

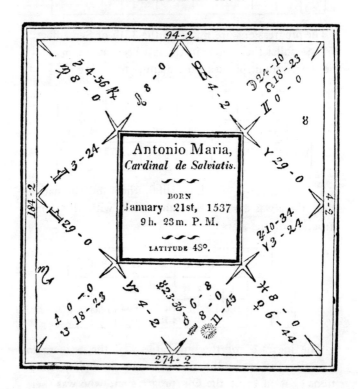

PRIMUM MOBILE.

	LATITUDES.				DECLINATIONS.		
♄	. .	1°	54'	N.	11°	31'	N.
♃	. .	1	20	S.	2	57	N.
♂	. .	0	3	S.	18	50	S.
☉	. .	0	0		17	20	S.
♀	. .	1	16	S.	10	15	S.
☿	. .	0	50	S.			
☽	. .	0	31	N.	23	54	N.

HE died, April 16, 1602, aged 65 years, 2 months, and 15 days. This nativity is among the seven examples which we have extracted from Maginus; and to 65 years and 3 months which the native lived, we have shewn that the ☽, by direction (who is hyleg), according to a right motion, came to the fixed star Cor Leonis, and to the parallel of declination of ♂ and the ☉; but, according to converse motion, to their □; which directions ought, doubtless, to be esteemed sufficiently powerful to infer a fatal sickness, especially in an old man. Now, after having well considered the matter, we add that the ☽, by converse motion, came to the mundane parallel of ♄, by exact calculation. Maginus takes the □ of ♄ to the horoscope in the equator, and Argol, to the same, adds the antiscion of ♂, both neglecting the ☽ being the significator, having dignity of life. The calculation of the ☽'s direction to the fixt star Regulus, and parallel declination of the ☉ and ♂, is as follows: The ☽'s declination is 23° 54', ascensional difference 24° 26', semi-diurnal arc 114° 26', the third part of which is 38° 9', the pole of the ninth house is 18°; the ☽'s right ascension is 83° 38', her distance from the *medium cœli* 10° 24'; therefore,

	D.	M.
As the third part of the semi-diurnal arc	38	0
is to the pole of the ninth house . . .	18	0
so is the ☽'s distance from the *medium cœli*	10	1
to her pole	4	0

To which the oblique ascension of the ☽'s ☊ is 265° 25': the oblique ascension of the ☊ of Regulus in that place is 326° 54'; from which, subtracting the former, leaves the arc of direction 61° 31', which, for the equation, I add to the ☉'s right ascension, which is 314° 13', and it makes 15° 44', answering to 17° 4' of ♈, to which the ☉, from the day of birth, arrives in 65 days and one-third, and points out 65 years and 4 months of his life; the ☽ in that place had 4° 32' north latitude, and, consequently, her declination was 18° 3', the ☉'s declination was 17° 20', and that of ♂ 18° 50'; the ☽ was therefore between the declination of the ☉ and ♂. Again, by reason of the magnitude of the ☉ and ☽'s bodies, and, also, on account of the parallax, the ☽ had already gained the ☉'s declination, and was declining from that of ♂, who, being combust, did not discover his effects; but the ☉, instead of him, according to the opinion of Cardan. The converse direction of the ☽ to the mundane parallel of ♄ is thus: The semi-diurnal arc of ♄ is 100° 58', his right ascension 157° 30', his distance from the *medium cœli* 63° 28', the ☽'s semi-diurnal arc 114° 26'; whence, if 100° 58' give 63° 28', 114° 26' will give 71° 56', which is the ☽'s secondary distance from the *medium cœli*, her primary is 10° 24'; which, subtracted, gives the arc of direction 61° 32'.

The ☽'s direction to the □ of the ☉, by converse motion is thus computed: The ☉'s semi-nocturnal arc is 106° 56', distance from the *imum cæli* 40° 11', the ☽'s semi-diurnal arc is 114° 26', which gives the ☽'s secondary distance from the seventh house 43°; the oblique ascension of the ☽'s ☍ is 288°; from which, subtracting the horoscope's oblique ascension, the ☽'s primary distance from the seventh house becomes 103° 58'; there remains, therefore, the arc of direction 60° 58'. The secondary directions are made on the 27th of March, 1537, 15ʰ 32' P. M. at which time the planets were posited in the following manner:

	☉	☽	♄	♃	♂	♀	☿	☋
Deg. of Lon.	♈ 17.0	♏ 4. 0	♍ 1.31	♈ 25.17	♓ 28.57	♉ 26.28	♉ 6. 0	♊ 14.15
Lat.		N. 3.17	N. 1.56	S. 1. 5	S. 0, 6	N. 0.49	S. 2. 0	

The ☽ and ☿ in an exact diametrical ☍ had the declination of ♄, both there and in the nativity. The progressions to the day of his death were as follow: For 65 years they are finished on the 25th of April, 1542, the ☽ continuing in ♍ 27°; for two months and a half the ☽ is posited in ♐ 17°, May 1, 1542.

	☉	☽	♄	♃	♂	♀	☿	☊
Deg. of	♉	♐	♏	♍	♏	♊	♊	♓
Lon.	20.4	17.0	4.28R	19.13R	8.18R	15.0R	7.16R	6.22
Lat.		S. 5. 0	N. 2.55	N. 1.45	S. 0.5	N. 4.34	N. 0.29	

It is remarkable, that all the planets are here retrograde, and, also, at his death, at which time they abound with diseases; on the 16th of April, 1602, the day he died, the stars remained in the following manner:

	☉	☽	♄	♃	♂	♀	☿	☊
Deg. of	♈	♒	♏		♍	♈	♉	♐
Lon.	25.45	18.40	28.17R	16.22R	3.25R	18.16R	13.54R	16.57
Lat.		S. 4.17	N. 2.56	N. 2. 4	N. 3. 0	N. 1. 0	S. 2.47	

There was a full ● on the 6th of April, the ☉ remaining upon his own place of the secondary direction. Therefore, on the day he died, ♄ entered from a □ the place of the ☽'s direction in the zodiac, and was posited in ☍ with nearly the same declination, ♄ in ☍ of the ☉'s progression; the ☾, by progression, came to ♂, and its own parallel; the ☽, on the day he died, was posited in a parallel near the □ of ♄ and ♂ of the progression; ♄, on the same day, was in a parallel of the ☉'s declination of the nàtivity, and of the place of the ☽'s direction in the zodiac.

On the 13th of December, 1583, when he was 46 years and near 11 months old, he was created a Cardinal; the ☉, by right direction, came to a parallel of ♃'s declination in ♓ 22° 35', which is the declination of ♃ 2° 57'.

Of the ☉.

The semi-nocturnal arc is	7ʰ	7'
Crepusculine arc	1	43
Obscure arc	5	24
Right ascension	314°	13
Distance from the *imum cœli* . . .	40	11

Of ♓ 22° 35.

The semi-nocturnal arc is	6ʰ	11'
Crepusculine arc	1	39
Obscure arc	4	32
Primary distance from the *imum cœli*	79°	10
Right ascension	353	12

The secondary distance is, therefore, 33° 44', which, subtracted from the primary, leaves the arc of direction 45° 26', which, added to the ☉'s right ascension, which is 314° 13', makes the sum 359° 39', answering to 29° 30' of ♓, at which the ☉, from the day of birth, arrives in 48 days; but the effect anticipated this direction 8 months: If, however, the place of ♃ be true, as to longitude and latitude, or otherwise, because the luminaries are usually antecedent by reason of the magnitude of their bodies, in the directions to the parallels, as is seen in the other calculations, for the ☉, 3 years before, had, by converse direction, arrived at the ✱ of ♀, therefore, the difference of 8 months is but small. The horary times of ♀ are 16° 37′, her distance from the sixth house 1° 38′; for the oblique ascension of the ☍ of ♀ is 152° 24′; the ☉'s horary times are 17° 49′, whence arises his secondary distance 1° 45′ from the *imum cœli*, and, added to the primary, makes the arc of direction of the ☉, by converse motion, to the ✱ of ♀ *in mundo* 41° 56′. The secondary directions for 46 years, 10 months, and 10 days, are made on the 9th of March, 1537, with 6h 12′, P. M. under this constitution of the heavens:

	☉	☽	♄	♃	♂	♀	☿	☊
Deg. of Lon.	♓	♓	♍	♈	♓	♉	♈	♊
	29.0	4.30	2.40	20.52	14.20	4.30	14.0	15.50

The progressions for full 47 years depend on the 10th of November, 1548, when the ☽ was in ♈ 10°.

Therefore, one sign 24°, for the one month and 20 days, must be subtracted from the aforesaid place of the ☽, who will then be in ♒ 16°, and the rest disposed in the following manner:

	☉	☽	♄	♃	♂	♀	☿	☊
Deg. of Lon.	♏	♒	♎	♌	♑	♎	♏	♈
	24.0	16.0	22.2	28.8	10.56	17.56	5.45	5.0

PRIMUM MOBILE.

On the day of election, December 13, 1583, the Stars were thus posited:

	☉	☽	♄	♃	♂	♀	☿	☊
Deg. of Lon.	♐	♐	♓	♓	♐	♑	♐	♐
	20.36	13.4	17.0	20.4	25.24	7.6 R	10.28 R	11.46

There had preceded a full ●, the ☉ being in ♐ 7°, the ☽ in ♊ 7°, under the △ and ✶ of ♃ of the nativity.

You see, that the ☉, on the election day, was in the exact △ of ♃ of the secondary direction, and applied to the △ of the same in the progression; and, on the contrary, ♃, on the same day, was in △ to the ☉'s progression, and applied to the same of the secondary direction, which, indeed, is worthy of admiration. Add to this, that ♀, on the day he was made a Cardinal, was in ✶ of the ☽ in the secondary direction, and the ☽, on the same day, was posited in △ of ☿ of the secondary direction, for he was a very learned man.

In the secondary directions the ☽ is in ✶ of ♀; in the progression, in △ of ♀, which gave famous and good offices of friends; the ☉, on the day of election, was in ✶ of ♀ of the progressions, and in the △ of ☿ of the secondary directions.

230   PRIMUM MOBILE.

EXAMPLE XVII.

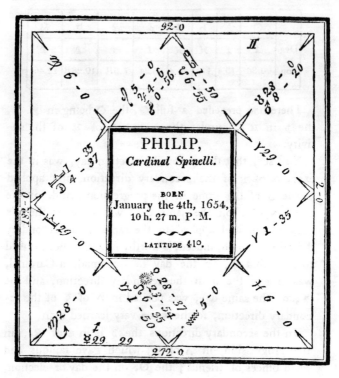

LATITUDES.				DECLINATIONS.		
♄	. .	0° 25'	N.	20° 26'	N.
♃	. .	0 42	N.	19 59	N.
♂	. .	1 26	N.	15 42	N.
☉	. .	0 0		21 34	S.
♀	. .	1 9	S.		
☿	. .	0 33	S.	24 4	S.
☽	. .	5 0	S.	6 25	S.

HE died, May the 26th, 1616, aged 52 years, 4 months, and 12 days, at which time the ☽, who is moderator of life, as being the conditionary luminary in the centre of the horoscope, came, by right direction, to a parallel of ♄'s declination in ♏ 15° 48′, where she is in 3° 53′ south latitude, the declination of which place is 20° 20′; a parallel of ♃ succeeds, but because there is, at the same time, a mundane parallel of ♂ to the ☽, and she, by a converse motion in □ to ♂, ♃ could be of no service. The ☽'s direction to the parallel of ♄ is thus calculated: The ☽'s declination is 6° 25′, which, in the ecliptic, answers to ♎ 16°, whose nocturnal horary times are 15° 55′, which, doubled, make 31° 50′; the ☽'s oblique ascension in the horoscope is 187° 51′, from which there remains her distance from the east 5° 51′; the pole of the second house is 30°, therefore the difference of the poles of the first and second is 11°.

If therefore the double horary times of the ☽ 31ʰ 50′ gives the polar difference of the 1st and 2d 11° 0 the ☽'s distance from the east . . . . 5 51 gives . . . . 2 0 and there remains the ☽'s pole 39, to which pole her oblique ascension is 187° 28′.

The oblique ascension of 15° 48′ of ♏, with 3° 33′ south latitude, is 239° 32′, from which, subtracting the ☽'s oblique ascension, there remains the arc of direction 52° 4′, which, for the equation, add to the ☉'s right ascension, which is 295° 47′, and it makes

347° 51', answering to 16° 45' of ♓, to which the ☉ arrives in 52 days and a quarter, which denotes so many years.

The ☽'s right direction to the mundane parallel of ♂ is thus: The ☽'s semi-nocturnal arc is 6ʰ 22', its distance from the east 5° 51'; the oblique ascension of the ☍ of ♂, taken in the horoscope, is 229° 32'; from which, subtracting the oblique ascension of the horoscope, there remains the primary distance of ♂ from the west 47° 32'.

Therefore, as the ☽'s semi-nocturnal arc . 6ʰ 22'
is to her distance from the east . . . . 5° 51
so is ♂'s semi-nocturnal arc 5ʰ 8
to his secondary distance from the west . 4° 38

which, added to the primary, as this is under the earth, and the other above, makes the arc of direction 52° 10'. The ☽ at the same time came, by a converse motion, to the □ of ♂.

As the semi-diurnal arc of ♂ . . . . 6ʰ 57'
is to his distance from the west . . . . 47° 32
so is the ☽'s semi-diurnal arc 5ʰ 38
to her secondary distance from *medium cœli* 38° 32

Her primary distance from *medium cœli* is 90° 16', for her right ascension is 182° 16'; subtracting, therefore, the secondary distance from the primary, there remains the arc of direction 51° 44'. The secondary directions are made on the 25th of February, with 19ʰ P. M., the ☽ remaining in 8° of ♍.

	☉	☽	♄	♃	♂	♀	☿	☊
Deg. of	♓	♍	♋	♋	♊	♈	♈	♑
Lon.	17.0	8.0	28.56	28.2	4.16	4.52	2.16	4.16

The progressions for 52 years complete, fall on the 19th of March, 1568; whilst the ☽ continued in ♐ 19°; for 4 months and a third she came to ♉ 9°, on the 30th of the same month, when the planets were in the following position:

	☉	☽	♄	♃	♂	♀	☿	☊
Deg. of	♈	♉	♍	♐	♋	♓	♈	♎
Lon.	19.50	9.0	22.46	8.18	26.32	6.34	26.35	15.9
Lat.		S. 2.2	N. 2.38	N. 1.14	N. 2.23	N. 1.30		

On the day he died, May the 26th, 1616, these were the places of the planets:

	☉	☽	♄	♃	♂	♀	☿	☊
Deg. of	♊	♎	♉	♐	♉	♉	♉	♓
Lon.	4.58	7.45	4.27	26.9	5.58	2.54	19.1	13.57
Lat.		S. 2.2	S. 2.2	N. 1.9	S. 0.10	S. 1.34	S. 3.5	

The ☽ was in the secondary direction, in □ to ♂;

and, on the day he died, the ☉ entered the place of ♂, and in □ to the ☽. The ☉, by progression, leaving the parallel of ♄, applied to the □ of ♂, who was in ☍ of the ☉'s place of the nativity: on the same day, ♄ and ♂ entered upon the ☽'s progression; the ☽, likewise, on that day, with the declination of ♄'s progression, goes to the ☍ of the ☉ and □ of ♂'s progression; but what is most important, is, that the ☉, on the fatal day, entered upon ♂ in the secondary direction; but, from the ☉'s situation, the times of the effects are first principally defined, and then from the ☽.

In the 41st year and two months of his age, that is, in 1605, Argol says he was dangerously ill, and lays down the manner of his death, by supposing it to be from the ascendant directed to the □ of ♃; but we say, from the ☽ to an ☍ of ♂. The ☽'s oblique ascension is 187° 28′ to the pole 39°; and the oblique ascension of the ☍ of ♂ is 228° 36′; from which, subtracting the former, leaves the arc of direction 41° 8′, which, equated in our way, denotes 42 years, though the effect was very slow; if only the place of ♂ be true, for other tables place him in ♉ 9°, but the difference is but trifling; and if the direction is made to the ☍ in the zodiac it will be found to precede. The ☽ also, by a converse direction, reached the mundane parallel of ♂.

As the semi-diurnal arc of ♂ . . . . 6ʰ 57′
is to his distance from the west . . . 47° 32
so is the semi-diurnal arc of the ☽ . . 5ʰ 38
to her distance from the east . . . 38° 32
which, added to her primary distance . 5 51
makes the arc of direction 44 23

But, if this figure be altered one degree, this direction agrees nearly.

The secondary directions fall on the 14th of February, 1564; the ☽ remaining in ♈ 13°, that is to say, 14^h 27′, P. M. At his death, ♂ was found in ♈ 18° upon this place of the ☽, she being in ☍ to ♄, and in the declination of ♂ of these motions.

The progressions are made on the 5th of May, 1567, whilst the ☽ was in ♈ 10°, applying to ♂, he being in ♈ 15°, and in the same place at his death; the ☽, therefore, had arrived at the ☍ of her radical place. On the 5th of March, preceding his death, there was a full ☉ in ♍ 14° upon ♄ of the progression, and in parallel there of ♂, according to the doctrine of Ptolemy, in the last chapter of his 4th Book; and, that you may not look upon this as a dream, if you observe, in these examples, the equal progression now commonly used, you will find little or no agreement between them; so that you may perceive they are altogether false and useless.

In the 41st year, when the native was created a Cardinal, the *medium cœli*, having stopt first at a ☌ of ♃, came afterwards to the biquintile of ♃, who assumed the nature of ♃ from that biquintile ray, and partly of ♀ from the parallel of the declination. ☿ remained very strong in the centre of the *imum cœli*, when the satellites of the luminaries were very fortunate, the ☉ of ♀, the ☽ of ♃ from the ✶. The declination of ☿ is 24° 4′, ascensional difference 22° 50′, and semi-nocturnal arc 112° 50′; the fifth part of which is 22° 34′, and, doubled, are 45° 8′; the right ascension of ☿ is 270°

22′, whence his distance from the *imum cæli* becomes 1° 38′, which, subtracted from the geminated fifth part of ☿'s semi-nocturnal arc, there remains the arc of direction 43° 30′, which, equated in our way, denotes 41 years: but, if the nativity be increased 1°, as aforesaid, the time agrees exactly. Argol places ☿ in 8° of ♒: in this he must certainly be mistaken.

Moreover, the ☉ had arrived at the sesqui-quadrate of ♃ by a converse motion: the oblique ascension of ♃ to the pole of the eleventh house 16°, is 120° 43′; the oblique ascension of the ☉'s ☍ to the same pole is 109° 21′; this, subtracted from the former, leaves the ☉'s distance from the ☍ of ♃ 11° 22′. The ☉'s horary times are 18° 19′, which, triplicated, are 54° 57′; and as the distance of the sesqui-quadrate ray from the ☍ are the triplicate horary times; from this, therefore, subtracting the ☉'s distance from the ☍ of ♃, leaves the arc of direction 43° 35′. The secondary directions fall on the 14th of February, 1564, when the ☉ was in the exact biquintile of ♃, and the ☽ in △.

EXAMPLE XVIII.

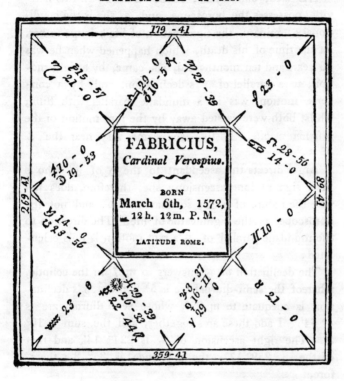

LATITUDES.				DECLINATIONS.
♄	. . 2° 40′	N.		14° 2′ S.
♃	. . 1 1	S.		
♂	. . 3 28	N.		
☉	. . 0 0			
♀	. . 0 34	S.		
☿	. . 2 46	N.		
☽	. . 3 8	N.		20 0 S.

HE died, January 27, 1639. The ☽, in this nativity, possesses the horoscope, and, as she is the conditionary luminary, the signification of life belongs to her. At the time of his death, which happened when he was 66 years and ten months old, she came, by a right motion, to a parallel of ♄'s declination, and, by a converse motion, was in a mundane parallel with him; whilst both were carried away by the rapt motion of the *primum mobile*. Lastly, she came very near the ☌ of ♂.

Argol directs the ascendant to the △ of ♂, who is in a sign of long ascension; she, therefore, does not take the nature of a ☐; so that the ☽, and not the horoscope, is the significator of life. The direction to the mundane parallel of ♄'s rapt motion is thus calculated:

The declination of ♄ answers to ♏ 7° in the ecliptic, whereof the semi-diurnal arc is $5^h\ 9'$; the ☽'s declination is adequate to ♏ 29°, whose semi-diurnal arc is $4^h\ 54'$. I add these arcs together, and the sum is $10^h\ 3'$. The right ascension of ♄ is 224° 14′, and that of the ☽ 259° 17′; the difference is 35° 3′; therefore,

As the sum of the semi-diurnal arcs . . 10^h 3′
is to the semi-diurnal arc of ♄ 5 9
so is the difference of right ascension . 35° 3
to the secondary distance of ♄ from the
   medium cœli 17 58

The primary distance of ♄ is 44° 33′, which is to be added to the 17° 58′, because ♄ moves from the ascendant to the descendant parts, and makes the arc of direction 62° 31′, which, for the equation, add to the ☉'s right ascension, which is 356° 50′, and it makes 59° 21′, answering to 1° 30′ of ♊, to which the ☉ arrives in 66 days and 20 hours, which denotes the age of 66 years and 10 months.

The ☽ to the parallel of the declination of ♄; the ☽'s oblique ascension under the pole of Rome is 278° 16′, to which I add the arc of direction 62° 31′, which makes 340° 47′; I look for this in the same table, near the end of the sign ♒, where the ☽ gains near 2° south latitude, and I find it in ♒ precisely 23° 14′, of which place, with 2° south latitude, the declination is 15° 42′, and that of ♄ 14° 2′; so that the ☽ had not yet exactly reached the declination of ♄, either because the places of ♄ and the ☽ are not yet exactly true, or that the luminaries in the directions to the parallels of declination always precede, as we have said, in producing the effects, the true time of the parallel; or, lastly, because the preceding directions and agreement of the other motions were urgent, which frequently happens.

The ☽ to the ☌ of ♂. The pole of ♂ is 9°, his oblique ascension 196° 39′; the ☽'s oblique ascension under that pole is 262° 32′; from which, subtracting the former, leaves the arc of direction 65° 53′; so that the ☽ was but 3° distant from ♂.

The secondary directions happened on the 12th of May, 1572, at 8^h 5′ P. M. when the stars were thus posited:

	☉	☽	♄	♃	♂	♀	☿	☊
Deg. of	♊	♊	♏	♈	♍	♋	♊	♋
Lon.	1.40	12.0	10.44	19.46	29.6	7.0	9.0	25.30
Lat.		S. 3.25	N. 2.51	S. 1.10	N. 0.41	N. 1.44	S. 0.39	

The progressions are made the 1st of August, 1577, whilst the ☽ was in ♓ 22°.

	☉	☽	♄	♃	♂	♀	☿	☊
Deg. of	♌	♓	♑	♍	♌	♋	♌	♈
Lon.	18.20	22.0	5.54	15.2	21.39	26.47R	17.57R	14.31
Lat.		S. 1.54	N. 0.40	N. 1. 4	N. 0. 6	S. 4.49	S. 3.38	

January 27th, 1639, the day he died, the planets were placed in the following manner:

	☉	☽	♄	♃	♂	♀	☿	☊
Deg. of	♒	♏	♒	♐	♈	♒	♒	♐
Lon.	7.31	22.40	9.11	1.52	4.30	2.12	26.22	26.29
Lat.		S. 2.48	S. 0.45	N. 0.53	S. 0.13	S. 1.55	N. 0. 8	

The preceding day there was a □ of the ☽, the ☉ remaining in ♒ 7°, in the □ of ♄'s secondary direction, and the ☽ in 7° of ♏ upon ♄, and with the declination of his primary directions, viz. that of ♄ of the nativity. On the day he died, the ☽ passed from ♄'s radical place to the □ of the ☉, and ♂'s progression; who, with ☿ retrograde, were conjoined in ☍ to the ☽'s place in the right direction, who, in the secondary direction, being posited in opposition to her radical place, made the year climacterical; and likewise in the progression was posited in the □ of the radical place; but the preceding □ of the luminaries, as it happened there in an hostile aspect of ♄, who was in a parallel of the declination and ☌ of the ☉ and □ of the ☽; and lastly, the enemies configurated to the place of the ☽'s direction, who is hyleg; and ♂ in ♈ 5° from the fourth house of the nativity, afflicted the ☽ in her radical place, it is very evident, to her it belonged to produce the effects denoted by the direction of the same to the aspects of ♄. These agreements are, indeed, truly worthy of admiration!

EXAMPLE XIX.

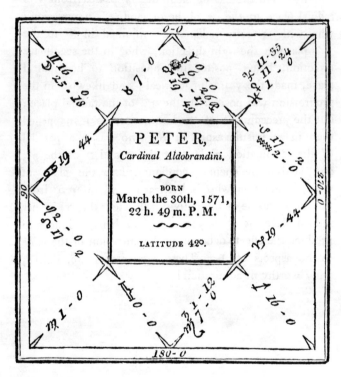

LATITUDES.				DECLINATIONS.		
♄ . .	2°	58′	N.	9°	6′	S.
♃ . .	0	54	S.	8	5	S.
♂ . .	0	0		7	46	N.
☉ . .	0	0		7	34	N.
♀ . .	2	47	N.	4	44	S.
☿ . .	1	13	S.			
☽ . .	3	56	S.			

PRIMUM MOBILE. 243

HE died the 10th of March, 1621, aged 49 years, 11 months; was elected a Cardinal in January, 1592, being at that time nearly 20 years and 10 months old.

Argol speaks of this nativity in the last edition of "CRITICAL DAYS," page 184. He places the ☽ in ♉ 25°, and directs the horoscope to its □ in the 50th year, rejecting the ☉, to whom belongs the signification of life; but the ☽, according to the common Tables and Ephemeris, is posited in ♊ 25°, and then that direction will not be the □, but the ✶. Now we, in imitation of Ptolemy, make the ☉ entirely aphæta, who, in 49 years and 11 months, comes to the mundane parallel of ♄, both by a right and converse motion. A calculation of the right direction is thus: The ☉'s declination is 7° 34', ascensional difference 6° 52', semi-diurnal arc 96° 52', right ascension 17° 47', distance from the *medium cœli* 17° 47'; ♄'s declination 9° 6', ascensional difference 8° 18', semi-nocturnal arc 98° 18', right ascension 210° 6', primary distance from the *imum cœli* 30° 6'; these produce ♄'s secondary distance 18° 3'; this, added to the primary, makes the arc of direction 48° 9', which, added to the ☉'s right ascension, makes 65° 56', answering to 7° 45' of ♊, to which the ☉ arrives in 50 days, which gives 50 years.

The converse direction is thus:

As ♄'s semi-nocturnal arc	98°	18'
is to his distance from the *imum cœli* .	30	6
so is the ☉'s semi-diurnal arc . . .	96	52
to his secondary distance	29	40

244   PRIMUM MOBILE.

which, with the primary, makes the arc of direction 47° 27′. But you are to observe, that the ☉, when in ☌ with ♂, applies to a parallel of the declination of ♄; wherefore as aphæta, he denotes the corrupt qualities of the body and shortness of life; especially, as from the *medium cœli* he, by a □ ray, afflicted the horoscope.

The secondary directions happen on the 19th of May, 1571, with 20ʰ 49′, P. M. under the following disposition of the stars:

	☉	☽	♄	♃	♂	♀	☿	☋
Deg. of Lon.	♊ 8 0	♈ 29.0	♎ 28.0	♓ 20.30	♉ 26.0	♈ 25.53	0. 0	♌ 14.27
Lat.		S. 4.50	N. 2.53	S. 1.13	S. 0.2	S. 1.23	S. 0.12	

The progressions for full 50 years are made on the 15th of April, 1575; therefore, for 49 years and 10 months, those progressions are made on the 11th of April, the ☽ remaining in ♉ 6°; the other as you may see under:

	☉	☽	♄	♃	♂	♀	☿	☋
Deg. of Lon.	♉ 0.50	♉ 6. 0	♐ 19.0	♋ 5. 2	♉ 26.37	♉ 11.18	♉ 20.21	♉ 29.5
Lat.		S. 1.57	N. 1.48	0. 0	N. 0. 8	S. 0.25	N. 1.30	

February 10, 1621, the day he died, the stars were thus placed:

	☉	☽	♄	♃	♂	♀	☿	☋
Deg. of Lon	♒ 22.11	♎ 20.38	♊ 29.53	♉ 12.59	♏ 11.13	♑ 14.28	♑ 25.58	♐ 10.0
Lat.		S. 3.46	S. 0.39	S. 0.46	N. 1.40	S. 0.34	S. 1.35	

In the secondary direction the ☽ was in ☍ to ♄, as well there, as from the nativity: on the day of death ♄ was upon ☽ in the nativity, the ☉, by progression, in ☍ of ♄'s radical place; the ☉, on the day he died, in the □ of ♂ of the progression.

In the progression, the ☽ was in the same parallel of ♄'s declination, and nearly so on the day of his death: on the contrary, the ☽ on the same day was found upon ♄ of the secondary direction. And is this not wonderful?

Before his death there was an ☍ of the luminaries, the ☉ in ♒ 18°, and the ☽ in ♌ 18°, in □ to ♂ of the progression and secondary directions.

The nonutility of the common progression is easily perceptible.

In the 21st year, the ☉, by direction, came to the ✶ of ♃ and ♀.

EXAMPLE XX.

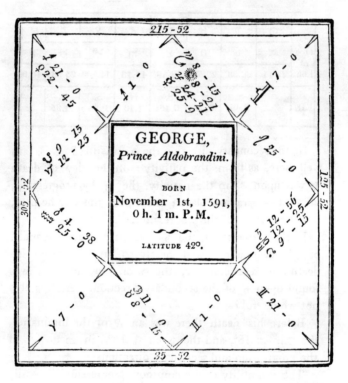

LATITUDES.				DECLINATIONS.		
♄	. . 1°	28′	S.	21°	3′	N.
♃	. . 0	58	N.	17	59	S.
♂	. . 1	55	S.	21	5	S.
☉	. . 0	0		14	20	S.
♀	. . 3	36	S.			
☿	. . 3	12	S.	22	13	S.
☽	. . 4	17	S.	11	7	N.

HE died May 16, 1637, at the age of 45 years, 6 months, and 15 days.

In his nativity the ☉ becomes entirely hyleg, and not the ascendant, according to Argol; for he is on the cusp of the *medium cœli*, and at the time of death, in 45 years and a half, came, by right direction, to ♐ 24° 50′, where he is afflicted by the ☽'s sesqui-quadrate, having, for some time before, been under a parallel declination of ♄ and ♂, and likewise in a ☐ of ♂ *in mundo*, to which the ☉ from 0° of ♐ applied, but, from a ☌ with ♀ and the terms of the favourable planets, he was preserved: besides, it is to be observed, that both the luminaries were moved, by converse direction, to a mundane ☐ of ♄, who in the nativity afflicted the horoscope from the ☍ and the luminaries by a ☐ ray *in mundo*, and being posited on the cusp of the seventh, he denoted a short life with bad health, and had not ♀, in exact mundane ✶, assisted the ☉ in its radical place, the native would never have lived so long. Lastly, there was an application of the ☉ by converse motion to the parallel of ♂ *in mundo*, whilst both were carried away by the rapt motion of the *primum mobile*. The calculation is thus: The ☉'s semi-diurnal arc is $5^h\ 7'$, ♂'s declination answers to 4° 30′ of ♐, whose semi-diurnal arc is $4^h\ 39'$; I add these arcs together, and the sum is $9^h\ 46'$: the ☉'s right ascension is 215° 58′, and that of ♂ 307° 28′, from which I subtract the ☉'s right ascension, and the right difference between them is 91° 30′. Now say,

As the sum of both semi-diurnal arcs . 9ʰ 46′
is to the ☉'s semi-diurnal arc 5 7
so is the difference of right ascension . 91° 30
to the ☉'s sec. distance from *medium cœli* 47 56
which, added to the primary, makes the arc of direction 48° 2′, which for the equation add to the ☉'s right ascension, and the sum is 264°, answering to 24° 30′ of ♐, to which the ☉, from the day of birth, arrives in 45 days, which denotes so many years.

In this example, as well as others, is proved the measure of directions which we make use of; for, if we add to the ☉'s right ascension 45° 30′, according to the common method, we make the sum 261° 28′, equal to ♐ 22° 10′, where ♀'s parallel is, who doubtless would have preserved him; and as our measure of the directions brings the ☉ farther, to 24° 30′, and ♀ being in 3° 36′ south latitude, she was already separated from the ☉, and constituted in the terms of ♄.

The secondary directions fall on the 16th of December 1591, with 13ʰ, P. M. at which time the places of the stars were as follow :

	☉	☽	♄	♃	♂	♀	☿	☋
Deg. of Lon.	♐ 24.40	♑ 6 0	♋ 10.29	♐ 4.33	♓ 7.13	♒ 1.38 R	♐ 8.26	♋ 6.49
Lat.		N. 0. 4	S. 1.32	N. 0.57	S. 0.52	N. 1. 5	N. 0.40	•

The progressions for 45 years and a half, exact, are

made on the 7th of July, 1595, the ☽ being in 18° 59′ of ♋; to these I add 16° 30′ for the half month, and the ☽ is posited in ♌ 4° 30′; but the rest, on the 8th of July, 1595, are as follow:

	☉	☽	♄	♃	♂	♀	☿	☊
Deg. of Lon.	♋	♌	♌	♈	♈	♊	♋	♈
	15.0	4.30	22.45	3. 8	19.20	7. 0	20.0	27.56
Lat.		N. 4.58	N. 0.38	S. 1.25	S. 2.11	S. 1.48	N. 1.22	

On the day he died, May 16, at 1h 5′, the planets remained thus:

	☉	☽	♄	♃	♂	♀	☿	☊
Deg. of Lon.	♉	♒	♑	♍	♊	♉	♉	♑
	26.0	22.0	25.18	25.24	6.52	10.46	19.15	28.3
Lat.		N. 2. 2	N. 0. 1	N. 1.29	N. 0.32	S. 1.17	S. 0.42	

In the secondary directions the ☽ was with the ☊ in ☍ to ♄, and the ☉ nearly in the parallel of the declination of ♄; and these luminaries, by the same secondary direction on the day he died, entered a similar parallel of ♄ and ♂.

In the progression the ☉ in □ of ♂ continued upon ♄'s radical place; the ☽ in ☍ of ♂'s radical place, exactly: on the day of his death the ☉ was in □ of ♄

250   PRIMUM MOBILE.

of the progression, and, on the contrary, ♄ in ☍ with the parallel of the ☉'s progression; ♂ had likewise the same declination with him; on the above day the ☽ was found in the exact ☍ of ♄ of the progression.

The luminaries had alternately the □ on that day, with many other attestations of the infortunes; so that the effect was not frustrated.

EXAMPLE XXI.

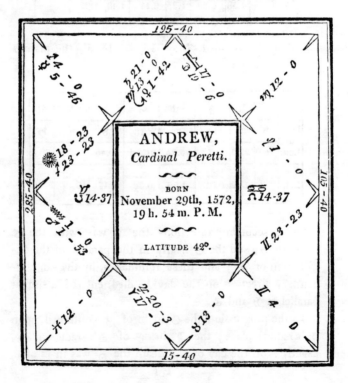

PRIMUM MOBILE.

	LATITUDES.			DECLINATIONS.		
♄	. . 1°	59'	N.	16°	7'	S.
♃	. . 1	22	S.	6	36	N.
♂	. . 1	18	S.	21	4	S.
☉	. . 0	0		23	1	S.
♀	. . 2	49	N.	9	29	S.
☿	. . 0	53	N.	20	27	S.
☽	. . 4	59	N.	2	51	S.

IN this nativity, if the ascendant had 18° 37′ of ♐, according to the explanation of Argol, we freely confess if the ☉ were hyleg, no direction of his would agree with the time of the native's death.

For the direction's arc for 56 years 8 months, is 61° 15′, the ☉'s oblique ascension is 279° 41′; to which, if we add the direction's arc 61° 15′, the sum is 340° 56′; answering to ♒ 27° in the same table, obnoxious to none of the malefics.

Wherefore, as in this nativity the ☉ begins to be separated from the horoscope, if, to the time in the nativity, a quarter of an hour is added, which is probable and likely to be true, because of the usual difference between the solar and civil horology, the prorogatory dignity of life is taken away from the ☉, as he has now left the horoscope, and is transferred entirely to the ☽; which that it is so, is confirmed by the agreements of the ☽'s directions with the time of death, as will be presently evident.

The native died the 4th of August, 1629, aged 56 years and 8 months, at which time the ☽ came, by a right direction, to a parallel declination of ♂ ; the parallel of ☿ preceding near 21° 25′ of ♐ when the ☽ gains 2° North latitude, and declination 21° 13′. But because about the tropics the declination suffers very little variation ; so that the ☽, for some preceding degrees, participated of the parallel of ♂ ; a subsequent △ of ♃ preserved him, and also from his ☌ with the ☉ ; but the △ of ♃ began now to cease, and the ☽ entered the terms of ♄. Lastly, there was, by converse direction, a mundane parallel of ♂ to the ☽ ; the effect of this parallel of ♂ to the ☽ immediately appeared ; and at the same time the ☽, by a converse motion, came to the ☍ of ♂ ; and seeing so many agreements on the part of the ☽ concur, of consequence the signification of life belongs to her.

We have said, that the arc of direction for 56 years and 8 months is 61° 15′. Now the ☽, in 56 days and 16 hours from the nativity, arrives at ♒ 16° 8′, whose right ascension is 318° 37′, from which subtracting the ☉'s right ascension, 257° 22′, there remains the arc of direction, 61° 15′, which is due to the aforesaid years ; the ☽'s right ascension is 199° 31′, to which adding 61° 15′, the sum is 260° 46′ ; this, in the tables of right ascension, answers to ♐ 21° 25′, under the column of latitude 2° north, which the ☽ gains there, and where she is posited in the declination of ♂.

The calculation of the converse direction to the mundane parallel of the same is thus : The ☽'s declination, 2° 51′, answers to ♎ 7° in the ecliptic, whose semidiurnal arc is 5ʰ 50′; the declination of ♂, 21° 4′,

answers to ♑ 26°, whose semi-diurnal arc is 4ʰ 39'.
I add these arcs together, and the sum is 10ʰ 29'. The
right ascension of ♂ is 304° 35': from which, subtracting the ☽'s right ascension, there remains the right
difference between them, 105° 4'; therefore,

As the sum of the semi-diurnal arcs . . 10ʰ 29'
is to the ☽'s semi-diurnal arc 5 50
so is the right ascensional difference . . 105° 4
to the ☽'s secondary distance 58 28
which, added to the primary 3 51
makes the arc of direction 62 19

greater than that above taken by one degree; so that
this direction succeeded the year, and also the ☍ of ♂,
if the places of the ☽ and ♂ be true.

The converse direction to the ☍ of ♂ is thus calculated: The elevation of the pole of the second house
is 31°; but as ♂ hath 1° 18' south latitude, and is 1°
distant below the cusp, the elevation of his pole is 30°,
under which ♂'s oblique ascension is 315°; but the
oblique ascension there of the ☽'s ☍ is 17° 59', from
which, subtracting that of ♂, leaves the arc of direction
62° 50'.

Argol says that the native was sick in the 44th year
and a half of his age; at that time the ☽ came, by
converse motion, to a mundane ☐ of ♄; which direction, if you would see, is thus: The first number is the
semi-diurnal arc of ♄; the second his distance from the
east by the oblique ascension of the horoscope; the
third is the ☽'s semi-diurnal arc; and the fourth number will be her secondary distance from the *medium*

cœli, which added to the primary, and the direction's arc equated, for the 44th year and a half, is 48° 47′ ; but the luminaries seem very frequently to precede, in their effects, the intimate application of the direction, especially in the parallel, as has been frequently mentioned.

The secondary directions happen on the 25th of January, 1573, with the hours 12, from meridian, under the following construction of the stars :

	☉	☽	♄	♃	♂	♀	☿	☊
Deg. of Lon.	♒ 16.30	♏ 12.36	♏ 26.24	♈ 25.9	♓ 17.0	♑ 4. 0	♓ 6. 0	♋ 11.50
Lat.		N. 4.17	N. 2.10	S. 1.20	S. 0.10	N. 2. 8	N. 1.53	

The progressions are made on the 30th of June, 1577, the stars in the position following :

	☉	☽	♄	♃	♂	♀	☿	☊
Deg. of Lon.	♋ 17.20	♑ 18.0	♑ 8. 4	♍ 3.50	♋ 29.58	♌ 11.49	♌ 12.24	♈ 16.22
Lat.		N. 4.17	N. 0.46	N. 1. 9	N. 1.14	S. 0.40	N. 0.15	

PRIMUM MOBILE.

On the 4th of August, the day of his death, the stars were as under:

	☉	☽	♄	♃	♂	♀	☿	☊
Deg. of Lon.	♌ 11.57	♒ 15.38	♎ 18.41	♒ 1.10	♊ 3.40	♌ 18.1	♍ 3.14	♊ 29.0
Lat.		S. 3.38	N. 2.24	S. 0.44	S. 0.43	N. 1.26	S. 2.39	

On the day he died, there was a full ☽ in the □ and parallel of ♄ in the radix, and in his place of the secondary directions, in which ♂ was, in □ of the ☉ and parallel of the ☽. On the same day ♄ was in □ of the ☉ and ☽ of the progression, and exactly upon the place of the ☽ in the radix; and ♂ on that day had a parallel declination in the place of the ☽'s right direction; ♀ had the ✶ to the ☽ in the nativity, but was combust. On the above day, the ☉ was in an exact parallel declination of ♄ of the secondary direction, and the ☽ entered the same parallel.

You see, Reader, how various and mutual the agreements are, both active and passive, and yet how exact. In the 24th year, the time he was made a Cardinal, the ☉ came to the quintile of ♀ in the zodiac, near 13° 42′ of ♑, which hath the same declination with the ☉ in the nativity, the direction is easy, viz. by the right ascensions; for as many days as the ☉ was arriving at 13° 42′ of ♑, so many years do they denote; the number of days is 24; besides, the ☉ applied at the same time to the quintile of ♃ *in mundo*, which is thus calculated:

I divide ♃'s nocturnal horary times 13° 58' by 5°, the quotient is 2° 48', which, added to his nocturnal horary times, make 16° 46', which are the 5th part of ♃'s semi-nocturnal arc.

I direct ♃ to the □ of the ☉ in the world thus:

If the horary times of ☉	11ᵈ	15'
give his distance from the East . . .	5	59
What will ♃'s horary times give . . .	13	58
Answer, ♃'s secondary distance from the *imum cœli*	'7	25

The right ascension of ♃ is 19°, whence his primary distance from the *imum cœli* is 3° 20'; which, added to the secondary, makes the arc of direction of the ☉ to the □ of ♃ 10° 45': to this I add a 5th part of ♃'s semi-nocturnal arc, taken as before 16° 46', and the sum is 27° 31', for the arc of direction of the ☉ to the quintile of ♃ *in mundo*, which turned into time, gives 25 years nearly.

In this nativity, is to be observed a very noble Satellitum of the luminaries, particularly of the ☉, who was in the △ of ♃ and ✶ of ♀, viz. in the world to ♀; for ♀, in such a ✶, confers very great honours on the ☉. See in other examples brought by Argol in the Cardinals Lenius, Lanfranche, Borromeus; in George Prince Aldobrandine, Charles I, Gonzago Duke of Mantua, Dominic Molinus, Barnard Vamarius, and others.

The secondary directions are made on December 23,

1572, with 7^h 54′, P. M. and the progression on the 25th of October, 1574, almost in the meridian, in which the luminaries were alternately in △, and both in exact △ of ♃. On the 5th of June, when he was elected, the luminaries were posited alternately in △, and were found in △ of ♀ of the progression, the ☉ in parallel of ♃, &c.

Argol directs the *medium cœli* to the ✶ of ☿ [1] for the 24th year; but the ✶ falls in ♎ 5° 46′, which precedes, not succeeds, the *medium cœli;* and the right ascension of the ✶ of ☿, where it is taken 213° 24′, is 5° 46′ of ♏, and not ♎.

[1] Argol takes the *medium cœli* to the ✶ of ☿ in the zodiac, which cannot be admitted, as the angles cannot be directed to zodiacal aspects. And, in this instance, he has mistaken his own theory.

EXAMPLE XXII.

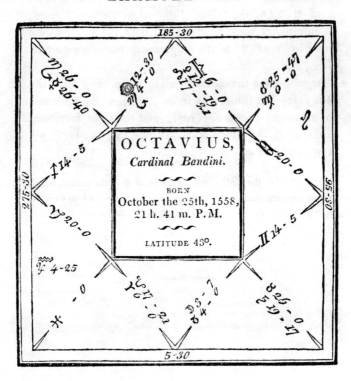

LATITUDES.		DECLINATIONS.
♄ .. 2° 28′ S.		15° 13′ N.
♃ .. 1 5 S.		20 16 S.
♂ .. 1 19 N.		
☉ .. 0 0		15 38 S.
♀ .. 1 46 N.		
☿ .. 1 45 S.		

HE died August 1, 1629, aged 70 years and 9 months; was created a Cardinal on the 5th of June, 1596, at the age of 37 years and 7 months.

In this nativity, which is explained by Argol, ♀ is to be placed in ♎ 12o, not 21°; he directs the ascendant to the ☐ of ♄ in the zodiac; but, as the rays to the angles in the zodiac are rejected by us for very plain reasons, and also by Ptolemy; and on the other hand, the ☉'s arc of direction corresponds very well with the proper ☐ *in mundo*, whereby both the prerogatory virtues, *viz.* one by a right direct motion, and the other by a converse, is injured, especially by the subsequent parallels of ♄ *in mundo*, as will appear by calculating them.

Likewise, as the significator of life belongs to the ☉, that he may obtain this dignity, the time of birth must be lengthened some few minutes; wherefore we add to the given hour 18 minutes. At the time of his death the ☉ came to its own ☐ *in mundo;* the calculation whereof is easy; for the ☉'s semi-diurnal arc is 74° 54′, his horary times are 12° 29′. The ☉ likewise came by right motion to a mundane parallel of ♄.

As the horary times of the ☉ . . . . 12° 29′
to his distance from the *medium cœli* . 34 33
so is ♄'s horary times 12 33
to his secondary distance from the *imum cœli* 34 44

The right ascension of ♄ is 47° 31′; from which, subtracting the right ascension of the *imum cœli*, leaves the primary distance of ♄ from the *imum cœli* 42° 1′; which, added to the secondary, makes the arc of direction 76° 45′; lastly, the ☉, by converse motion, came to the mundane parallel of ♄.

For as ♄'s horary times 12° 33′ is to his distance from the *imum cœli* 42° 1′, so is the ☉'s horary times 12° 29′ to his secondary distance from the *medium cœli* 41° 48′; which, added to the primary, 34° 33′, makes the arc of direction 76° 21′. For the equation add the arc of direction to the ☉'s right ascension, and it makes 296° 24′, answering to 24° 29′ of ♑, to which, from the day of birth, the ☉ arrives in 70 days and 18 hours, which denotes 70 years and nine months. The secondary directions are made on the 14th of January, 1559, with the hours from meridian, 15° 23′, in this situation of the stars.

	☉	☽	♄	♃	♂	♀	☿	☊
Deg. of	♑	♐	♉	♒	♏	♑	♑	♈
Lon.	24.29	15.0	17.45	17.35	7.20	10.0	20.10	13.44

The progressions, for full 70 years, are made on the 23d of June, 1564, the ☽ remaining in ♑ 3°; for the other 9 months, we have the ☽ posited in ♎ 25° 30′; the rest, on the 15th of July, were as under:

	☉	☽	♄	♃	♂	♀	☿	☊
Deg. of	♌	♎	♌	♌	♌	♍	♌	♐
Lon.	2.27	25.30	8. 7	14.36	27.30	17.0	25.19	26.51
Lat.		S. 4.23	N. 0.30	N. 0.38	N. 0.17	N. 1.31	S. 2.48	

On the day of death, which was the 1st of August, 1629, the Stars were thus posited:

	☉	☽	♄	♃	♂	♀	☿	☋
Deg. of Lon.	♌ 9.5	♑ 10.0	♎ 18.29	♒ 1.25	♊ 1.43	♌ 14.20	♍ 3.32	♋ 0.41

On the day he died, the ☉ entered the progression of ♄, and in □ of the secondary direction of ♂; ♄, the ☽'s progression, and the □ of the ☉'s secondary direction; ♂ a parallel of the ☉'s secondary direction.

In 1596, aged 37 years and 7 months, he was made a Cardinal; the ☉ came, by a right direction, to the ✶ of ♃ *in mundo;* likewise, to the quintile of ♀, and parallel of the same, by a converse motion.

The direction to the ✶ of ♃ is thus calculated:

The ☉'s oblique ascension under the pole of the eleventh house 18°, is 225° 16', from which, subtracting the oblique ascension of that house, which is 215° 30', leaves the ☉'s distance from the eleventh house 9° 46'; therefore, ♃'s horary times 18° 21', will give his secondary distance from the East 14° 21'. The oblique ascension of ♃ in the horoscope is 327° 13'; from which, subtracting the horoscope's oblique ascension, leaves the primary distance of ♃ from the ascendant, 51° 43'; from this, subtracting the secondary distance, the remainder is the arc of direction, 37° 22'.

If you want the direction to the parallel of ♀, by converse motion, say, As the horary times of ♀ are to her distance from the *medium cœli,* so is the ☉'s horary times to its secondary distance; and adding the fourth number to the ☉'s primary distance, the sum will be the arc of direction.

The secondary directions fall on the 2d of December, 1558, with $11^h\ 41'$, P. M. in the following situation of the stars:

Deg. of Lon.	☉	☽	♄	♃	♂	♀	☿	☋
	♐	♍	♉	♒	♎	♏	♏	♈
	20.43	27.0	19.4	10.30	18.21	28.0	28.0	15.30

The progressions depend on the 8th of November, 1561, the ☽ remaining in ♐ 16°; the rest as under:

Deg. of Lon.	☉	☽	♄	♃	♂	♀	☿	☋
	♏	♐	♋	♉	♓	♎	♏	♒
	26.30	16.0	6.50	26.33	12.25	13.0	23.0	18.41

On the day of election, June the 5th, 1596, the stars were posited thus:

Deg. of Lon.	☉	☽	♄	♃	♂	♀	☿	☋
	♊	♎	♍	♉	♌	♋	♊	♈
	14.29	5.21	2.4	0.4	0.31	23.31	3.18	10.22

On the day of election the ☉ was posited in △ of ♃ of the secondary direction, and △ of ♀ of the progression. On the contrary, ♀, on the day he was elected, was posited in the △ of the ☉'s progression, and in the ✶ of the ☽'s secondary direction; and the ☉ in △ of ♀ of the nativity, there was a new ☽ on the 26th of May, in ♊ 5°, in △ of ♃'s radical place and secondary direction; the ☽, on the 5th of June, was upon ♀ and in △ of ♃, of the nativity, &c.

EXAMPLE XXIII.

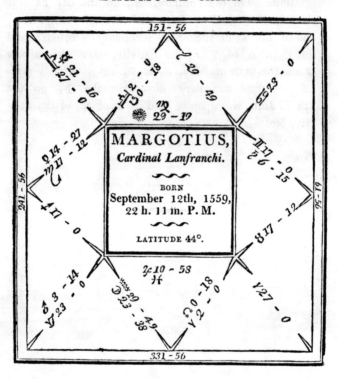

LATITUDES.			DECLINATIONS.
♄	1° 54′	S.	19° 33′ N.
♃	0 56	S.	
♂	2 48	S.	
☉	0 0		
♀	2 11	S.	18 20 S.
☿	1 10	S.	
☽	3 2	S.	16 35 S.

HE died the 30th of November 1611, aged 52 years, 2 months, 10 days. He was sent for in 1606 from Naples by Paul V, to be secretary to his grandson, Cardinal Burghesus. He was elected Cardinal on November 24, 1608.

Argol, in this nativity, as usual, directs the ascendant for the native's death; but the ☉ is undoubtedly hyleg, who, according to our method, falls on a parallel declination of the ☽; ♀ and ♄ following immediately after; and what is very remarkable, the ☉ with that declination, 16° 35', found the declination of Syrus, Aldebaran, Cauda, and very nearly Cor Leonis, four fixed stars of the first magnitude, of a hot and destructive nature. I have found, by observation, that this declination is possessed of a great force and virtue; so that if any significator obtains that declination, the signification is thereby greatly increased; good with the benign, and evil with the malignant. I have observed that ☿ with that declination gives acuteness to the mind and understanding; ♀, a desire for luxury and pleasure; ♂, anger, madness, boldness, temerity, &c.

The ☉ with this declination causes a warm pestilential air; he brings back the heat of summer about the beginning of November; and, when configurated with the malefics, raises storms at sea, spoils the fruits and wines, and produces on the earth vermin to destroy the seed. With the benefics, the contrary; he purifies the air, makes it productive, increases the buds, &c.; so that there seems to be great power in the declination of those stars.

But it is very evident that this right direction of the ☉ was alone sufficient; for in the nativity the ☉, who is hyleg, was surrounded by the enemies by both motions; in the zodiac, it applied very near to the □ of ♂, and *in mundo*, by converse motion, to the □ of ♄, and ♀ only, of the benefics gave any assistance by the mundane ✱, whereby she conferred great dignities; nevertheless, she being unfortunately situated in the sign ♏, her detriment, and under a parallel of ♄'s declination, who is in the western angle, where he is generally the cause of diseases: what ♀ denoted shewed it only to be corrupt, sickly, and of short duration. The ☉, directed to the △ of ♃, both ways, and ☌ of ♀, conferred very great honours on the native, and unexpected: he did not seek for honours, but was sought for to be promoted. But as the benefics were with violent fixed stars in the nativity, after the ☉ had passed through the rays of the favourable planets, and declined to the parallel of the malefics, the native died.

But I am of opinion that the secondary directions, with the other motions, contributed greatly to his death, as we shall observe.

The calculation of the ☉'s direction is thus:

The ☉'s pole is 16°, his oblique ascension there is 179° 18'; the oblique ascension of ♏ 15° 40', in which the ☽'s declination 16° 35' falls, is 228° 4', from which subtracting that of the ☉, there remains the arc of direction 48° 46', which for the equation add to the ☉'s right ascension, which is 179° 24', and it makes 228° 10', answering to 20° 40' of ♏, to which the ☉,

PRIMUM MOBILE.

from the day of birth, arrives in 52 days, which denotes 52 years nearly.

The secondary directions are made on the 4th of November 1559, three hours P. M.

	☉	☽	♄	♃	♂	♀	☿	☋
Deg. of Lon.	♏ 21.44	♑ 22.0	♊ 4.45	♓ 8.55	♒ 10.54	♎ 4.14	♏ 5.55	♓ 27.40
Lat.		S. 4.34	S. 2.17	S. 1.34	S. 1.20	S. 3.50	N. 1.48	

You see that the ☉ was exactly in a parallel of the declination of ♂, the ☽ in sesqui-quadrate of ♄, the ☉ likewise remaining in a parallel of ♄. The progressions fall on December the 2d, 1563.

	☉	☽	♄	♃	♂	♀	☿	☋
Deg. of Lon.	♑ 20.1	♋ 22.0	♌ 4.53	♌ 6.59	♉ 0.7	♐ 16.16	♐ 25.27	♑ 3.49
Lat.		S. 1.8	N. 0.18	N. 0.30	N. 0.48	N. 0.37	N. 1.30	

November 30, 1611, the day he died, the stars were posited in the manner following:

Deg. of Lon.	☉ ♐ 7.28	☽ ♎ 21.55	♄ ♒ 29.38	♃ ♌ 25.33	♂ ♍ 20.35	♀ ♐ 4.36	☿ ♍ 18.56	☊ ♊ 10.45
Lat.		N. 3.46	S. 1.6	N. 0.32	N. 0.5	N. 0.26	N. 0.18	

The ☉, on the day he died, was posited in ☌ of ♄'s radical place, and in ☌ of ♄'s secondary direction; the ☽ upon ☿, and in □ of his secondary directions and progression; ♄, on the same day, was in □ to the ☉'s secondary direction, and upon the ☽ in the radix, and ♂ upon the secondary direction of the ☉, and ☿ in ☌ with him near the place of the primary directions, and in □ of the ☽'s radical place; on the day of his illness, the ☉ was upon the place of the primary directions, and the ☽ in □ of ♂'s progression.

Thus you see a mutual permutation of the ingressions.

EXAMPLE XXIV.

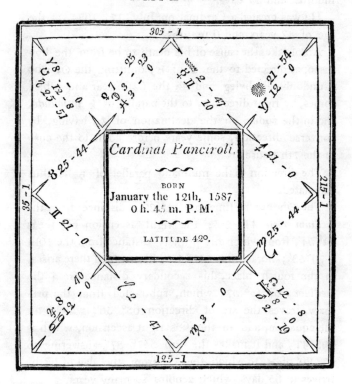

LATITUDES.		DECLINATIONS.
♄ .. 2° 25′ S.		7° 38′ N.
♃ .. 0 34 S.		
♂ .. 2 28 N.		1 21 S.
☉ .. 0 0		
♀ .. 0 13 S.		
☿ .. 1 26 S.		
☽ .. 3 9 N.		7 25 S.

HE died the 3d of September 1651, aged 64 years, 7 months, and 20 days.

He was created a Cardinal on July 17, 1634, at the age of 47 years and 6 months.

Argol takes the cause of his death to be from the horoscope, directed to the □ of ♄, omitting the ☉, who is undoubtedly hyleg, and in the 64th year and a half comes, by right direction, to the parallel of ♄ *in mundo*, and in the zodiac to the declination of ♂, having, by converse direction, some years before come to the cusp of the 7th house.

The direction to the mundane parallel of ♄ is thus calculated.

The ☉'s horary times are 11° 29′; distance from the *medium cœli* 11° 20′; the right ascension of ♄ is 24° 54′, from which his primary distance from the 10th is 79° 53′; horary times 16° 10′; from which there arises, in the fourth place, his secondary distance from the *medium cœli* 15° 57′, which, subtracted from the primary, leaves the arc of direction 63° 56′, which, for the equation, add to the ☉'s right ascension, which is 293° 41′, and it makes the sum 357° 37′, answering to 27° 20′ of ♓, to which the ☉, from the day of birth, arrives in 65 days, which denotes so many years.

The 9th house is elevated 17°; therefore

As the ☉'s double horary times . . 22^d 58′
is to the elevation of the 9th . . . 17   0
so is the ☉'s distance from the *medium*
cœli 11 20
to the ☉'s pole 8   0

To which, the oblique ascension of his ☌ is 110° 29′; to which I add the arc of direction 63° 56′, and the sum is 174° 25′, answering to 24° 15′ of ♍, in the tables of oblique ascension; so that the ☉ had arrived at ♓ 24° 15′, whose declination is 2° 18′, and that of ♂ 1° 21′, if his place is true by longitude and latitude; therefore, the ☉ applied to his declination within one degree, and the luminaries in the directions to the parallels, always anticipate their effects, as is seen in all these examples. The ☉, by converse motion, had departed from the west, and ♂, at the same time, was found at the centre of the *imum cœli* (i. e.) in a mundane □ ray to the ☉; with this same ray of ♂, the ☉ moved successively, and continued so; and this is worth observing, that any significator whatsoever, together with the other stars, whilst they are moved by a converse universal motion, change the aspect alternately, and, consequently, the mundane rays, as it likewise happens when they acquire parallels which we have already calculated.

But, because this happens insensibly, and such rays so acquired are generally lasting, we have not, for a long time, laid down a method to calculate them in the Canons, but any one may, from the tables of the houses, know the time of acquisition, and duration of these rays. As, in this example, the ☉, posited in the west, with ♑ 22°, in the *imum cœli*, are found ♎ 2°; and as the rays, thus acquired, are of a long continuance, they denote a certain universal disposition of the things signified, either good or bad, according to the nature of the aspecting stars, as it happened to this

Cardinal, who, some years before his death, was always sickly; and this observation is wonderful in the changes of the times and weather; for this principle Ptolemy adhered to in the *Almajest*, lib. viii, chap. 4. This doctrine he mentions in the Second Book of Judgments in the Chapter on the Nature of Events.

But, to our business; the secondary directions fall on the 17th of March, with 16ʰ 5′ P. M.

	☉	☽	♄	♃	♂	♀	☿	☊
Deg. of Lon.	♓ 26.30	♋ 0. 4	♉ 0.45	♋ 5.30	♍ 27.11R	♓ 11.33R	♓ 6.38	♎ 8.42
Lat.		S. 5. 0	S. 2.10	S. 0.18	N. 3.56	N. 5.30	S. 1.35	

The ☉ was found in ☍ of ♂ near his primary direction, under the declination of ♂ of the nativity, the ☽ in □ of ♂ of the nativity, and, therefore, the ☌ with him of ♃ availed nothing, nor the △ of ♀ and ☿, because ☿ had the declination of ♄, and being upon the ☽ of the nativity, was rather prejudicial; and as the ☽ was in 5° south latitude, she was at a great distance from ♃.

The progressions for full 64 years are finished on the 16th of March, 1592, whilst the ☽ lustrates 8° of ♉, where her vespertine distance from the ☉ is 42° nearly, the same as in the nativity; for the other 7 months I add 7 signs, and 17° 30′, and come to ♐ 25°. Lastly, for the 19 days, till the day of his death, I add 21°, and the ☽ is posited in ♑ 16°; the rest as follows:

	☉	☽	♄	♃	♂	♀	☿	☊
Deg. of	♈	♑	♋	♐	♉	♓	♐	♋
Lon.	15. 0	16. 0	6.14	19.22	24 0	1.40	19.0	1 1
Lat.		S. 1.18	S. 1. 4	N. 1.18	N. 0.11	S. 0.30	S. 2. 0	

September the 3d, 1651, the day he died, the stars were in the following order:

	☉	☽	♄	♃	♂	♀	☿	☊
Deg. of	♍	♉	♋	♐	♏	♌	♍	♈
Lon.	10.36	0.13	24.41	3. 1	21.37	18.45	14.43	22.3
Lat.		N. 0.42	S. 0.14	N. 0.29	S. 1.14	N. 0.56	N. 1.16	

On the day he died the ☉ was found with the declination of ♄ of the nativity, and almost of the secondary directions, and the ☽ also upon ♄ in the secondary directions exact; ♄ in ☍ to the ☽ and in □ of the ☉'s progression. Preceding his death, there was a full ☽, the ☉ remaining in an exact parallel of declination of ♄'s radical place, and secondary directions; ♂, on the same day, obtained the declination of the ☽'s secondary directions; ♄ was posited in ☍ of the ☉ of the nativity. You see a mutual transit, active and passive, of ♄ to the ☉.

274   PRIMUM MOBILE.

EXAMPLE XXV.

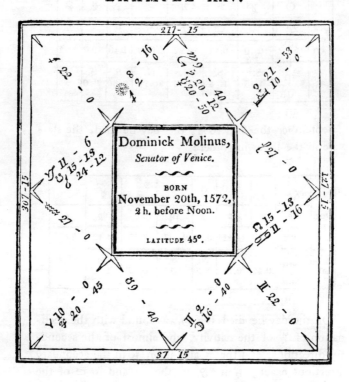

	LATITUDES.				DECLINATIONS.		
♄	. .	2°	2'	N.	15°	53'	S.
♃	. .	1	25	S.			
♂	. .	1	23	S.			
☉	. .	0	0		21	45	S.
♀	. .	2	3	N.			
☿	. .	1	49	N.	16	16	S.
☽	. .	2	23	S.	20	28	N.

PRIMUM MOBILE. 275

HE died November the 16th, 1635, 14 hours, P.M. aged 63 years, all but 14 days.

For this effect, Argol directs the ☉ to the antiscions of ♄ and ☿ ; but as these planets are in 2° north latitude, their declination becomes 16°, whereby they cut the ecliptic in 16° of ♒, and Argol takes the antiscion of ☿ in 9° 10′ of ♒. But we direct the ☉ to ♒ 16°, and then we shall see whether our method corresponds ; for, otherwise, in this example, we must comply with the opinion of others; *viz.* that the antiscions are not to be taken by preserving the latitude as we do, but wholly neglected according to their method.

The ☉'s direction to ♒ 16° is thus calculated :

The ☉'s horary times are 11° 6′, which, doubled, makes 22° 12′; the space of the eleventh house, lustrated by the ☉'s motion ; the pole of the eleventh house is 19°, and of the twelfth house 34°, the difference between them is 15°; the oblique ascension of the eleventh house is 247° 15′; the ☉'s oblique ascension is 254° 22′, therefore his distance from the eleventh house is 7° 7′. Therefore,

As the ☉'s double diurnal horary times   22° 12′
is to the difference of the poles   . . .   15   0
so is the ☉'s distance from the 11th house   7   7
to the ☉'s polar distance   5   0

which, added to the pole of the 11th, = 19, makes the ☉'s pole 24°, under which his oblique ascension is 256° 44′; the oblique ascension there of 16° of ♒ is 325° 51′, from which, subtracting that of the ☉, leaves the arc of direction 69° 7′, which, for the equation, add to the ☉'s right ascension, which is 246° 30′, and it makes 315° 37′, answering to 13° of ♒, to which the ☉, from the day of birth, arrives in 63 days, which denotes so many years. You see, therefore, gentle reader, that our method in this, as in all other examples, agrees perfectly well; therefore, the numbers of Argol's computations, in this one nativity, were merely a fortunate case that they agreed with the time of the effects.

The ☉, likewise, had arrived at its proper □ *in mundo* two years before, for the ☉'s semi-diurnal arc is 66° 36′; but when the significator does not change the hemisphere, the semi-diurnal or semi-nocturnal arc is the arc of direction of its proper □ *in mundo*, and, by his ray, both the prorogatory virtues are injured; *viz.* that in the *primum mobile* and that *in mundo*. Lastly, the ☉ arrived to the mundane parallel of the ☽, which is calculated thus: The ☉'s semi-diurnal arc is $4^h 26'$, distance from the *medium cœli* 29° 15′; the ☽'s semi-nocturnal arc is $4^h 33'$, from which arises her secondary distance from the *imum cœli* 30° 1′: this, added to the primary, which is 38° 31′, makes the arc of direction 68° 32′.

But, because the declination of the ☉ and ☽ is nearly the same, and the semi-diurnal arc of the ☉ and semi-nocturnal arc of the ☽ the same, the ☉, a little before, was, by converse motion, posited in the ☽'s mundane parallel: for

As the ☽'s semi-nocturnal arc . . . . 4^h 33′
is to her distance from the *imum cœli* . . 38° 31
so is the ☉'s semi-diurnal arc . . . . 4^h 26
to his secondary distance . . . . . . 37° 22

PRIMUM MOBILE.   277

which, added to the primary 29° 15′, makes the arc of direction 66° 47′. You may ask, Why he was not preserved, as the place of the parallels of ♄ and ☿ are nearly followed, by the ✶ ray of ♃ and △ of ♀? I answer, that they are first followed by the ☐ ray of ♄ and ☿; when, therefore, more testimonies of the malefics than of the benefics presented themselves, the malefics prevailed.

Hence we are taught, that the testimonies of the aspects may be multiplied by one and the same planet from which the quality of the effect is augmented, though that planet only is the cause of them; and so in all kinds of things.

The secondary directions happen on January the 21st, 1557, with 21ʰ P. M.

	☉	☽	♄	♃	♂	♀	☿	☊
Deg. of Lon.	♒	♍	♏	♈	♓	♐	♓	♋
	12.48	28.0	26.14	24.38	14.20	29.45	2.30	12.3
Lat.		N. 4.51	N. 2. 9	S. 1.22	S. 0.12	N. 2.23	N. 1.20	

The ☉ remains in an exact parallel of ♄'s declination, without any assistance from the benefics.

The progressions are made on the 24th of December, 1577.

	☉	☽	♄	♃	♂	♀	☿	☊
Deg. of Lon.	♑ 13.20	♋ 3.0	♑ 14.20	♎ 10.56	♏ 26.55	♐ 9.40	♐ 22.0	♈ 6.50
Lat.		S. 5.0	N. 0.20	N. 1.31	N. 0.11	N. 2. 9	0. 0	

The ☉ was in ☌ there with ♄; the ☽ in their ☍.

November the 16th, 1635, the day he died, the stars were posited thus:

	☉	☽	♄	♃	♂	♀	☿	☊
Deg. of Lon.	♏ 24.0	♒ 13.0	♑ 0.40	♍ 3.28	♍ 21.12	♏ 20. 0	♐ 14.40	♒ 26.37
Lat.		S. 1.10	N. 0.40	N. 0.57	N. 1.37	N. 0.45	S. 1.36	

He fell sick when the new ☽ was upon ♄ and ☿ of the nativity, and died when she came to the place of the ☉'s direction, who, on the day he died, was found upon ♄ of the secondary directions, and upon ♂ of the progressions, and the ☽ was posited in their ☐.

These agreements are wonderful. The year was also climactric, because the ☽, in the secondary direction, had stopped at the proper ☐ of her place in the nativity.

EXAMPLE XXVI.

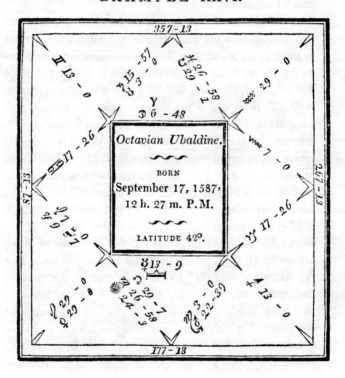

LATITUDES.				DECLINATIONS.	
♄	2°	30′	S.	14° 16′	N.
♃	0	31	S.		
♂	1	1	S.		
☉	0	0			
♀	1	11	N.		
☿	3	37	S.		
☽	0	42	S.	2 3	N.

HE died the 12th of August, 1632, aged 44 years and 11 months.

Argol directs the ascendant to the □ of ♂; whereas the ☽ is hyleg, who, according to our calculation, comes exactly to an ☍ of ♂. The ☽'s declination 2° 3′, answers to ♈ 5° in the ecliptic, whose horary times are 15° 18′, and, doubled, 30° 36′; the ☽'s right ascension is 6° 32′, from which her distance from the *medium cœli* becomes 9° 19′; the pole of the eleventh house is 17°, whence, by the golden rule, is had the ☽'s pole 5°, under which her oblique ascension is 6° 21′. The oblique ascension of ♂'s ☍ is 48° 11′, from which, subtracting that of the ☽, leaves the arc of direction 41° 50′, which, for the equation, add to the ☉'s right ascension, which is 174° 33′, and it makes 174° 33′, answering to 8° 47′ of ♏, to which the ☉, from the day and hour of birth, arrives in 45 days, which indicates so many years. The ☽, likewise, near 21° 15′ of ♉, came to the parallel declination of ♄, where, being in 4° south latitude, she gains the declination of ♄ 14° 16′, the oblique ascension of which place, according to latitude and longitude under the ☽'s pole, is 48° 38′, from which, subtracting the ☽'s oblique ascension, there remains the arc of direction 42° 17′. But, by converse motion, the ☽ applied to the mundane parallel of ♄; and if there was placed on the midheaven 2° 16′ of ♈, it answers exactly, for the right ascension of the midheaven would be 2° 5′; the declination of ♄ 14° 16′, answers to 8° of ♉ in the ecliptic, whose diurnal horary times are 17° 12′; the right ascension of ♄ is 44° 13′, from which his distance from the midheaven becomes 42° 8'; therefore,

As the horary times of ♄	17° 12'
is to his distance from the *medium cœli*	42 8
so is the horary times of the ☽	15 18
to her secondary distance	37 27
which added to the primary, which is	4 27
makes the arc of direction	41 54

so that this direction had not exactly arrived, but, nevertheless, it strongly co-operated with the other two above computed.

The secondary directions remained thus, November the 1st, 1587, at 10' P. M.

	☉	☽	♄	♃	♂	♀	☿	☋
Deg. of Lon.	♏ 8.35	♏ 26.0	♉ 13.9	♌ 15.22	♐ 25.20	♎ 26.30	♎ 25.0	♍ 26.37
Lat.		N. 4.20	S. 3. 3	N. 0.13	S. 0.28	N. 1. 11	N. 1. 7	

Thus, you see, the ☉ is between a parallel declination, and in ☍ to ♄; the ☽ nearly also with the declination of ♄. On the day of his death, the progressions are made on May 10, the stars being as under:

	☉	☽	♄	♃	♂	♀	☿	☋
Deg. of Lon.	♉ 15. 0	♎ 28. 0	♊ 26. 0	♏ 13.13	♑ 1.43	0.12	29.20	♋ 18.45
Lat.		N. 5. 0						

On the day of his death, August 12, 1632, the stars were thus posited; viz.

Deg. of Lon.	☉ ♌ 19.53	☽ ♋ 10.32	♄ ♏ 22.38	♃ ♉ 24.19	♂ ♎ 11.43	♀ ♌ 9.43	☿ ♌ 19.21	☊ ♉ 2.17
Lat.		N. 4. 37	N. 2. 0	S. 1. 4	N. 0. 9	N. 1.0	N. 1.22	

The ☉, on the day he died, was separated from ♃ in the secondary directions, and was posited in a parallel declination of ♄'s secondary direction; and *e contra* ♄, on the day he died, had the parallel of declination to the secondary direction, and, also, to the ☉'s progression; and ♄ was upon the ☽ of the secondary direction. In his sickness, the ☉ was found in the exact □ of ♄'s secondary direction, ♂ in ☍ of the ☽'s place in the nativity.

EXAMPLE XXVII.

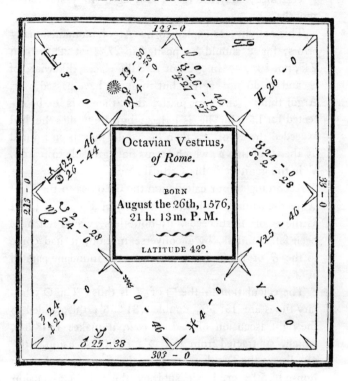

LATITUDES.

♄ . . 1° 3′ N.
♃ . . 0 43 N.
♂ . . 4 16 S.
☉ . . 0 0
♀ . . 0 50 N.
☿ . . 1 21 S.
☽ . . 0 31 N.

HE died, May the 1st, 1626, aged 49 years and 8 months.

This nativity, as explained by Argol, contains many errors, for ♃ should be posited in 27° (not 22°), ♄ in 24°, not 19°; ♂ in ♑, not ♎; the places, likewise, of ♀ and ☿ do not agree, but these we have passed over. Argol thinks, and very justly, that the ☉ is to be directed for life, for he is hyleg; but he wishes he had exceeded the ☌ of ♂, then he would have been injured by the ☌ of the ☽, which seems not agreeable to reason. Vide the geniture in his Critical Days.

According to our calculation the ☉ comes to the □ of ♂ in the zodiac, with the testimony of a ✶ of ♄; but as the ✶ of ♃ succeeds, it, doubtless, would not have been fatal, unless, by a converse motion, it had come to the ☍ of ♂, and, by direct, to the mundane parallel of ♂.

The calculation to the □ of ♂ is thus: The ☉'s horary times are 15° 59′, doubled 31° 58′; this, added to the right ascension of *medium cœli*, it makes 154° 58′, which, subtracted from the ☉'s right ascension, 164° 48′, leaves the ☉'s distance from the cusp of the eleventh house 9° 50′; or, if we subtract the oblique ascension of the eleventh house, 153° 0′, from the ☉'s oblique ascension there taken, which is 162° 50′, there remains the ☉'s distance 9° 50′; the pole of the eleventh house is 17°, of the twelfth house 31°, and their difference is 14°. Therefore,

As the ☉'s duplicate horary times . . . 31° 58'
is to the polar difference 14 0
so is his distance from the 11th house . . 9 50
to his polar distance from the 11th . . . 4 0

which, added to the pole of the eleventh house, 17°, the ☉'s pole becomes 21°, under which his oblique ascension is 162° 18'. The oblique ascension of the □ of ♂ in the ecliptic (upon which the ☉ is perpetually moved) is 207° 36'; from which, subtracting that of the ☉, leaves the arc of direction 45° 18', which, for the equation, add to the ☉'s right ascension, which is 164° 48', and it makes 210° 8', answering to 2° 20' of ♏, to which the ☉, from the day and hour of birth, arrives in 49 days and one-third nearly, which denotes so many years.

To the ☍ of ♂, by a converse motion, the calculation is easy.

The polar altitude of ♂ is 2°, under which his oblique ascension is 229° 26', and that of the ☉'s ☍, there is 345° 3', from which, subtracting the former, there remains the arc of direction 45° 37'.

To the mundane parallel of ♂ the calculation is thus:

The ☉'s horary times are 15° 59', distance from the *medium cœli* 41° 48', the declination of ♂ is 25° 18', ascensional difference is 25° 12', and, divided by 6, quotes 4° 12', to be added to the equator's horary times, and the horary times of ♂'s are 19° 12', from which are produced 50° 13', which is the secondary distance of ♂ from the *imum cœli;* his primary distance therefrom is 40° 30', for his right ascension is 298° 30', and the right ascension of the *imum cæli* is 308° 0′; subtracting, therefore, 4° 30′ from 50° 13′, leaves the arc of direction 45° 43′.

You see, therefore now, how well all the directions agree at the same time; so that it is no wonder the native was deprived of life. For the single direction to the □ of ♂, as has been said, does not seem sufficient. The secondary directions for 49 years and 8 months are made October 15, 1576, with 13ʰ P. M. nearly, under this position of the stars:

	☉	☽	♄	♃	♂	♀	☿	☋
Deg. of Lon.	♏ 3. 0	♌ 13.5	♐ 26.40	♍ 6.47	♒ 16.0	♏ 8.4	♏ 8.0	♈ 29 49
Lat.		N. 4.52	N. 0.51	N. 0.53	S. 3. 0	N. 0.50	S. 1. 0	

The ☽ is found in a parallel declination of ♂, and ♄ with the ☍ of ♂; the ✶ of ♃ to the ☉ could give no assistance, because ♃ is cadent, and the ray ✶ is very weak, especially when it is the principal ray, for which reason, Ptolemy, in the Chapter of Life, when he mentions the planets that are able to save in the occourses of the infortunes, does not name the ✶, but the □, △, and ☍; because the ✶ ray is feeble, particularly when it is less than 60°; neither could ♀ assist, as she was cadent from the house, and in a sign inimical to the ☉. Lastly, when the primary directions are strong for evil, the secondary rather co-operate for mischief, from the testimony of the malefics; and, on the contrary, they co-operate for good, if the primary are fortunate. The ☉ was likewise with the ☋.

The progressions were made September 2, 1580.

	☉	☽	♄	♃	♂	♀	☿	☊
Deg. of Lon.	♍	♋	♒	♐	♊	♎	♎	♒
	19.25	2. 0	11.3	6.17	7.20	19.38	12.43	14.46
Lat.		N. 3.25	S. 1. 2	N. 0. 41	S. 1. 1	S. 4.11	S. 2.13	

On the day he died, May 1, 1626, the stars were thus situated:

	☉	☽	♄	♃	♂	♀	☿	☊
Deg. of Lon.	♉	♋	♍	♎	♊	♉	♉	♍
	10.58	20.8	9. 5	24.2	29.1	9.43	22.44	0.51

On the day he died the ☉ was found in □ of ♂ of the secondary directions, and □ of ♄ of the progression; ♂ upon the ☽ of the progression. And it is to be observed, that for several months before, ♄ remained upon the ☉ of the nativity, and without doing any mischief, because ♃ was upon the ☉'s primary and secondary directions: but when he was separated by retrogradation, he left the ☉ in the power of an infortune, and there was a new ☽ before his death, in ♉ 6°, in the place of the ☍ to the ☉'s secondary direction, and in □ of the ☽ there, and in □ of ♄'s progression.

EXAMPLE XXVIII.

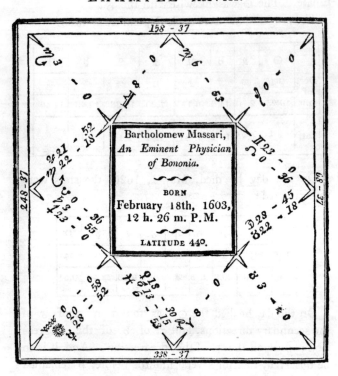

	LATITUDES.			DECLINATIONS.		
♄	2°	22'	N.	18°	40'	S.
♃	1	34	N.	16	47	S.
♂	0	9	S.	6	43	S.
☉	0	0		11	29	S.
♀	5	10	N.	0	22	S.
☿	1	43	S.	13	26	S.
☽	0	11	N.	20	7	N.

THE ☽ with the Pleiades, Hyades, Orion's Belt, and near the great Dog-star Sirius, the ☉ with Fomahaut.

He died February 18, 1655, at the 17th civil hour. This man was a professor of physic and philosophy in the college at Bononia, and of great repute. He argued very subtilely, and supported his arguments with the strongest reason. Being sent for by the principal great men of Italy for his advice when they were sick, he always returned loaded with honours and rich presents. He had a great knowledge of the mathematics. His liberality, particularly towards his friends, extended to profusion; in other things extremely prudent and sagacious. His house was ornamented with the most beautiful and valuable pictures, precious stones, gems, &c.; and he had filled his library with volumes of the best authors in philosophy, physic, mathematics, and astrology.

To business his application was unremitting: of his promises he was a careful observer. In short, the man was rich in every kind of virtue. He was born with his feet inverted, owing to the constitution of the ☽ in the western horizon with ☋ in a mundane □ of ♂, who passed through ♓, the sign of the feet, and in ☍ of ♄ in ♐, the sign of the thighs. On account of the friendship that subsisted between us, he desired me (for he was well acquainted with the common way) to calculate the directions of his nativity, which I very gladly performed, and the calculation of past accidents appeared to a minute; but I afterwards observed to the year 52, a direction of the ☽, who is hyleg to a parallel of ♄ in the zodiac, near ♋ 14° 15′, in south latitude 3° 28′, though indeed the declination of this place is 19° 13′ and ♄'s declination is 18° 40′; but I know that the luminaries in these parallels precede by their effects the intimate application; the ☽, by a converse motion, applied to the mundane parallel of ♂, whilst both were carried away by the rapt motion of the *primum mobile* round the world. Lastly, the ☽, by a right direction, came to the sesqui-quadrate of ♂ in mundo. And, indeed, as in every direction, the rays of the friends are subsequent, it might be thought these aspects would not prove fatal, yet he died on February 18, 1655, near the 17th hour, almost suddenly, having some days before received the holy sacrament, conscious of his impending unfortunate directions, and the unfortunate revolution which happened the day he died; and I think of some inward accident which forewarned him of his death, whence he is said to have feared the 18th, because, perhaps, on that day, by calculation, a crisis or judgment of some consequence would fall, for it is said he was sick the night before; however it be, he died the day he had predicted, to the grief of the whole city of Felsina. His auditors, for the love and estimation they bore their very learned preceptor, celebrated his funeral with great pomp and solemnity.

The arc of direction for 52 years is 47° 50′; for the ☉, after the nativity, arrives in 52 days to 21° 40′ of ♈, whose right ascension is 20° 1′, from which subtracting the ☉'s right ascension, which is 332° 11′, leaves the arc of direction 47° 50′. The direction of the ☽ to a parallel of ♄'s declination is thus calculated:

The oblique ascension of the ☽'s ☍ in the horoscope is 257° 10′, from which subtracting the horoscope's oblique ascension, leaves the ☽'s distance from the west 8° 33′; the pole of the second house is 38°; therefore the difference of the poles of the 7th and 8th houses is 11°. The ☽'s diurnal horary times are 18° 27′; which doubled produce 36° 54′; for the ☽'s declination is equal to ♉ 29° 30′ in the ecliptic: Now therefore

As the ☽'s diurnal horary times . . . 36° 54′
is to the polar difference of the 7th and
  8th houses 11   0
so is the ☽'s distance from the west . . 8 33
to the ☽'s polar distance 3   0
which added to the pole of 8th 38   0

her pole then becomes 41°, under which the oblique ascension of her ☍ is 255° 0′, to which I add the arc of direction 47° 50′, and the sum is 302° 50′, answering in the same table to ♑ 14° 15′ with the north latitude, which the ☽ gains in the place of the ☍ to him, viz. 3° 28′; therefore the ☽ came to ♋ 14° 15′ in 3° 28′ south latitude, where she gains a declination of 19° 13′, that is 33′ greater than that of ♄: but as the ☽ lessened her declination, she therefore applied.

The calculation of the ☽'s converse direction to the mundane parallel of ♂, whilst both were carried away by the rapt motion of the *primum mobile*, is thus:

The ☽'s semi-nocturnal arc is 69° 17′, that of ♂

96° 33', which added together are 165° 50'. The ☽'s right ascension is 56° 28', that of ♂ is 344° 28', which, subtracted from the former, leaves the ☽'s right distance from ♂ 71° 50': the ☽'s primary distance from the *imum cœli* is 77° 51': therefore

    As the sum of the arc's . . . . . 165° 50'
    is to the ☽'s semi-nocturnal arc . . . 69 17
    so is her right distance from ♂ . . . 71 50
    to her secondary distance 30   1

which subtracted from the primary, leaves the arc of direction 47° 50'; and if you have a mind to calculate it by logarithms, the minutes of the first numbers are 9950', where the logarithm is 3.99782; the minutes of the second are 4157', logarithm 3.61878; and the minutes of the third are 4510', and logarithm 3.63447. I add these two last together, and the sum is 7.25326, from which I subtract the first, and the remaining logarithm is 3.25544, which gives 1801', or 30° 1'.

The ☽'s direction to the sesqui-quadrate of ♂ *in mundo*, by right motion, is thus calculated:

I first direct to his □ *in mundo* thus:

    As the ☽'s diurnal horary times . . . 18° 27'
    is to her distance from the west . . .   8 33
    so is ♂'s nocturnal horary times . . . 16   5
    to his distance from the *imum cœli* . .   7 27

which is to be subtracted from the primary. But as the primary distance of ♂ is less by 5° 41', therefore ♂ precedes this □ 1° 46'. In this case I first triplicate ♂'s horary times, which must be added to the □'s ray, that we may form the sesqui-quadrate, and I have

PRIMUM MOBILE. 293

48° 15', from which I subtract 1° 46', which ♂, by his □, precedes the ☽, and there remains the ☽'s arc of direction to the sesqui-quadrate of ♂ 46° 29'; therefore this ray of ♂ had preceded a year, or more, at which time, as he related to me, he suffered very great troubles of mind.

The secondary directions are made on April 11, 1603, 12 h. 26 m. P. M.

	☉	☽	♄	♃	♂	♀	☿	☊
Deg. of Lon.	♈ 21.37	♈ 26.0	♎ 3.45	♏ 29.57	♑ 22.47	♓ 10.22	♈ 21R44	♏ 27.53
Lat.		N. 2.39	N. 2.42	N. 1.53	S. 0. 3	N. 1.56	N. 2.37	

You see the ☉ is in ☌ with ♂, and separating from the sesqui-quadrate of ♄, and the ☽ under the ☉'s rays in ♈ in ☌ with ♂; and ☿ was with the luminaries retrograde; which denotes an apoplexy, so that it is very probable the native died of that disease; for the place of the ☽'s right direction concurs with the sesqui-quadrate of ☿ in the zodiac exactly by calculation, and was the more fatal, as it was also in the terms of ☿.

The progressions happen on May 3, 1607.
The planets as follow:

	☉	☽	♄	♃	♂	♀	☿	☊
Deg. of	♉	♌	♑	♓	[illegible]	♉	♊	♍
Lon.	13.0	11.40	19R34	28.27	8. 0	29. 0	3. 0	9. 17
Lat.		S. 2.21	N. 1.10	S. 0.56	N. 0. 8	N. 0.16	N. 2. 4	

He died on February 18, 1655, the planets being found as under:

	☉	☽	♄	♃	♂	♀	☿	☊
Deg. of	♒	♌	♍	♓	♐	♓	♒	♒
Lon.	29.48	1.14	6.55	27.53	10.40	1. 5	17.7	15.6
Lat.		N. 1.13	N. 1.48	S. 1. 9	N. 0 30	S. 1.27	S. 1.30	

It is worth observing, that the native died nearly at the hour of the ☉'s revolution, in which he had the declination of ♄; and the ☽ that of ♂; and ♀ was separated from the ☉; and the ☽ was also in a parallel declination of ♂'s progression; ☿ in ☍ of the ☽, □ and parallel of the ☉'s progression, also ☽ in parallel declination of ♄'s progression, and ♂ with the ☽'s anaretic declination.

The magistracy in this nativity is denoted by ♀ oriental in ☌ with ♂ in the southern circle, both angular and in their dignities, and conciliated to the ☽ by the ray quintile; vide Ptolemy, Cap. de Opificio. "*Si ♀ & ☿ simul officiis moderandis præficiuntur, &c. medicamentarios, Medicos, &c.*" But it was the more excellent from the △ of ♃ constituted on the cusp of the ascendant and oriental. Ptolemy in the same place says, "*Nam orientalia cum sunt, aut in angulis, opificia sua, authoritate & fama minime caritura, &c. & superata à beneficis, magna significant opera, illustria, lucrosa, inculpabilia, venusta, &c.*" This one nativity, in preference to numberless others which I have calculated, I thought proper to insert here, that the memory of a man so famed for virtue and erudition might survive among the living, who in his lifetime, by his profession and friendly offices, studied only the good of his fellow creatures.

EXAMPLE XXIX.

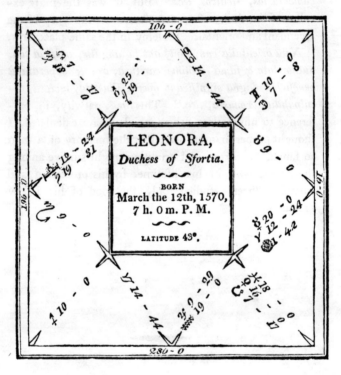

LATITUDES.				DECLINATIONS.		
♄	. .	2° 47′	N.	5°	5′	S.
♃	. .	0 49	S.	18	44	S.
♂	. .	3 38	N.	16	25	N.
☉	. .	0 0		1	2	S.
♀	. .	1 14	S.	6	17	N.
☿	. .	1 37	N.			
☽	. ,	5 0	S.	16	38	N.

SHE died December 17, 1634, aged 64 years and 9 months, nearly.

In this nativity, as explained by Argol, he places ♀ in ♒ and ☿ in ♓, but she ought to be in ♓ and he in ♈. He directs the ascendant to the ☍ of the ☽, as if she was anareta, though she rather appears to be the significator of life, and her directions agree very well; for the ☽, by right direction, in 64 years and 9 months, comes to a parallel declination of ♂, near 5° 30′ of ♌, where the ☽ is in 2° 40′ south latitude, and gains a declination 16° 22′; and that of ♂ 16° 25′.

The calculation is thus: the ☽'s declination, which is 16° 38′, answers to ♉ 16° in the ecliptic, whose horary times are 17° 42′, which doubled, make 35° 24′, the space of the ☽'s house; the oblique ascension of the third house is 256°. The oblique ascension of the ☽'s ☍ to the pole of the third house, which is 18°, is 251° 44′; therefore the ☽'s distance from the cusp of the 9th house is 4° 16′, and her polar elevation 20°, under which the oblique ascension of her ☍ is 252° 24′; the oblique ascension of ♒ 5° 30′, with 2° 40′ north latitude under the same pole is 313° 22′; from which, subtracting the former, leaves the arc of direction 60° 58′, which, for the equation, add to the ☉'s right ascension, which is 1° 34′, and it makes 62° 30′, answering to 4° 32′ of ♊, to which the ☉ arrives in 64 days and 18 hours, which denotes 64 years and 9 months.

And because the ☽'s declination in the nativity is 16° 38′, which is nearly the same that she obtains in the place of direction, the arc of direction may be likewise had by the right ascension. The right ascension of the ☽ is 66° 10′; the right ascension of ♌ 5° 30′, with 2° 40′ south latitude, is 127° 12′; from which, subtracting that of the ☽, there remains the arc of direction 61° 2′, greater by 4′ than the other, by means of some difference of the ☽'s declination and the place of the occourse.

At the same time the ☽, by a direct direction, came to the mundane parallel of ♄, for the ☽'s declination in the ecliptic answers to ♉ 16°; whose horary times are 17° 42′; her distance from the *medium cœli* is 39° 50′; ♄'s declination 5° 5′, answers to ♎ 13° in the ecliptic, whose diurnal horary times are 14° 12′. From these, by the Golden Rule, are produced ♄'s secondary distance from the *medium cœli* 31° 57′; his primary distance from the 10th is 93° 4′ (for ♄'s right ascension is 199° 4′), and subtracting the primary distance from the secondary, leaves the arc of direction 61° 7′: this direction was succeeded by the ☽ to the mundane parallel of ☿, who was endued with the nature of ♄.

By converse direction the ☽ had arrived at the ☍ of ♄ 4 years before: ♄'s pole is 39°; under which his oblique ascension is 203° 13′; the oblique ascension of the ☽'s ☍ under ♄'s pole, is 260° 10′; which therefore being subtracted, leaves the arc of direction 56° 57′.

Retention of urine is denoted by ♀, lady of the ascendant in the 6th house, and in parallel of ♄'s declination in the horoscope, posited in the sign of the reins and kidnies; the ☽ was also in a parallel of declination with ♂, and in mundane □ with ♀ in the 6th house.

The secondary directions happen May 16, 1570, near ½ hour P. M.

	☉	☽	♄	♃	♂	♀	☿	☊
Deg. of	♊	♎	♎	♒	♍	♊	♉	♍
Lon.	4.40	18.30	15.54	16.45	5. 0	6. 0	16.20	4. 0
Lat.		N. 3.30	N. 2.50	S. 0.37	N. 1. 0	S. 0.20	S. 2.20	

Observe that ♀ is combust of the ☉ and in □ of ♂, and with the hyades; the ☽ is in the sesqui-quadrate of the ☉ and ♀, and parallel declination of ♄, and in the preceding ☌, ♃ assisted with his △ ray.

The progression for full 65 years falls on June 13th, 1575, the ☽ remaining in 7° of ♍, and the ☉ in 1° of ♋. But there is a deficiency of 3 months and 6 days; for the three months I subtract 3 signs 7°, and go back with the ☽, so that she is posited in ♊ 0°. Lastly, I subtract 6° for the same number of days, and the ☽ is posited in ♉ 24°; the rest of the planets as under:

	☉	☽	♄	♃	♂	♀	☿	☊
Deg. of	♊	♉	♐	♋	♋	♋	♊	♉
Lon.	24.20	24.0	15.40	15.18	3.32	19.38	3.48	26.12
Lat.		S. 0.11	N. 1.48	N. 0. 6	N. 0. 8	N. 1.30	S. 2. 0	

The ☉ was in an exact parallel declination of ♂, ♀

also with the declination of ♂, and the ☽ in ☐ of ♂ of the nativity.

December 17th, 1634, the day she died, the stars were found as under:

	☉	☽	♄	♃	♂	♀	☿	☋
Deg. of Lon.	♐ 25.39	♏ 20.0	♐ 24.10	♌ 2.54	♎ 28.4	♒ 12.51	♑ 15.31	♓ 16.52
Lat.		S. 4.27	N. 1. 2	N. 0.31	S. 1.16	S. 1.53	S. 1. 2	

The ☉ is conjoined to ♄ in the ☍ of his progression, and ♄ in ☍ exactly to the ☉'s progression; the ☽ remaining with the declination of ♄ in ☍ of his progression, and in the sesqui-quadrate of ♂, when he was separated from the △ of ♃. There was a full ● December 5th before her death, the ☉ remaining upon ♄ of the progressions.' Both the luminaries were found in parallel declination of the malefics; the ☽ stopped at the ☐ of ♂ in the nativity on the day of death, and ♃, by retrogradation, separated from the place of the ☽'s right direction.

EXAMPLE XXX.

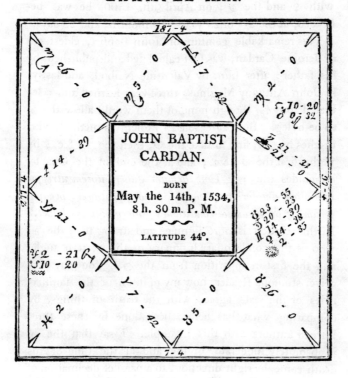

	LATITUDES.			DECLINATIONS.		
♄	0°	26′	S.	21°	22′	N.
♃	0	6	N.	19	36	S.
♂	0	51	N.	20	57	N.
☉	0	0		20	44	N.
♀	2	17	N.	24	55	N.
☿	1	52	N.	21	31	N.
☽	3	50	S.	19	21	N.

MEDUSA's head on the cusp of the seventh house, with ♀ and the ☽; on April 9th, 1560, he was beheaded, at the age of 25 years, 10 months, and 26 days.

This remarkable geniture of John Baptist, eldest son of Jerome Cardan, was first calculated and published by his father; after him, by Valentine Naibod, and lastly, by John Anthony Maginus, three very learned and celebrated authors, though none of them would allow the ☽ to be hyleg. But, agreeable to Ptolemy's method, who teaches by day, first to take the ☉, then the ☽, &c.; by night, first the ☽, &c.; and at the end of the Chapter concludes thus: "*Tunc demum gubernatorem utrisque luminibus anteferimus, quando honorificentiorem occupat locum, & ad utrasque conditiones gubernandi ius habet.*" In this case ☿ is more dignified and strong than the ☽, who is the conditionary luminary in the western angle, and the first in apparition from the ☉. You may perceive, studious Reader, how my opinion of the familiarities of the stars agrees with the truth of things, by comparing what has before been done by these three learned authors with this Example. I say that the ☽ is absolutely moderator of life, and at the time of his death came, by right direction, to a parallel declination of the ☉, near 13° 50' of ♋, where having obtained 2° south latitude, her declination is 20° 50'. Next follows the ☌ of ♄, and the parallel of ♃'s declination; but he being very unfortunate, and not agreeing with the signs of the luminaries, threatened (according to Ptolemy) the anger of the Prince, and the sentence of the judges, who in Cap. de Morte saith thus: "*Quod si & ♃ testificetur*

♂ *simul pravitatem indutus, illustri rursus mortis genere decedunt, condemnatione nimirum, & ira principium, ac regum;"* for ♃ is occidental, retrograde, peregrine, with ☍, and in ☌ of ♂, with the declination of ♄.

The ☽, too, by converse direction, came to the mundane parallel of ♄, succeeded also by that of ♂ and ♃. The arc of direction for 25 years 11 months, is 26° 32'; for the ☉, from the day of birth, in the space of 25 days 22 hours, arrives at 27° 17' of ♊, whose right ascension is 87° 2'; from which, subtracting the right ascension of the ☉, which is 60° 30', there remains the arc of direction 26° 32'.

The oblique ascension of the ☽'s ☍ under the pole 44° (for the ☽ is on the cusp of the seventh house) is 279° 37'; to which, adding the arc of direction 26° 32', makes 306° 9'; which, in the same table of oblique ascension, answers to 13° 30' of ♑, with 2° north latitude; the declination of which place is 20° 50'. Parallels about the tropics are of long duration, and their effects more fully appear, when the other motions of direction, both direct and converse, the secondary directions, progressions, ingresses, &c. agree with them. The calculation of the ☽'s converse direction to the mundane parallel of ♄ will be thus: The declination of ♄, 21° 22', is equal to ♋ 24° in the ecliptic, whose diurnal horary times are 18° 42'; the oblique ascension of his ☍ in the horoscope is 315° 26'; from which subtracting the horoscope's oblique ascension, there remains ♄'s distance from the west 38° 32'.

The ☽'s declination, 19° 21', is reduced to ♉ 26° in the ecliptic, whose nocturnal horary times (for the ☽ is posited below the earth) are 11° 42′; the oblique ascension of the ☽'s ☍ is 279° 37′, from which, subtracting the horoscope's oblique ascension, leaves her primary distance from the west 2° 33′; therefore

As the diurnal horary times of ♄ . . . 18ᵈ 42′
is to his distance from the west . . . 38 22
so is the ☽'s nocturnal horary times . 11 42
to her secondary distance from the west 24 0

which added to the primary, as the ☽ in the nativity is above the earth, and by the direction posited below, makes the arc of direction 26° 33′.

The secondary directions happen on the 9th of June, 1534, 4ʰ 10′ P. M. at which time the planets were found as follows:

	☉	☽	♄	♃	♂	♀	☿	☋
Deg. of Lon.	♊ 27.22	♊ 3.37	♋ 26.31	♒ 0R.16	♌ 13.59	♊ 1R.36	♊ 23R.22	♌ 9. 2
Lat.		S. 4.33	N. 0.13	S. 0.21	N. 0.34	S. 1. 1	S. 4.20	

The progressions fall on June 17th, 1536; the ☽ remaining in ♊ 20°, and the rest as under:

	☉	☽	♄	♃	♂	♀	☿	☋
Deg. of Lon.	♋ 5. 0	♊ 20. 0	♌ 21.31	♈ 12.45	♍ 2.20	♊ 6.10	♊ 28.0	♊ 29.56
Lat.		S. 0.52	N. 1.12	S. 1.31	N. 0.34	S. 1.23	N. 0.50	

On the day of his death, April the 9th, 1560, the stars were thus found:

Deg. of Lon.	☉	☽	♄	♃	♂	♀	☿	☊
	♈	♎	♊	♈		♓	♈	♓
	29.29	14.54	6.51	8.17	0.37	17.27	23.46	19.21
Lat.		S. 2.9	S. 1.26	S. 1.6	N. 0.13	S. 0.20	S. 1.10	

In the secondary direction the ☽ had a declination 16° 17', and that of ♂ was 17° 15', and the ☽ was near Aldebaran and Medusa's head. The day he died, both the malefics were found upon this place of the ☽ in ♊ 4°. Besides, the ☉, by secondary direction, was in ☌ with ☿ retrograde, who having a declination of 19°, and communicating to ♂ from the parallel, transferred the enmity of ♂ to the ☉, who, on the day of his death, was found in the □ of ♄'s secondary direction, and in the □ of ♂ of the nativity, and in □ of ♃'s secondary direction unfortunate.

In the progression the ☽ was found upon her place of the nativity in ☌ with ☿, under the ☉'s rays near Medusa's head; and the day he died, ♂ had a parallel of declination to her. The same day she applied to the □ of ♄'s radical place, the ☉ was in △ of ♂ of the progression, and in parallel declination, exactly to minutes, viz. 11° 14'. According to Ptolemy, *Cap. de Vita*, it is observable that in this geniture nearly all the planets have the same declination, ♃ in obedience and ♀ under the ☉ beams; ♄ and ♂ are elevated above ☉, who is falling from the angle of the 7th into the 6th, but they are succedent in the 8th, the house of death, which is terrible. Whenever the malefics are found in the 8th, and afflicting the luminaries, especially the conditionary, so that nevertheless if they are well situate and powerful, their strength is of no avail when a violent death is threatened, and the more so if the places of both the malefics agree with the nature of the signs and the fixed stars, and the luminaries are found in the same horary circle with the malefics, as in this case the ☽ descends with Caput Medusæ. See Ptolemy, Chap. of Death.

He was beheaded for poisoning his wife; that being the usual mode of executing malefactors, at that time, in that country.

DIGNITIES OF THE PLANETS IN THE SIGNS.

Signs.	Houses.	Exaltation.	Triplicities.	EGYPTIAN TERMS.									
♈	♂ D.	☉	☉ ♃	6	♃	12	♀	20	☿	25	♂	30	♄
♉	♀ N.	☽	♀ ☽	8	♀	14	☿	22	♃	27	♄	30	♂
♊	☿ D.		♄ ☿	6	☿	12	♃	17	♀	24	♂	30	♄
♋	☽	♃	♂ ♀ ☽	7	♂	13	♀	19	☿	26	♃	30	♄
♌	☉		☉ ♃	6	♃	11	♀	18	♄	24	☿	30	♂
♍	☿ N.	☿	♀ ☽	7	☿	17	♀	21	♃	28	♂	30	♄
♎	♀ D.	♄	♄ ☿	6	♄	14	☿	21	♃	28	♀	30	♂
♏	♂ N.		♂ ♀ ☽	7	♂	11	♀	19	☿	24	♃	30	♄
♐	♃ D.		☉ ♃	12	♃	17	♀	21	☿	26	♄	30	♂
♑	♄ N.	♂	♀ ☽	7	☿	14	♃	22	♀	26	♄	30	♂
♒	♄ D.		♄ ☿	7	☿	13	♀	20	♃	25	♂	30	♄
♓	♃ N.	♀	♂ ♀ ☽	12	♀	16	♃	19	☿	28	♂	30	♄

Rays of the Signs.										Rays of the Houses.									
	✱	□	△	☍		✱	□	△	☍		✱	□	△	☍		✱	□	△	☍
♈	♒ ♊	♑ ♋	♐ ♌	♎	♎	♌ ♐	♋ ♑	♊ ♒	♈	1	3 11	4 10	5 9	7	7	9 5	10 4	11 3	1
♉	♓ ♋	♒ ♌	♑ ♍	♏	♏	♍ ♑	♌ ♒	♋ ♓	♉	2	4 12	5 11	6 10	8	8	10 6	11 5	12 4	2
♊	♈ ♌	♓ ♍	♒ ♎	♐	♐	♎ ♒	♍ ♓	♌ ♈	♊	3	5 1	6 12	7 11	9	9	11 7	12 6	1 5	3
♋	♉ ♍	♈ ♎	♓ ♏	♑	♑	♏ ♓	♎ ♈	♍ ♉	♋	4	6 2	7 1	8 12	10	10	12 8	1 7	2 6	4
♌	♊ ♎	♉ ♏	♈ ♐	♒	♒	♐ ♈	♏ ♉	♎ ♊	♌	5	7 3	8 2	9 1	11	11	1 9	2 8	3 7	5
♍	♋ ♏	♊ ♐	♉ ♑	♓	♓	♑ ♉	♐ ♊	♏ ♋	♍	6	8 4	9 3	10 2	12	12	2 10	3 9	4 8	6

CANON.

Of the Part of Fortune.

WHEN this work was finished, the very illustrious D. ADRIAN NEGUSANTIUS, of Fanum, a man, not only very well versed in Astrology, according to the true doctrine of Ptolemy, but, also, in Physics and the sublime secrets of Nature, having transmitted to me a method to calculate the ⊕ perfectly agreeable to reason and experience, I thought proper to set it down here, word for word, that every one might see a secret in this art, invented by so great a man, truly worthy the pen of the greatest Astrologers; for I willingly confess, that, with regard to the ⊕, I have laboured a long time, and have not been able hitherto to find any truth in it.

"The ⊕ (says he), if we may credit the precepts of Ptolemy, who asserts that it has the same position to the ☽ as the ☉ has to the horizon *(Quadripart.* Book III, chap. xii), ought to be described and defined in the lunar parallels; for neither, if it be constituted in the ecliptic, according to the intentions of the common Astrologers, or in the ☽'s orbit, as was the opinion of a very eminent professor, will it be found to preserve that order and similitude which the respective conversions of two luminaries, both diurnal and annual, denote." This man subscribes to the truth of every thing I lately mentioned in my Celestial Philosophy, wherein I said, that the ⊕ moves upon the orbit or way of the ☽'s latitude, and, therefore, not in the ecliptic.

But as I have shewn that the distances and rays to the angles are, by no means, made in the zodiac, but upon the parallel of every star, he argues, and, indeed, very ingeniously, that the ☉, in like manner, is elongated from the East, viz. upon his parallel; and, also, the ☽, who has not by any other method nor way different than when the ☉ is in the horizon, by her real presence, posited the place of ⊕; for no other fundamental principle is seen to constitute this part in nature, unless by such an assignation and impression of virtue, exhibited by the ☽, at ☉ rise. When this learned man adds, " For when the ☉ comes to the Cardinal Sign of the East, then it is necessary the ☽ be found in its horizon; afterwards, in an equal space of time, the ☉ digressing, he is removed from it according to his ascension;" wherefore, if we study the matter with accuracy, we shall find that, entirely in the same manner as the ☉ departs from the East, the ☽ is likewise separated from the ⊕, that is, both upon their parallels, so that as many degrees as the ☉, in his parallel circle, is elongated from the East, so many is the ☽ in her parallel, distant from the ⊕: whence it follows, that the true place of ⊕ does not always remain in the zodiac, but always under the ☽'s parallel circle, that is, with the ☽'s declination the same both in number and name, and, therefore, the ⊕ does not receive any aspects from the stars in the zodiac, but only *in mundo*. We may make a calculation of the ⊕ several ways, but it will be shorter, as well as easier, if, in the diurnal geniture, the ☉'s true distance from the East is added to the ☽'s right ascension, and, in the nocturnal, subtracted, for the number thence arising will be the place and right ascension of ⊕: and it always has the same declination with the ☽, both in number and name, wherever it is found. Again, let the ☉'s oblique ascension, taken in the ascendant, be subtracted always from the oblique ascension of the ascendant, as well in the day as in the night, and the remaining difference be added to the ☽'s right ascension, the sum will be the right ascension of ⊕, which will have the ☽'s declination. There are likewise other methods to take the place of ⊕. He, who has a mind to make its directions, will accomplish it only by the motions in the world, that is, to the aspects *in mundo;* and, indeed, it appears that the conversions of both the luminaries agitate the ⊕ by the two motions, since, if the luminaries are carried together by the motion of the *primum mobile*, then the ⊕ remaining immoveable in its horary circle of position, waiting for the coming and rays of the opposite stars, will be directed by a right motion; but, by a converse motion, if the ☉ be constituted immoveable, and the ☽ preceding as usual. ⊕ will, by the rapt motion, be devolved to the bodies and rays of the promittors: but as it may very reasonably be doubted whether the ⊕ institutes the directions by converse motion, I will omit speaking of this till another time, and, in the interim, see what experience says. This is worth observing, that if ⊕ does not consist in the zodiac, it is, nevertheless, directed to the parallels of the stars in the *primum mobile*, together with the ☽, whose declination it is always known to follow, and which they vary continually and successively; therefore, when the ☽ comes to the declination of any star, she produces a double effect, according to the proper signification of every one portended in the geniture, because she then falls together with ⊕ on the parallel of the same star: an invention truly ingenious; for, as the ☉, by his motion in the zodiac, successively changes his parallel, and, therefore, that relative point of his rising in the horoscope, so likewise the ☽, whilst she, by a right direction, lustrates the zodiac, and varies her parallels, seems therefore of consequence to draw to her declination the point of existence of ⊕. All these things, however, I confess must be confirmed by examples and experience.

And, as the same Negusantius transmitted to me some things which he found relating to this in the Commentaries of George Valla, on the Quadripartite, which appear to the mind of this learned author, I therefore subjoin the following:

"But, that the ⊕ (says Valla) is the nocturnal and lunar horoscope, is manifest from what Ptolemy says; for the ☽ will have the same ratio of parts to the part of Fortune, and the same figuration, as the ☉ has to the horoscope:" and that every one may know that this figuration and ratio of the distance of the luminaries must be taken in the parallels of the luminaries, he adds,

"It will be likewise plainer still, if we follow the same method by the Canons, as in the horoscope; for it will be found again, that the horoscope is the Part of Fortune, for, adding the part of the ☽ in the diurnal nativities, and, in the nocturnal, by taking the ascensionary times of the opposites, we multiply the hours, and compounding the produced number with the ascensions, look in their climates, where the number falls, and there we say is the lunar horoscope." The ascensionary times and hours are nothing but the times of the parallels, whereon the luminaries are moved by an universal motion, and effect their distances from the Cardinals and other Houses, and, consequently also, configurations, as I have evidently demonstrated in the Celestial Philosophy. And the climates are distinguished by parallels to the equator, as has been observed; therefore they are taken, by this author, for the parallels, which he explains in these words: "In like manner we shall find, from a measurement from the ☉ to the ☽, that whatever ratio and figuration the ☉ has to the eastern horizon, the same has the ☽ to ⊕;" for, indeed, the luminaries, and all the stars, form no other distances from the horoscope and houses, except upon every one of their parallels, and, as has been said, by the horary and ascensionary times. Ptolemy speaks expressly of this in the Chapter of Life, whence Valla reasonably infers, " the figuration of ⊕ to the ☽, taken in this manner, will be the same as the horoscope to the ☉; and, on the contrary, whatever figuration the ☉ has to the horoscope, the same will be that of the ☽ to ⊕. In like manner, for the same reason, both will be the same as the other; that is, as many parts as the ☉ was distant from the horoscope, so many was the ☽ from ⊕," viz. always upon their parallels, and by the ascensionary times in them. To prevent any one supposing this doctrine fictitious and void of experience, and that the method of calculating might not be obscured, I have subjoined one example, in preference to others, which I myself have observed, which you have in the nativity of Francis, the infant son of D. Camillius Piazole, a native of Padua.

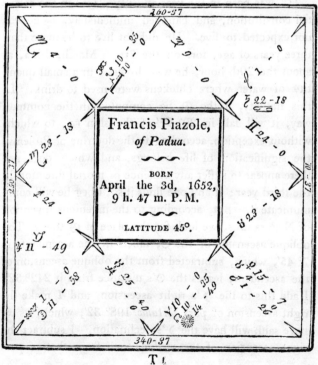

Francis Piazole, *of Padua.*

BORN
April the 3d, 1652,
9 h. 47 m. P. M.

LATITUDE 45°.

	LATITUDES.	DECLINATIONS.
♄	0° 19′ N.	21° 59′ N.
♂	0 3 S.	11 59 N.
☽	4 14 S.	21 19 S.

	R. A.	H. T.
♄	114 9	18 57 D.
♂	29 17	12 57 N.
☽	315 40	18 51 N.
⊕	198 32	11 9 D.

HE was born in the year and day placed in the celestial constitution, and baptized immediately, as he was not expected to live. He did not live to be more than three years of age, for, on the 7th of March, 1655, at about the 20th hour, he was drowned in a small quantity of water where chickens were used to drink. In this nativity, if the ⊕ be computed in the common way, it will fall in 20° 27′ of the sign ♍; to which, without exception, according to the doctrine of Ptolemy, the signification of life belongs, and which does not there appear to suffer any violence or mortal direction in the third year; if any one finds it so, I beg he will communicate it. But, according to the ingenious invention of Negusantius, we look for the place of ⊕ thus: The oblique ascension of the ☉, taken in the ascendant, is 7° 45′, which, subtracted from the oblique ascension of the ascendant, leaves the ☉'s distance from it 242° 52′: I add this to the ☽'s right ascension, and I make the right ascension of *pars fortunæ* 198° 32′, which, as we have said, will have the ☽'s declination. I subtract the right ascension of the *medium cœli* from that of *pars fortunæ*, and its distance therefrom is 37° 55′; and, as its horary times are 11° 9′, it doubtless remains about the middle of the eleventh house, where ♂'s ☍ and ♄'s ▫ cosmical ray *in mundo* fall. But let us calculate these rays exactly:

    As the horary times of *pars* ⊕ . . . 11° 9′
    is to its distance from the *medium cœli* . 37 55
    so is ♂'s horary times 12 57
    to his secondary distance from the *imum cœli* 44 2

his primary distance is 48° 40′; from which, subtracting the secondary, leaves the arc of direction of *pars* to ♂'s ☍, 4° 38′.

Again. The semi-diurnal arc of *pars* is 66° 54′, and is taken from the horary times multiplied by 6; therefore, if from the semi-diurnal arc is subtracted its distance from the *medium cœli*, there will remain its distance from the horoscope 28° 59′. Now, I say,

    As the horary times of *pars fortunæ* . . 11° 9′
    is to its distance from the horoscope . . 28 59
    so is ♄'s horary times 18 57
    to his secondary distance from the *medium cœli* 49 16

from which, subtracting the primary, which is 46° 28′, leaves the arc of direction of *pars fortunæ* to the cosmical ▫ of ♄ 2° 48′. But the ⊕ remained about the beginning of ♏, ♄ in the eighth house, the ☽ in ♒, and both the ☽ and ⊕ under a parallel of ♄'s declination, and ⊕ applied to the hostile rays of the malefics, which threatens drowning, according to the doctrine of Ptolemy, in the chapter of death.

What wonder, therefore, if this unhappy infant met

with the abovementioned fate, and came into the world attended with nothing but sickness?

It is rather wonderful he survived; the reason he did, was, perhaps, owing to the cosmical parallel of ♃ concurring to that part; which, if any chooses, he may calculate, and will find it follow.

But, ♃ being so very unfortunate, and alone, against two enemies, could be of no service; and, it is worthy of observation, that, at the 20th hour of the 7th of March, in which this infant was drowned, ♂ went over the middle of the fifth house, that is, in ♉ of the mundane place of the ⊕, and ♄ was in the middle of the second, in □ of the same; so that we know there was no other place of the ⊕, except that which we have calculated: and this method, concerning it, is certainly conformable to reason, and also experience.

Receive, my very courteous reader, this secret in Astrology, as truly worthy, and not taken from the common professors of this art, but freely communicated by the truly learned Negusantius.

And, may the conclusion of the whole work turn to the praise of ALMIGHTY GOD.

ADIEU.

From what has been said in this Canon, and its exemplification, the following conclusions are to be drawn as to ⊕, viz. That ⊕ is the mundane place of the ☽ at ☉ rise; and, consequently, has the ☽'s declination, both in quantity and denomination. And if ⊕ remains in the same hemisphere as the ☽, it has the ☽'s arc and horary times; but, if the ☽ and ⊕ are in different hemispheres, ⊕ will have the complement of the arc and horary times of the ☽.

The ⊕ cannot be directed *in mundo* converse, because it is not affected by the rapt motion; nor can it be directed to the aspects in the zodiac, either direct or converse, except only the zodiacal parallels, and, of them, only such as the ☽ falls upon, and at the same time with the ☽. The ⊕ hath no determinate latitude, but its latitude is constantly varying, and it is rarely, by position, in the ecliptic; and whatever configuration the ☉ has to the ascendant, the same has the ☽ to the ⊕, as Ptolemy declares in Lib. III, cap. xiii, Quad. by Leo Allatius, page 184. *" Hanc itaque ⊕ vero, quæ semper die, ac nocte colligitur; ut quam habet rationem, & positum ☉ ad horoscopum, eandem habeat ☽ & ad ⊕ sit veluti lunaris horoscopus."* And which is most elegantly and demonstrably proved by Cardan, in his Commentary upon the Quadripartite, folio edition, printed at Basil in 1578, page 359, which, for its peculiar beauty and simplicity, I will here insert, with the diagram by which its relative situation is proved by mathematical demonstration.

Cardan says, " If the ☽ is going from the ☌ to the ☍ of the ☉,
" then the ☽ follows the ☉, and ⊕ is always under the earth,
" from the ascendant; but if the ☽ has passed the ☍, she goes
" before the ☉, and ⊕ is before the ascendant, and always above
" the earth. Which is thus shewn:

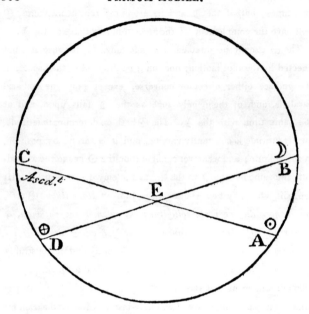

"Let the ☉ be in A, the ☽ in B, and draw the line AC, from
"the ☉ to the ascendant, and, from the ☽, BD equal to AC:
"then it is demonstrated in the third of the Elements of Euclid,
"that the arc BD is equal to the arc AC. Subtract AD, which
"is common to both, and there remains AB, equal to CD: there-
"fore, the distance of the ☽ from the ☉, being added to the
"ascendant, there arises the place of ⊕, which is the place where
"the ☽ reflects the ☉'s rays, equal to that with which the ☉ irra-
"diates the ascendant; therefore the place of ⊕ is had, by adding
"the distance of the ☽ from the ☉, to the ascendant." By which
it appears, that Cardan had a good general idea of ⊕, but his error,
in computing its place, arose from his taking it in the ecliptic instead
of taking it upon the parallel of the ☽'s declination.

Addenda.

URBAN THE EIGHTH.

(FROM THE AUTHOR'S CELESTIAL PHILOSOPHY.)

THIS curious nativity being referred to, by the Author, in Canon XXXVIII, page 108, it was deemed proper to subjoin it to the present work, as an illustration of that Canon.

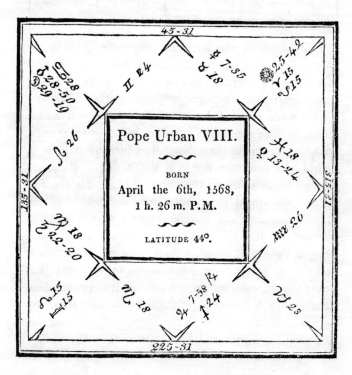

P.	Latitudes.		Arcs.		Horary Times.		Rt. Ascension.	
♄	2°	37' N.	84°	53'	14°	8'	173°	58'
♃	1	15 N.	110	24	18	23	246	23
♂	2	13 N.	112	53	18	49	121	24
☉	0	0	99	26	16	38	23	49
♀	0	3 S.	83	50	13	57	344	43
☿	0	7 N.	103	39	17	17	35	11
☽	4	50 S.	106	50	17	48	120	26

THE cause of this fortunate constitution, is, by the common professors, unanimously asserted to be, Cor Leonis in the ascendant and in △ with the ☉, from the ninth house, in the sign ♈; but neither have any weight with me, for I can affirm, of my own knowledge, to have seen many genitures of unfortunate men, with Cor Leonis in the ascendant and tenth, and the ☉ beheld, by fortunate rays, in the zodiac. But, according to my opinion, the principal cause was the fortunate position of the luminaries, the satellites of the ☉ being benefics, and angular; for the ☉ is in ✶ to ♀ *in mundo* (as it is in the first, and many of the examples brought by Argol, which I have long ago examined), and also in zodiacal parallel with ♀, by reason it has nearly the same declination: moreover, it is in mundane parallel with ♃, namely, at the same distance from the *medium cœli* that ♃ is from the *imum cœli*, and applies to a sesqui-quadrate and biquintile of ♃ in the zodiac. Lastly, it is in △ to Cor Leonis, with which it is fa-

PRIMUM MOBILE. 321

vourably conjoined in the zodiac, and effects, with the same, all the rest of the familiarities. The ☽ is upon the cusp of the twelfth house, with the fixed stars Canis Major and Minor, in parallel with ♃ and ☿, in the zodiac, ♀ is descending with Lucida Fidiculæ to a quintile with the *medium cœli;* to which the ☉, by converse direction, arrived in 56 years. At 76 years and 3 months, the ☉ came to the west, and it happened that ♀ was interposed, which added some small time, but ♄'s ☍ succeeding, diminished more than ♀ added; then ♃'s △ from the cusp of the third house, superadded more time than was diminished by ♄. Lastly, ♂ lustrates a greater space, by his quintile ray from the *medium cœli,* than all the rest, whence he diminishes more than all the others. ☿, who is mixed with the ✶ of ♀, and sesqui-quadrate of ♄, neither gives nor takes away by his ✶.

The calculation of the Directions by Canon XXXVIII.

	ARCS.	
♀'s ☌ to the west	23°	2'
♄'s ☍ to ditto	33	20
♃'s △ to ditto	57	38
♂'s □ to ditto	75	53
☉'s ☌ to ditto	77	44

Proportional Parts.

♀, As 167° 40' : 13° 57' :: 23° 2' : 1° 54' +.
♄, As 169 46 : 14 8 :: 33 20 : 2 37 —.
♃, As 220 48 : 18 23 :: 57 38 : 4 47 +.
♂, As 225 46 : 18 49 :: 75 53 : 6 16 —.

U u

$♃ + ♀ = 6° 41'$. $♄ + ♂ = 8° 53'$; their difference $= 2° 12'$ to be subtracted from the ☉'s arc to the west $= 77° 44'$, and there remains the arc of direction of the ☉ to the west, diminished by the addition and subtraction of the fortunate and unfortunate stars $= 75° 32'$. For the equation, I add this arc to the ☉'s right ascension, and the sum is $99° 21'$, answering to $8° 35'$ of ♋, to which the ☉ arrives in 76 days and a quarter. At which place is found the □ of ♂ to the west, just before the ☉ descended, that is, nearly $2°$, and is a great proof that I am right in my opinion.

Urban the Eighth was a Florentine, and succeeded Gregory the Fifteenth in the Papal Chair. At the time of his election disputes ran so extremely high, that ten cardinals lost their lives on this occasion. In the year 1626, Urban had the honour of consecrating St. Peter's church at Rome, which was performed with pomp and splendour equal to the magnificence of the structure. That the grandeur of the apostolical chair might be the more advanced, in 1631, he gave to the cardinals the title of Eminence, forbidding them to acknowledge any other appellation. There was a conspiracy against his life in 1633, but which was detected, and its authors punished. In 1634, he issued a bull, compelling the cardinals and bishops to residence. Prideaux, in his Introduction to History, says, that the cardinals had long wished for a vacancy by the death of Urban, and were afraid he would have outsat St. Peter. He was a man of great abilities, and a good poet.

TABLES

OF

𝔇𝔢𝔠𝔩𝔦𝔫𝔞𝔱𝔦𝔬𝔫, 𝔑𝔦𝔤𝔥𝔱 𝔄𝔰𝔠𝔢𝔫𝔰𝔦𝔬𝔫,

ASCENSIONAL DIFFERENCE,

CREPUSCULINES,

AND

PROPORTIONAL LOGARITHMS,

FOR COMPUTING

THE ARCS OF DIRECTION.

Introduction to the tables

It should be noted that the tables included with this, the 1814 edition are not those of the original 1657 edition of *Tabulae Primi Mobilis*. As the translator, John Cooper, explains on page *vi* of his introduction, they were considered too inaccurate for reproduction. In consequence he replaced them with the best tables available in 1814. However, rather than omit them entirely as being unrepresentative of Placido, the first pages of each section have been retained.

PRIMUM MOBILE,

TABLES

OF

DECLINATION.

North Latitude.

♈	0		1		2		3		4		5		6		7		8		9		
	D.	M.	D.	M.	D.	M.	D.	M.	D.	M.	D.	M.	D.	M.	D.	M.	D.	M.	D.	M.	
0	23	32	24	32	25	32	26	31	27	32	28	32	29	32	30	32	31	32	32	32	30
1	23	31	24	31	25	31	26	31	27	31	28	31	29	31	30	31	31	31	32	31	29
2	23	31	24	31	25	31	26	32	27	31	28	31	29	31	30	31	31	31	32	31	28
3	23	30	24	30	25	30	26	30	27	30	28	30	29	30	30	30	31	30	32	30	27
4	23	28	24	29	25	28	26	28	27	28	28	28	29	28	30	28	31	28	32	28	26
5	23	26	24	26	25	26	26	26	27	26	28	26	29	26	30	26	31	26	32	26	25
6	23	23	24	23	25	23	26	23	27	22	28	22	29	22	30	22	31	22	32	22	24
7	23	20	24	20	25	20	26	20	27	19	28	19	29	19	30	19	31	19	32	19	23
8	23	17	24	17	25	17	26	16	27	16	28	16	29	16	30	16	31	16	32	15	22
9	23	13	24	13	25	13	26	13	27	12	28	12	29	12	30	12	31	12	32	12	21
10	23	9	24	9	25	9	26	9	27	8	28	8	29	8	30	8	31	8	32	8	20
11	23	4	24	4	25	4	26	4	27	2	28	3	29	3	30	3	31	3	32	3	19
12	22	59	23	59	24	59	25	59	26	58	27	58	28	58	29	57	30	57	31	57	18
13	22	53	23	53	24	53	25	53	26	54	27	52	28	52	29	51	30	51	31	51	17
14	22	47	23	47	24	46	25	46	26	46	27	45	28	45	29	45	30	44	31	44	16
15	22	41	23	41	24	40	25	40	26	40	27	39	28	39	29	39	30	38	31	38	15
16	22	34	23	34	24	33	25	33	26	33	27	32	28	32	29	32	30	31	31	31	14
17	22	27	23	27	24	26	25	2	26	25	27	25	28	24	29	24	30	24	31	23	13
18	22	19	23	19	24	18	25	18	26	17	27	16	28	16	29	16	30	15	31	15	12
19	22	10	23	10	24	9	25	8	26	8	27	7	28	6	29	6	30	5	31	5	11
20	22	2	23	2	24	1	25	0	25	59	26	58	27	57	28	57	29	56	30	55	10
21	21	53	23	52	24	51	25	50	26	49	27	48	28	48	29	47	30	46			9
22	21	43	22	43	23	42	24	41	25	40	26	39	27	38	28	38	29	37	30	36	8
23	21	33	22	33	23	32	24	31	25	30	26	29	27	28	28	28	29	27	30	25	7
24	21	23	22	22	23	21	24	20	25	19	26	18	27	17	28	16	29	15	30	14	6
25	21	13	22	11	23	10	24	9	25	8	26	7	27	6	28	5	29	4	30	3	5
26	21	1	22	0	22	59	23	58	24	57	25	56	26	55	27	54	28	53	29	52	4
27	20	50	21	48	22	47	23	46	24	45	25	44	26	43	27	42	28	41	29	40	3
28	20	38	21	36	22	35	23	34	24	33	25	32	26	30	27	29	28	28	29	27	2
29	20	26	21	23	22	22	23	21	24	20	25	19	26	17	27	16	28	15	29	14	1
30	20	13	21	12	22	10	23	9	24	7	25	6	26	4	27	3	28	1	28	59	0
																					♍

PRIMUM MOBILE.

TABLES

OF

DECLINATION.

South Latitude.

♋	0		1		2		3		4		5		6		7		8		9		
	D.	M.	D.	M.	D.	M.	D.	M.	D.	M.	D.	M.	D.	M.	D.	M.	D.	M.	D.	M	
0	23	32	22	32	21	32	20	32	19	32	18	32	17	32	16	32	15	32	14	32	30
1	23	31	22	31	21	31	20	31	19	31	18	31	17	31	16	31	15	31	14	31	29
2	23	31	22	31	21	31	20	31	19	31	18	31	17	31	16	31	15	31	14	31	28
3	23	30	22	30	21	30	20	30	19	30	18	30	17	30	16	30	15	30	14	30	27
4	23	28	22	28	21	28	20	28	19	28	18	28	17	28	16	28	15	28	14	28	26
5	23	26	22	26	21	26	20	26	19	26	18	26	17	26	16	26	15	26	14	26	25
6	23	23	22	23	21	23	20	23	19	23	18	23	17	23	16	23	15	23	14	23	24
7	23	20	22	20	21	20	20	20	19	20	18	20	17	20	16	20	15	20	14	20	23
8	23	17	22	17	21	17	20	17	19	17	18	17	17	17	16	17	15	17	14	17	22
9	23	13	22	13	21	13	20	13	19	13	18	13	17	13	16	13	15	14	14	14	21
10	23	9	22	9	21	9	20	9	19	9	18	9	17	10	16	10	15	10	14	10	20
11	23	4	22	4	21	4	20	4	19	5	18	5	17	5	16	5	15	6	14	6	19
12	22	59	21	59	20	59	19	59	19	0	18	0	17	0	16	1	15	1	14	1	18
13	22	53	21	53	20	53	19	53	18	54	17	54	16	54	15	55	14	55	13	55	17
14	22	47	21	47	20	47	19	47	18	48	17	48	16	48	15	49	14	49	13	49	16
15	22	41	21	41	20	41	19	41	18	42	17	42	16	42	15	43	14	43	13	43	15
16	22	34	21	35	20	35	19	35	18	36	17	36	16	36	15	37	14	37	13	37	14
17	22	27	21	28	20	28	19	28	18	29	17	29	16	29	15	30	14	30	13	30	13
18	22	19	21	20	20	20	19	21	18	21	17	21	16	21	15	22	14	23	13	23	12
19	22	10	21	11	20	11	19	12	18	13	17	13	16	13	15	14	14	15	13	15	11
20	22	2	21	3	20	4	19	4	18	5	17	5	16	5	15	6	14	7	13	7	10
21	21	53	20	54	19	55	18	56	17	57	16	57	15	58	14	58	13	59	12	59	9
22	21	43	20	44	19	45	18	46	17	47	16	47	15	48	14	48	13	49	12	49	8
23	21	33	20	34	19	35	18	36	17	37	16	37	15	38	14	39	13	40	12	40	7
24	21	23	20	24	19	25	18	26	17	27	16	28	15	28	14	29	13	30	12	31	6
25	21	13	20	14	19	15	18	16	17	17	16	18	15	19	14	20	13	21	12	22	5
26	21	1	20	2	19	3	18	4	17	5	16	7	15	8	14	9	13	10	12	11	4
27	20	50	19	51	18	52	17	53	16	54	15	56	14	57	13	58	12	59	12	0	3
28	20	38	19	39	18	40	17	41	16	42	15	44	14	45	13	46	12	47	11	48	2
29	20	26	19	27	18	28	17	29	16	30	15	32	14	33	13	34	12	35	11	37	1
30	20	13	19	14	18	15	17	17	16	18	15	19	14	20	13	21	12	23	11	24	0

PRIMUM MOBILE.

TABLES

OF

RIGHT ASCENSION.

North Latitude.

♈	0		1		2		3		4		5		6		7		8		9	
	D.	M.	D.	M.	D.	M.	D.	M.	D.	M.	D.	M.	D.	M.	D.	M.	D.	M.	D.	M.
0	0	0	359	37	359	13	358	49	358	25	358	1	357	37	357	13	356	48	356	23
1	0	55	0	6	0	8	359	44	359	20	358	58	358	32	358	8	357	43	357	18
2	1	50	1	27	1	3	0	39	0	15	359	51	359	27	359	3	358	38	358	13
3	2	45	2	22	1	58	1	34	1	10	0	46	0	22	359	58	359	34	359	9
4	3	40	3	17	2	53	2	29	2	5	1	41	1	17	0	53	0	29	0	4
5	4	35	4	12	3	48	3	24	3	0	2	36	2	12	1	48	1	24	0	59
6	5	30	5	7	4	43	4	19	3	55	3	31	3	7	2	43	2	19	1	54
7	6	25	6	2	5	38	5	14	4	50	4	26	4	2	3	38	3	14	2	49
8	7	21	6	57	6	33	6	9	5	45	5	21	4	57	4	33	4	9	3	44
9	8	16	7	52	7	28	7	4	6	40	6	16	5	52	5	28	5	4	4	39
10	9	11	8	47	8	23	7	59	7	35	7	11	6	47	6	23	5	59	5	34
11	10	6	9	42	9	18	8	55	8	31	8	7	7	43	7	19	6	55	6	30
12	11	2	10	38	10	14	9	51	9	27	9	3	8	39	8	15	7	51	7	26
13	11	57	11	33	11	9	10	46	10	22	9	58	9	34	9	10	8	46	8	22
14	12	53	12	29	12	5	11	42	11	18	10	54	10	30	10	6	9	42	9	18
15	13	48	13	25	13	1	12	38	12	14	11	50	11	26	11	2	10	38	10	14
16	14	44	14	20	13	57	13	34	13	10	12	46	12	22	11	58	11	34	11	10
17	15	40	15	16	14	53	14	30	14	6	13	42	13	18	12	54	12	30	12	6
18	16	31	16	12	15	49	15	26	15	2	14	39	14	15	13	51	13	27	13	3
19	17	35	17	8	16	45	16	22	15	58	15	35	15	11	14	47	14	23	13	59
20	18	27	18	4	17	41	17	18	16	54	16	31	16	7	15	43	15	20	14	56
21	19	23	19	0	18	37	18	14	17	51	17	28	17	4	16	41	16	17	15	53
22	20	20	19	57	19	33	19	11	18	48	18	25	18	1	17	38	17	14	16	50
23	21	16	20	53	20	30	20	8	19	45	19	22	18	58	18	35	18	11	17	47
24	22	12	21	50	21	27	21	5	20	42	20	19	19	55	19	32	19	8	18	44
25	23	9	22	47	22	24	22	2	21	39	21	16	20	52	20	29	20	5	19	41
26	24	6	23	44	23	21	22	59	22	36	22	13	21	50	21	27	21	3	20	39
27	25	2	24	41	24	19	23	57	23	34	23	11	22	48	22	25	22	1	21	37
28	25	59	25	38	25	16	24	54	24	31	24	9	23	46	23	23	22	59	22	35
29	26	57	26	35	26	13	25	51	25	29	25	7	24	44	24	21	23	57	23	34
30	27	54	27	33	27	11	26	49	26	27	26	5	25	42	25	19	24	56	24	52

PRIMUM MOBILE.

TABLES
OF
RIGHT ASCENSION.

South Latitude.

♈	0		1		2		3		4		5		6		7		8		9	
	D.	M.	D.	M.	D.	M.	D.	M.	D.	M.	D.	M.	D.	M.	D.	M.	D.	M.	D.	M.
0	0	0	0	23	0	47	1	11	1	35	1	59	2	23	2	47	3	12	3	36
1	0	55	1	18	1	42	2	6	2	30	2	54	3	18	3	42	4	6	4	30
2	1	50	2	13	2	57	3	1	3	25	3	49	4	13	4	37	5	1	5	25
3	2	45	3	8	3	32	3	56	4	20	4	44	5	8	5	32	5	56	6	20
4	3	40	4	3	4	2	4	51	5	15	5	39	6	3	6	27	6	51	7	15
5	4	35	4	58	5	22	5	46	6	10	6	34	6	58	7	22	7	46	8	9
6	5	30	5	54	6	18	6	42	7	6	7	30	7	53	8	17	8	41	9	4
7	6	25	6	49	7	13	7	37	8	1	8	25	8	48	9	12	9	36	9	59
8	7	21	7	44	8	8	8	32	8	56	9	20	9	43	10	7	10	30	10	53
9	8	16	8	40	9	4	9	28	9	51	10	15	10	38	11	2	11	25	11	48
10	9	11	9	35	9	59	10	23	10	46	11	10	11	33	11	57	12	19	12	42
11	10	6	10	30	10	54	11	18	11	41	12	5	12	28	12	52	13	14	13	37
12	11	2	11	25	11	49	12	13	12	36	13	0	13	23	13	47	14	9	14	32
13	11	57	12	20	12	44	13	8	13	31	13	55	14	18	14	41	15	4	15	27
14	12	53	13	16	13	39	14	3	14	26	14	50	15	13	15	36	15	59	16	21
15	13	48	14	12	14	35	14	58	15	21	15	45	16	8	16	31	16	54	17	16
16	14	44	15	7	15	30	15	53	16	16	16	40	17	3	17	26	17	49	18	11
17	15	40	16	2	16	25	16	48	17	11	17	35	17	58	18	21	18	44	19	6
18	16	35	16	58	17	21	17	44	18	7	18	30	18	53	19	16	19	39	20	1
19	17	31	17	54	18	17	18	40	19	2	19	25	19	48	20	11	20	34	20	56
20	18	27	18	50	19	13	19	36	19	58	20	21	20	43	21	7	21	29	21	51
21	19	23	19	46	20	9	20	23	20	54	21	17	21	39	22	2	22	24	22	46
22	20	20	20	42	21	5	21	28	21	50	22	12	22	34	22	57	23	19	23	41
23	21	16	21	38	22	1	22	24	22	46	23	8	23	30	23	52	24	14	24	36
24	22	12	22	35	22	57	23	20	23	42	24	4	24	26	24	48	25	10	25	32
25	23	9	23	31	23	53	24	16	24	38	25	0	25	21	25	43	26	5	26	27
26	24	6	24	28	24	50	25	12	25	34	25	55	26	17	26	39	27	0	27	22
27	25	2	25	25	25	47	26	9	26	30	26	52	27	13	27	35	27	56	28	17
28	25	59	26	22	26	43	27	5	27	26	27	48	28	9	28	30	28	51	29	12
29	26	5	27	19	27	40	28	1	28	22	28	44	29	5	29	26	29	47	30	8
30	27	51	28	16	28	37	28	58	29	19	29	40	30	1	30	22	30	43	31	4

PRIMUM MOBILE.

TABLES
OF
ASCENSIONAL DIFFERENCE

For finding the Oblique Ascension or Descension, Semidiurnal or Nocturnal Arcs or Horary Times, for any Degree of Latitude.

Ele. P.i.	1		2		3		4		5		6		7		8		9		10	
D.	D.	M	D.	M	D.	M	D.	M	D.	M	D.	M	D.	M	D.	M	D.	M	D.	M
1	0	1	0	2	0	3	0	4	0	5	0	6	0	7	0	8	0	9	0	11
2	0	2	0	4	0	6	0	8	0	10	0	13	0	15	0	7	0	19	0	21
3	0	3	0	6	0	9	0	13	0	16	0	19	0	22	0	25	0	29	0	32
4	0	4	0	8	0	13	0	17	0	21	0	25	0	30	0	34	0	38	0	42
5	0	5	0	10	0	16	0	21	0	26	0	32	0	37	0	42	0	48	0	53
6	0	6	0	13	0	19	0	25	0	32	0	38	0	44	0	51	0	57	1	4
7	0	7	0	15	0	22	0	30	0	37	0	44	0	52	0	59	1	7	1	14
8	0	8	0	17	0	25	0	34	0	42	0	51	0	59	1	8	1	16	1	25
9	0	9	0	19	0	29	0	38	0	48	0	57	1	7	1	16	1	26	1	36
10	0	11	0	21	0	32	0	42	0	53	1	4	1	14	1	25	1	36	1	47
11	0	12	0	23	0	35	0	47	0	58	1	10	1	22	1	34	1	46	1	58
12	0	13	0	25	0	38	0	51	1	4	1	17	1	30	1	43	1	56	2	9
13	0	14	0	28	0	42	0	56	1	9	1	23	1	37	1	52	2	6	2	20
14	0	15	0	30	0	45	1	0	1	15	1	30	1	45	2	1	2	16	2	31
15	0	16	0	32	0	48	1	4	1	21	1	37	1	53	2	10	2	26	2	42
16	0	17	0	34	0	52	1	9	1	26	1	44	2	1	2	19	2	36	2	54
17	0	18	0	37	0	55	1	14	1	32	1	50	2	9	2	28	2	47	3	5
18	0	19	0	39	0	59	1	18	1	38	1	57	2	17	2	37	2	57	3	17
19	0	21	0	41	1	2	1	23	1	44	2	4	2	25	2	46	3	8	3	29
20	0	22	0	44	1	6	1	27	1	49	2	12	2	34	2	56	3	18	3	41
21	0	23	0	46	1	9	1	32	1	55	2	19	2	41	3	6	3	29	3	53
22	0	24	0	49	1	13	1	37	2	2	2	26	2	50	3	15	3	40	4	5
23	0	25	0	51	1	17	1	42	2	8	2	33	2	59	3	25	3	51	4	18
24	0	27	0	53	1	20	1	47	2	14	2	41	3	9	3	35	4	3	4	30
25	0	28	0	56	1	24	1	52	2	20	2	49	3	17	3	45	4	14	4	43
26	0	29	0	59	1	28	1	57	2	27	2	56	3	26	3	56	4	26	4	56
27	0	31	1	1	1	32	2	3	2	33	3	4	3	35	4	6	4	38	5	9
28	0	32	1	4	1	36	2	8	2	40	3	12	3	45	4	17	4	50	5	23
29	0	33	1	7	1	40	2	13	2	47	3	20	3	54	4	28	5	2	5	37
30	0	35	1	9	1	44	2	19	2	54	3	29	4	4	4	39	5	15	5	51
31	0	36	1	12	1	48	2	24	3	1	3	37	4	14	4	51	5	28	6	5
32	0	37	1	15	1	53	2	30	3	8	3	46	4	24	5	2	5	41	6	20

Stars Declinations.

PRIMUM MOBILE.

TABLES
OF
ASCENSIONAL DIFFERENCE

For finding the Oblique Ascension or Descension, Semidiurnal or Nocturnal Arcs or Horary Times, for any Degree of Latitude.

Ele. Pol. D.	1 D. M.	2 D. M.	3 D. M.	4 D. M.	5 D. M.	6 D. M.	7 D. M.	8 D. M.	9 D. M.	10 D. M.
33	0 39	1 18	1 57	2 36	3 15	3 55	4 34	5 14	5 54	6 35
34	0 40	1 21	2 2	2 42	3 23	4 4	4 45	5 26	6 8	6 50
35	0 42	1 24	2 6	2 48	3 31	4 13	4 56	5 39	6 22	7 6
36	0 44	1 27	2 11	2 55	3 39	4 23	5 7	5 52	6 36	7 22
37	0 45	1 30	2 16	3 2	3 47	4 33	5 11	6 5	6 51	7 38
38	0 47	1 34	2 21	3 8	3 55	4 45	5 30	6 18	7 6	7 55
39	0 49	1 37	2 26	3 15	4 4	4 53	5 42	6 32	7 22	8 13
40	0 50	1 41	2 31	3 22	4 13	5 4	5 55	6 46	7 38	8 31
41	0 52	1 44	2 37	3 29	4 22	5 15	6 8	7 1	7 55	8 49
42	0 54	1 48	2 42	3 37	4 31	5 26	6 21	7 16	8 12	9 8
43	0 56	1 52	2 48	3 44	4 41	5 38	6 34	7 32	8 30	9 28
44	0 58	1 56	2 54	3 52	4 51	5 50	6 49	7 48	8 48	9 48
45	1 0	2 0	3 0	4 1	5 1	6 2	7 3	8 5	9 7	10 9
46	1 2	2 4	3 7	4 9	5 12	6 15	7 18	8 22	9 29	10 31
47	1 4	2 9	3 13	4 18	5 23	6 28	7 34	8 40	9 47	10 54
48	1 7	2 13	3 20	4 27	5 35	6 42	7 50	8 59	10 8	11 18
49	1 9	2 18	3 27	4 37	5 47	6 57	8 7	9 19	10 30	11 42
50	1 12	2 23	3 35	4 47	5 59	7 11	8 25	9 39	10 53	12 8
51	1 14	2 28	3 43	4 57	6 12	7 27	8 43	10 0	11 17	12 35
52	1 17	2 34	3 51	5 8	6 26	7 44	9 3	10 22	11 42	13 3
53	1 20	2 39	3 59	5 19	6 40	8 1	9 23	10 45	12 8	13 32
54	1 23	2 45	4 8	5 31	6 55	8 19	9 44	11 9	12 35	14 3
55	1 26	2 52	4 18	5 44	7 11	8 38	10 6	11 35	13 4	14 35
56	1 29	2 58	4 27	5 57	7 27	8 58	10 29	12 2	13 35	15 9
57	1 32	3 5	4 38	6 11	7 44	9 19	10 54	12 30	14 7	15 45
58	1 36	3 12	4 49	6 26	8 2	9 41	11 20	13 0	14 41	16 23
59	1 40	3 20	5 0	6 41	8 22	10 4	11 48	13 32	15 17	17 4
60	1 44	3 28	5 12	6 57	8 43	10 29	12 17	14 5	15 55	17 47
61	1 48	3 37	5 25	7 15	9 5	10 56	12 48	14 45	16 36	18 33
62	1 53	3 46	5 39	7 33	9 28	11 24	13 21	15 20	17 20	19 22
63	1 58	3 56	5 54	7 53	9 53	11 54	13 57	16 1	18 7	20 15
64	2 3	4 6	6 10	8 15	10 20	12 27	14 55	16 45	18 57	21 21

(Stars Declinations.)

PRIMUM MOBILE.

TABLE

OF

THE POLES OF THE HOUSES,

According to PTOLEMY.

Latitude.	11th and 3d Poles.	12th and 2d Poles.	Latitude.	11th and 3d Poles.	12th and 2d Poles.
D.	D. M.	D. M.	D.	D. M.	D. M.
1	0 20	0 40	31	11 25	21 58
2	0 40	1 19	32	11 52	22 47
3	1 0	1 59	33	12 19	23 35
4	1 19	2 40	34	12 48	24 24
5	1 38	3 20	35	13 17	25 13
6	1 57	4 0	36	13 46	26 4
7	2 19	4 41	37	14 17	26 55
8	2 39	5 22	38	14 49	27 46
9	2 59	6 3	39	15 20	28 38
10	3 21	6 43	40	15 52	29 33
11	3 42	7 24	41	16 25	30 25
12	4 4	8 5	42	16 59	31 22
13	4 24	8 45	43	17 36	32 16
14	4 44	9 26	44	18 13	33 13
15	5 5	10 8	45	18 50	34 11
16	5 27	10 49	46	19 28	35 9
17	5 49	11 31	47	20 7	36 8
18	6 11	12 13	48	20 49	37 8
19	6 33	12 56	49	21 33	38 10
20	6 55	13 39	50	22 17	39 11
21	7 17	14 22	51	23 4	40 16
22	7 41	15 5	52	23 51	41 20
23	8 55	15 49	53	24 40	42 26
24	8 29	16 34	54	25 34	43 32
25	8 53	17 19	55	26 29	44 41
26	9 11	18 4	56	27 25	45 51
27	9 43	18 50	57	28 21	47 0
28	10 8	19 35	58	29 25	48 13
29	10 34	20 22	59	30 30	49 26
30	11 0	21 9	60	31 39	50 42
	9 & 5	8 & 6		9 & 5	8 & 6

PRIMUM MOBILE.

A

TABLE OF TWILIGHT,

Shewing the Crepusculine Circles for the Latitude of 44 Degrees.

Pa.	0		♋ 10		20		0		♌ 10		20		0		♍ 10		20		30	
3	5	9	5	6	4	59	4	50	4	41	4	30	4	22	4	16	4	13	4	10
4	6	55	6	52	6	42	6	30	6	16	6	3	5	59	5	43	5	38	5	34
5	8	42	8	39	8	26	8	11	7	52	7	34	7	19	7	9	7	2	6	58
6	10	32	10	26	10	11	9	52	9	30	9	8	8	49	8	36	8	27	8	21
7	12	24	12	17	11	59	11	36	11	9	10	43	10	20	10	4	8	52	9	45
8	14	19	14	12	13	51	13	22	12	50	12	19	11	52	11	32	11	18	11	9
9	16	17	16	9	15	44	15	11	14	32	13	55	13	24	13	0	12	44	12	33
10	18	18	18	7	17	38	16	58	16	14	15	33	14	56	14	29	14	10	13	58
11	20	23	20	9	19	35	18	53	17	59	17	12	16	30	15	59	15	37	15	23
12	22	31	22	17	21	38	20	45	19	47	18	53	18	6	17	30	17	4	16	48
13	24	45	24	28	23	45	22	40	21	37	20	35	19	42	19	1	18	32	17	13
14	27	5	26	44	25	14	24	44	23	30	22	19	21	19	20	33	20	1	19	39
15	29	32	29	10	28	10	26	49	25	24	24	6	22	59	22	6	21	30	21	4
16	32	7	31	45	30	32	28	59	27	23	25	54	24	38	23	41	22	59	22	32
17	34	46	34	27	33	2	31	16	29	25	27	45	26	20	25	19	24	30	23	59
18	37	32	37	16	35	40	33	38	31	30	20	38	28	0	26	55	26	3	25	26
	30		♊ 20		10		0		♉ 20		10		0		♈ 20		10		0	

Pa.	0		♎ 10		20		0		♏ 10		20		0		♐ 10		20		30	
3	4	10	4	12	4	13	4	19	4	26	4	35	4	41	4	48	4	52	4	55
4	5	34	5	35	5	37	5	44	5	53	6	5	6	13	6	22	6	28	6	30
5	6	58	6	58	7	1	7	9	7	20	7	34	7	44	7	56	8	3	8	5
6	8	21	8	21	8	25	8	34	8	47	9	3	9	15	9	28	9	37	9	40
7	9	45	9	44	9	48	9	56	10	13	10	31	10	45	11	0	11	10	11	13
8	11	9	11	7	11	13	11	21	11	39	11	59	12	14	12	31	12	42	12	45
9	12	33	12	31	12	36	12	46	13	4	13	25	13	42	14	1	14	13	14	16
10	13	58	13	55	13	59	14	12	14	29	14	52	15	11	15	30	15	44	15	48
11	15	23	15	19	15	23	15	35	15	51	16	17	16	49	16	59	17	14	17	18
12	16	48	16	43	16	47	16	59	16	19	18	42	18	6	18	28	18	43	18	47
13	18	13	18	7	18	10	18	22	18	45	19	9	19	32	19	56	20	12	20	17
14	19	39	19	31	19	33	19	46	20	12	20	36	20	59	21	24	21	41	21	46
15	21	4	20	55	20	55	21	8	21	34	22	1	22	25	22	51	23	9	23	13
16	22	32	22	19	22	20	22	33	22	55	23	26	23	51	24	17	24	36	24	42
17	23	59	23	44	23	44	23	57	24	19	24	51	25	17	25	44	26	3	26	7
18	25	26	25	9	25	8	25	20	25	43	26	15	26	42	27	10	27	30	27	37
	30		♓ 20		10		0		♒ 20		10		0		♑ 20		10		0	

PRIMUM MOBILE.

A TABLE OF HOUSES,

For the Latitude of 51 Degrees 32 Minutes,
According to PTOLEMY.

Time from noon.		10 ♈	11 ♉	12 ♊	Ascen. ♋		2 ♌	3 ♍	Time from noon.		10 ♉	11 ♊	12 ♋	Ascen. ♌		2 ♍	3 ♎
H.	M.	gr	gr	gr	Gr.	M.	gr	gr	H.	M.	gr	gr	gr	Gr.	M.	gr	gr
0	0	0	9	22	26	42	12	3	1	52	0	9	17	16	31	4	29
0	4	1	10	23	27	23	13	3	1	55	1	10	18	17	11	5	29
0	7	2	11	24	28	2	14	4	1	59	2	11	19	17	51	6	♎
0	11	3	12	25	28	48	15	5	2	3	3	12	19	18	31	7	1
0	15	4	13	25	29	21	15	6	2	7	4	13	20	19	12	8	2
0	18	5	14	26	0 ♌	1	16	7	2	11	5	14	21	19	52	9	2
0	22	6	15	27	0	40	17	8	2	15	6	15	22	20	32	9	3
0	26	7	16	28	1	20	18	8	2	19	7	16	22	21	13	10	4
0	29	8	17	29	2	0	18	9	2	23	8	17	23	21	54	11	5
0	33	9	18	♋	2	39	19	10	2	26	9	18	24	22	35	11	6
0	37	10	19	1	3	19	20	11	2	30	10	19	25	23	16	12	7
0	40	11	20	1	3	59	20	12	2	34	11	20	25	23	57	13	8
0	44	12	22	2	4	38	21	13	2	38	12	21	26	24	38	14	9
0	48	13	23	3	5	17	22	14	2	42	13	22	27	25	19	14	10
0	51	14	24	4	5	57	23	15	2	46	14	23	28	26	0	15	11
0	55	15	25	5	6	36	23	15	2	50	15	24	29	26	42	16	12
0	59	16	26	6	7	15	24	16	2	54	16	25	29	27	24	17	13
1	3	17	27	6	7	55	25	17	2	58	17	26	♌	28	6	18	13
1	6	18	28	7	8	35	26	18	3	2	18	26	1	28	47	18	14
1	10	19	29	8	9	14	26	19	3	6	19	27	2	29	30	19	15
1	14	20	♊	9	9	53	27	19	3	10	20	28	3	0 ♍	13	20	16
1	18	21	1	10	10	34	28	20	3	14	21	29	3	0	55	21	17
1	21	22	2	10	11	12	28	21	3	18	22	♋	4	1	37	22	18
1	25	23	3	11	11	52	29	22	3	22	23	1	5	2	20	22	19
1	29	24	4	12	12	32	♍	23	3	26	24	2	6	3	2	23	20
1	33	25	5	13	13	12	1	24	3	31	25	3	7	3	46	24	21
1	36	26	6	14	13	52	1	25	3	35	26	4	7	4	29	25	22
1	40	27	7	14	14	32	2	25	3	39	27	5	8	5	12	26	23
1	44	28	7	15	15	12	3	26	3	43	28	6	9	5	55	27	24
1	48	29	8	16	15	51	4	27	3	47	29	7	10	6	39	27	25
1	52	30	9	17	16	31	4	28	3	51	30	8	11	7	22	28	25

APPENDIX TO

A TABLE OF HOUSES,

For the Latitude of 51 Degrees 32 Minutes,

According to PTOLEMY.

Time from noon.		10 ♊	11 ♋	12 ♌	Ascen. ♍		2 ♍	3 ♎		Time from noon.		10 ♋	11 ♌	12 ♍	Ascen. ♎		2 ♎	3 ♏
H.	M.	gr	gr	gr	gr.	m.	gr	gr	H.	M.	gr	gr	gr	gr.	m.	gr	gr
3	51	0	8	11	7	22	28	25	6	0	0	6	6	0	0	24	24
3	55	1	9	12	8	0	29	26	6	4	1	7	7	0	47	25	25
4	0	2	10	12	8	50	♎	27	6	9	2	8	8	1	33	26	26
4	4	3	10	13	9	34	1	28	6	13	3	9	9	2	19	27	27
4	8	4	11	14	10	18	2	29	6	17	4	10	10	3	5	27	28
4	12	5	12	15	11	3	2	♏	6	22	5	11	10	3	51	28	29
4	16	6	13	16	11	47	3	1	6	26	6	12	11	4	27	29	♐
4	21	7	14	17	12	31	4	2	6	31	7	13	12	5	23	♏	1
4	25	8	15	17	13	16	5	3	6	35	8	14	13	6	9	1	2
4	29	9	16	18	14	1	6	4	6	39	9	15	14	6	55	2	3
4	33	10	17	19	14	46	7	5	6	41	10	16	15	7	40	2	4
4	38	11	18	20	15	31	8	6	6	48	11	16	16	8	26	3	4
4	42	12	19	21	16	16	8	7	6	52	12	17	16	9	12	4	5
4	46	13	20	21	17	1	9	8	6	57	13	18	17	9	57	5	6
4	51	14	21	22	17	46	10	9	7	1	14	19	18	10	41	6	7
4	55	15	22	23	18	31	11	10	7	5	15	20	19	11	28	7	8
4	59	16	23	24	19	17	12	11	7	9	16	21	20	12	14	8	9
5	3	17	24	25	20	4	13	12	7	14	17	22	21	12	59	8	10
5	8	18	25	26	20	49	14	13	7	18	18	23	22	13	45	9	11
5	12	19	25	27	21	35	14	14	7	22	19	24	22	14	30	10	12
5	16	20	26	28	22	20	15	14	7	27	20	25	23	15	14	11	13
5	21	21	27	28	23	6	16	15	7	31	21	26	24	15	59	12	14
5	25	22	28	29	23	51	17	16	7	35	22	27	25	16	44	13	15
5	29	23	29	♍	24	37	18	17	7	39	23	28	26	17	29	13	16
5	34	24	♌	1	25	25	19	18	7	44	24	29	27	18	14	14	17
5	38	25	1	2	26	9	20	19	7	48	25	♍	28	18	58	15	18
5	43	26	2	3	26	55	20	20	7	51	26	1	28	19	42	16	19
5	47	27	3	4	27	41	21	21	7	56	27	2	29	20	26	17	20
5	51	28	4	4	28	27	22	22	8	0	28	3	♎	21	10	18	20
5	56	29	5	5	29	13	23	23	8	5	29	4	1	21	54	18	21
6	0	30	6	6	30	0	24	24	8	9	30	5	2	22	38	19	22

PRIMUM MOBILE.

A TABLE OF HOUSES,

For the Latitude of 51 Degrees 32 Minutes,

According to PTOLEMY.

☉ in ♌								☉ in ♍						
Time from noon.	10 ♌	11 ♍	12 ♎	Ascen. ♎		2 ♏	3 ♐	Time from noon.	10 ♍	11 ♎	12 ♏	Ascen. ♏		2 ♐	3 ♑
H. M.	gr	gr	gr	gr.	m.	gr	gr	H. M.	gr	gr	gr	gr.	m.	gr	gr
8 9	0	5	2	22	38	19	22	10 8	0	2	26	13	30	13	20
8 13	1	5	3	23	22	20	23	10 12	1	3	26	14	9	14	21
8 17	2	6	3	24	5	21	24	10 16	2	4	27	14	49	15	22
8 21	3	7	4	24	48	22	25	10 20	3	5	28	15	29	16	23
8 25	4	8	5	25	32	23	26	10 24	4	5	29	16	9	16	24
8 29	5	9	6	26	19	23	27	10 28	5	6	29	16	48	17	25
8 34	6	10	7	26	58	24	28	10 31	6	7	♏	17	28	18	26
8 38	7	11	8	27	42	25	29	10 35	7	8	1	18	9	19	27
8 42	8	12	8	28	23	26	♐	10 39	8	9	2	18	43	20	28
8 46	9	13	9	29	6	27	1	10 42	9	10	2	19	27	20	29
8 50	10	14	10	29	48	27	2	10 46	10	1	3	20	0	21	♒
8 54	11	15	11	0♏	30	28	3	10 50	11	11	4	20	48	22	1
8 58	12	16	12	1	13	29	4	10 54	12	12	4	21	26	23	2
9 2	13	17	12	1	55	♐	4	10 57	13	13	5	22	5	24	3
9 6	14	18	13	2	36	1	5	11 1	14	14	6	22	4	24	4
9 10	15	18	14	3	18	2	6	11 5	15	15	7	23	24	25	5
9 14	16	19	15	4	0	2	7	11 9	16	16	7	24	4	26	6
9 18	17	20	16	4	41	3	8	11 12	17	17	8	24	43	27	8
9 22	18	21	16	5	21	4	9	11 16	18	17	9	25	23	28	9
9 26	19	22	17	6	4	5	10	11 20	19	18	10	26	1	29	10
9 30	20	23	18	6	45	5	11	11 23	20	19	10	26	41	♑	11
9 34	21	24	19	7	26	6	12	11 27	21	20	11	27	22	0	12
9 38	22	25	19	8	6	7	13	11 31	22	21	12	28	1	1	13
9 41	23	26	20	8	47	8	14	11 34	23	22	13	28	40	2	14
9 45	24	27	21	9	28	9	15	11 38	24	23	13	29	20	3	15
9 49	25	28	22	10	8	9	16	11 42	25	23	14	29	49	4	16
9 53	26	28	23	10	48	10	17	11 45	26	24	15	0♐	39	5	17
9 57	27	29	23	11	29	11	18	11 49	27	25	15	1	19	5	18
10 1	28	♎	24	12	9	12	19	11 53	28	26	16	2	2	6	19
10 5	29	1	25	12	50	12	20	11 56	29	26	17	2	39	7	20
10 8	30	2	26	13	30	13	20	12 0	30	27	17	3	10	8	21

APPENDIX TO

A TABLE OF HOUSES,

For the Latitude of 51 Degrees 32 Minutes,

According to PTOLEMY.

☉ in ♎.								☉ in ♏.							
Time from noon	10 ♎	11 ♎	12 ♏	Ascen. ♐		2 ♑	3 ♒	Time from noon	10 ♏	11 ♏	12 ♐	Ascen. ♐		2 ♒	3 ♓
H. M.	gr	gr	gr	gr.	m.	gr	gr	H. M.	gr	gr	gr	gr.	m.	gr	gr
12 0	0	27	17	3	15	8	21	13 51	0	22	10	25	15	10	27
12 4	1	28	18	3	59	9	22	13 55	1	23	11	26	5	11	28
12 7	2	29	19	4	49	10	24	13 59	2	24	11	26	50	12	♈
12 11	3	♏	20	5	20	11	25	14 3	3	25	12	27	47	14	1
12 15	4	1	20	6	2	12	26	14 7	4	26	13	28	59	15	2
12 18	5	1	21	6	43	13	27	14 11	5	26	14	29	29	16	4
12 22	6	2	22	7	24	14	28	14 15	6	27	15	0 ♑	24	18	5
12 26	7	3	23	8	5	15	29	14 19	7	28	15	1	18	19	6
12 29	8	4	23	8	46	16	♓	14 22	8	29	16	2	13	20	8
12 33	9	5	24	9	28	17	2	14 26	9	♐	17	3	10	22	9
12 37	10	6	25	10	10	18	3	14 32	10	1	18	4	6	23	10
12 40	11	6	25	10	52	19	4	14 34	11	2	19	5	3	25	11
12 44	12	7	26	11	35	20	5	14 38	12	2	20	6	1	26	13
12 48	13	8	27	12	18	21	6	14 42	13	3	20	7	0	28	14
12 51	14	9	28	12	59	22	7	14 46	14	4	21	8	0	29	15
12 55	15	10	28	13	43	23	9	14 50	15	5	22	9	2	♓	17
12 59	16	11	29	14	26	24	10	14 54	16	6	23	10	6	3	18
13 3	17	11	♐	15	10	25	11	14 58	17	7	24	11	9	4	19
13 6	18	12	1	15	54	26	12	15 2	18	8	25	12	14	6	21
13 10	19	13	1	16	39	27	13	15 6	19	9	26	13	21	8	22
13 14	20	14	2	17	23	28	15	15 10	20	9	27	14	29	9	23
13 18	21	15	3	18	8	29	16	15 14	21	10	27	15	37	11	24
13 21	22	16	4	18	54	♒	17	15 18	22	11	28	16	46	13	26
13 25	23	16	4	19	39	1	18	15 22	23	12	29	17	58	14	27
13 29	24	17	5	20	26	2	20	15 26	24	13	♑	19	1	16	28
13 33	25	18	6	21	14	4	21	15 31	25	14	1	20	27	17	29
13 36	26	19	7	22	1	5	22	15 35	26	15	2	21	43	19	♉
13 40	27	20	7	22	49	6	23	15 39	27	16	3	23	3	21	2
13 44	28	21	8	23	37	7	25	15 43	28	17	4	24	4	22	3
13 48	29	21	9	24	20	8	26	15 47	29	18	5	25	48	23	5
13 52	30	22	10	25	15	10	27	15 51	30	19	6	27	10	26	6

PRIMUM MOBILE.

A TABLE OF HOUSES,

For the Latitude of 51 Degrees 32 Minutes,

According to PTOLEMY.

☉ in ♐								☉ in ♑							
Time from noon.	10 ♐	11 ♐	12 ♑	Ascen. ♑		2 ♓	3 ♉	Time from noon.	10 ♑	11 ♑	12 ♒	Ascen. ♈		2 ♉	3 ♊
H. M.	gr	gr	gr	gr.	m.	gr	gr	H. M.	gr	gr	gr	gr.	m.	gr	gr
15 51	0	18	6	27	10	26	6	18 0	0	18	13	0	0	17	11
15 55	1	19	7	28	27	28	7	18 4	1	20	14	2	37	19	13
16 0	2	20	8	0 ♒	6	♈	9	18 9	2	21	16	5	19	20	14
16 4	3	21	9	1	37	1	10	18 13	3	22	17	7	55	22	15
16 8	4	22	10	3	11	3	11	18 17	4	23	19	10	29	23	16
16 12	5	23	11	4	48	5	12	18 22	5	24	20	13	2	25	17
16 16	6	24	12	6	27	7	14	18 26	6	25	22	15	37	26	18
16 21	7	25	13	8	8	9	15	18 30	7	26	23	18	7	28	19
16 25	8	26	14	9	52	11	16	18 35	8	27	25	20	35	29	20
16 29	9	27	16	11	40	12	17	18 39	9	29	27	23	0	♊	21
16 33	10	28	17	12	30	14	18	18 44	10 ♒	28	25	22	1	22
16 38	11	29	18	15	20	16	20	18 48	11	1	♓	28	43	2	23
16 42	12	♑	19	17	16	18	21	18 52	12	2	2	0 ♉	0	4	24
16 46	13	1	20	19	15	20	22	18 57	13	3	3	2	16	5	25
16 51	14	2	21	21	17	21	23	19 1	14	4	5	4	27	6	26
16 55	15	3	22	23	20	23	25	19 5	15	6	7	6	33	8	27
16 59	16	4	24	25	32	25	26	19 9	16	7	9	8	39	9	28
17 4	17	5	25	27	44	27	27	19 14	17	8	10	10	43	10	29
17 8	18	6	26	29	58	28	28	19 18	18	9	12	12	42	11	♋
17 11	19	7	27	2 ♓	17	♉	29	19 22	19	10	14	14	40	12	1
17 16	20	8	29	4	38	2	♊	19 27	20	12	16	16	31	13	2
17 20	21	♒	7	0	3	1	19 31	21	13	18	18	20	14	3
17 25	22	10	1	9	24	5	2	19 35	22	14	19	20	5	16	4
17 30	23	11	3	11	53	7	3	19 39	23	15	21	21	52	17	5
17 34	24	12	4	14	23	8	5	19 44	24	16	23	23	33	18	6
17 38	25	13	5	16	59	10	6	19 48	25	18	25	25	13	19	7
17 43	26	14	7	19	36	11	7	19 52	26	19	27	26	49	20	8
17 47	27	15	8	22	5	13	8	19 56	27	20	28	28	22	21	9
17 51	28	16	10	24	39	14	9	20 0	28	21	♈	29	53	22	10
17 56	29	17	11	27	20	16	10	20 5	29	23	1	1 ♊	23	23	11
18 0	30	18	13	30	0	17	11	20 9	30	24	2	2	50	24	12

A TABLE OF HOUSES,

For the Latitude of 51 Degrees 32 Minutes,
According to PTOLEMY.

Time from noon.	10 ♒	11 ♒	12 ♈	Ascen. ♊		2 ♊	3 ♋	Time from noon.	10 ♓	11 ♈	12 ♉	Ascen. ♋		2 ♋	3 ♌
H. M.	gr	gr	gr	gr.	m.	gr	gr	H. M.	gr	gr	gr	gr.	m.	gr	gr
20 9	0	24	4	2	50	24	12	22 8	0	3	20	4	45	20	8
20 13	1	25	6	4	14	25	12	22 12	1	4	21	5	35	21	8
20 17	2	27	7	5	37	26	13	22 16	2	6	23	6	23	22	9
20 21	3	28	9	6	58	27	14	22 20	3	7	24	7	12	23	10
20 25	4	29	11	8	17	28	15	22 24	4	8	25	8	0	23	11
20 29	5	♓	13	9	33	29	16	22 27	5	9	26	8	48	24	12
20 34	6	2	14	10	49	♋	17	22 31	6	10	28	9	35	25	13
20 38	7	3	16	12	3	1	18	22 35	7	12	29	10	22	26	14
20 42	8	4	18	13	14	2	19	22 39	8	13	11	11	7	26	14
20 46	9	6	19	14	24	3	20	22 42	9	14	1	11	52	27	15
20 50	10	7	21	15	32	3	21	22 46	10	15	2	12	37	28	16
20 54	11	8	23	16	40	4	21	22 50	11	17	3	13	22	29	17
20 58	12	9	24	17	46	5	22	22 54	12	18	4	14	7	29	18
21 2	13	11	26	18	55	6	23	22 57	13	19	5	14	54	♌	19
21 6	14	12	28	19	56	7	24	23 1	14	20	6	15	35	1	19
21 10	15	13	29	20	58	8	25	23 5	15	21	7	16	17	2	20
21 14	16	15	♉	22	0	9	26	23 9	16	23	8	17	1	2	21
21 18	17	16	2	23	0	10	27	23 12	17	24	9	17	44	3	22
21 22	18	17	4	23	59	10	28	23 16	18	25	10	18	26	4	23
21 26	19	19	5	24	58	11	28	23 20	19	26	11	19	9	5	24
21 30	20	20	7	25	55	12	29	23 23	20	27	12	19	52	5	24
21 34	21	22	8	26	51	13	♌	23 27	21	29	13	20	23	6	25
21 38	22	23	10	27	47	14	1	23 31	22	♉	14	21	14	7	26
21 41	23	24	11	28	41	15	2	23 34	23	1	15	21	56	7	27
21 45	24	25	13	29	36	15	3	23 38	24	2	16	22	37	8	28
21 49	25	26	14	0♋	29	16	4	23 42	25	3	17	23	18	9	28
21 53	26	28	15	1	22	17	4	23 45	26	4	18	23	59	9	29
21 57	27	29	16	2	14	18	5	23 49	27	5	19	24	39	10	♍
22 1	28	♈	18	3	4	19	6	23 53	28	6	20	25	21	11	1
22 5	29	2	19	3	56	19	7	23 56	29	8	21	26	2	12	2
22 8	30	3	20	4	45	20	8	24 0	30	9	22	26	42	12	3

Speedily will be published,

A New Translation of PTOLEMY's QUADRIPARTITE, with Notes and Observations, by the Editor of this Edition of Placidus de Titus.

Davis and Dickson, Printers,
St. Martin's-le-Grand, London.